# REVISITING 1956

# REVISITING 1956

## B. R. AMBEDKAR AND STATES REORGANISATION

SUDHA PAI
AVINASH KUMAR

*With a Foreword by*
SUKHADEO THORAT

Orient BlackSwan

REVISITING 1956: B. R. AMBEDKAR AND STATES REORGANISATION

**ORIENT BLACKSWAN PRIVATE LIMITED**

*Registered Office*
3-6-752 Himayatnagar, Hyderabad 500 029, Telangana, India
e-mail: centraloffice@orientblackswan.com

*Other Offices*
Bengaluru, Bhopal, Chennai, Guwahati, Hyderabad, Jaipur, Kolkata, Lucknow, Mumbai, New Delhi, Noida, Patna, Visakhapatnam



First published in 2014
Reprinted in 2015, 2018



ISBN 978-93-5287-388-3

*Maps cartographed by*
Sangam Books (India) Private Limited, Hyderabad

028060

*Typeset in Dante MT 10.5/13 by*
Jojy Philip, New Delhi 110 015

*Printed in India at*
Glorious Printers, Delhi

*Published by*
Orient Blackswan Private Limited
3-6-752 Himayatnagar, Hyderabad 500 029, Telangana, India
e-mail: info@orientblackswan.com

# Contents

# Tables and Maps

## Tables



## Maps

# Abbreviations

| | |
|---|---|
| BLA | Bombay Legislative Assembly |
| CAD | Proceedings of the Constituent Assembly of India Debates |
| CWC | Congress Working Committee |
| GoM | Group of Ministers |
| ILP | Indian Labour Party |
| INC | Indian National Congress |
| MP | Madhya Pradesh |
| NWFP | North-West Frontier Provinces |
| SCs | Scheduled Castes |
| SCFI | Scheduled Caste Federation of India |
| SRC | States Reorganisation Commission |
| TRS | Telangana Rashtra Samithi |
| UDF | United Democratic Front |
| UPA | United Progressive Alliance |

# Foreword

## Making Ambedkar Visible

*Revisiting 1956* focuses on the contribution of Dr B. R. Ambedkar on the ever-important question of state reorganisation in India, a question that emerged immediately after Independence. Ambedkar, in an academically and politically active life of about thirty-five years from the 1920s to 1956, contributed on all issues that were important, and decisively helped in shaping the social, economic and political character of India during the most crucial period of its history. During this period, the struggle for freedom was fought and Independence realised in 1947, and the process of framing the Constitution which began in the early 1920s finally led to the 1935 Act and later to the adoption of the Indian Constitution in 1950. The minority issue, which resulted in the partition of British India, was at its peak. The question of women also figured prominently, which led to the Hindu Code Bill for equal rights to women. Above all, the economic and social framework for India was laid down. And, it is also during this period that Ambedkar emerged in the political scene and led a powerful political and social movement for the depressed classes. Ambedkar's canvas of national engagement and influence is vast; it includes contributions in Constitution-making, the problem of minorities and Partition, problem of Hindu women, development strategy for India, water, power and labour policy, and above all, the issue of the reform of the Hindu social order and the problem of untouchables for which he dedicated most of his life.

Ambedkar had also written on a number of other issues that emerged in the post-Independence period. And among them, the question of reorganisation of the Indian states remains very relevant even today. Ambedkar wrote at length and provided alternative views on this question. However, when it comes to the recognition of Ambedkar's academic contributions, he generally stands ignored on a number of issues, if not all. His writings do not find a visible place in schools, colleges, universities and research institutes across India. The man who fought against caste discrimination became the victim of his own cause. The same is the case with respect to Ambedkar's contribution on the question of reorganisation of states in India.

Ambedkar made significant contributions through a series of writings in the 1940s and the 1950s on this question. Barring a few exceptions, his contribution remains invisible. The authors of this book write,

> While much has been written on Ambedkar's views on caste and identity, Buddhism, and the lower castes movements led by him, his views on the issue of states reorganisation have not attracted serious scholarship. While the controversy over states reorganisation has attracted many native and foreign observers since the 1950s, barring a few, most have ignored Ambedkar's views on the subject. … Surprisingly, even after the revival of interest in the ideas of Ambedkar in the 1990s, scholars have seldom mentioned his contribution on the subject.

The authors then go on to present some recent studies that gave attention to the views of Ambedkar on states reorganisation. However, as they point out, a complete picture of Ambedkar's views on the subject is still not available. This neglect, in the first place, provided the justification for starting this project.

As a part of an ongoing research programme on Ambedkar, the Indian Institute Dalit Studies (IIDS) approached Professor Pai and Dr Kumar to examine Ambedkar's contribution to the subject of states reorganisation. We are fortunate that they agreed to pen this book.

What is the purpose and relevance of this book? This book in some respect is different from other similar works. It has two parts. In the first part, the authors present an analysis of Ambedkar's writings on states reorganisation, and their contemporary relevance. In the second part, they present all these writings in the original. This includes tracts, articles, speeches and books that Ambedkar wrote on the issue of reorganisation of the states in the 1940s and the 1950s when the existing Indian states were being reorganised.

In its content, this volume does, as the authors put it, 'revisit the mid-1950s when states reorganisation took place, the principles on which this was undertaken, the views of various national leaders and the contentious debates in various public forums regarding reorganisation.' The authors particularly analyse the core of Ambedkar's thoughts on the question of the 'principles' and the 'criteria' on which reorganisation could take place. These criteria proposed by Ambedkar emerged from his critique of the States Reorganisation Commission (SRC) which emphasised statehood primarily on linguistic basis. He favoured multiple criteria and developed, what I would call, 'Language Plus Approach'. They carefully analyse the significance of the criteria developed by Ambedkar: size, economic viability, equality of all citizens (particularly, social minorities), federal balance and language. In Ambedkar's view, while language and culture constitute important components in formation of a state—as a common language and culture enable social homogeneity—language alone is not sufficient for the creation of states. The size of the state is equally important as the second criterion. But size is also closely linked with the third criterion, viability. The criterion of viability relates to the economic aspect. Since in Ambedkar's view size and viability are closely linked, economic viability should form one of the important criteria for state formation. Viability was interpreted with respect to the revenue of the state, which should be adequate enough to run the administration efficiently and enable the state to ensure expenditure on the basic needs of the people. Besides size and economic viability, Ambedkar attached great significance to another criterion: the safeguards against dominance of a communal majority over linguistic or socially-disadvantaged minorities. This would imply that while carving out states, religious, social and linguistic groups should not be reduced to small numbers and get exposed to the dominance of the communal majority. The proper population balance between the majority and the minority then becomes important in the creation of a state. Ambedkar felt that in 'smaller states,' the provision of equality and social justice for minorities, particularly the Scheduled Castes, will be possible. Another criterion that Ambedkar suggested was the maintenance of federal balance. He argued that federal balance will be feasible if the states are of 'similar size' and this similarity would avoid the possibility of dominance by large states. Dominance-free federation is essential in a culturally and regionally diverse country like India. The last criterion relates to the divisive use of language. While he favoured language as one of the criteria for the creation of states (unlike the SRC, however, he favoured more than one state with the same language to discourage any possibility of regionalism), Ambedkar also warned against the divisive role of language. He suggested safeguards against a conflict between the national language and the official language of each state, and a conflict between the official language of the state and the language of the majority in the state. Ambedkar also suggested that the language of each province should not be its official language.

Thus, while the SRC had reduced the complex issue of reorganisation of states to one immutable criterion of language, Ambedkar dealt with the underlying complexities of the issue in its multiple dimensions, indicated relevant multiple criteria, and also suggested alternative schemes different from SRC recommendations. Ambedkar, thus, favoured small but economically viable states. Since 'smallness' is a relative concept, when these small and viable states are carved out, it has to be ensured that they are of more or less the same size to enable federal balance. This will also prevent bigger states from enjoying a dominant position vis-a-vis the small ones.

The book thus analyses this complex issue and brings greater clarity by discussing Ambedkar's thoughts in a simple and lucid manner. The book also analyses Ambedkar's views on actual attempts of state formation in the cases of Maharashtra, Andhra, Karnatak, Uttar Pradesh, Bihar and Madhya Pradesh. The authors also discuss the recent effort to create Telangana out of Andhra Pradesh.

Insofar as the book includes the original writings of Ambedkar on the issue of reorganisation of states and also an analysis of these writings, it provides a complete and comprehensive treatment of the issue in the same volume. Readers can access Ambedkar's original writings and also a scholarly analysis of his thoughts. I feel that the book is going to be of immense use to researchers policy-makers and the government alike on an issue that continues to burn at regular intervals. The authors deserve appreciation for undertaking this exercise for us.

New Delhi
25 April 2014

Sukhadeo Thorat
Professor, Jawaharlal Nehru University
Chairman, Indian Council of Social Science Research
Managing Trustee, IIDS

# Preface

While much has been written on Ambedkar's views on caste and identity, Buddhism, and the lower castes movements led by him, his views on the issue of states reorganisation have not attracted serious scholarship. While the controversy over states reorganisation has attracted many Indian and foreign observers since the 1950s, barring a few, most have ignored Ambedkar's views on the subject. This volume is an attempt at revisiting the mid-1950s when the first round of states reorganisation took place, the principles on which this was undertaken, the views of various national leaders and the contentious debates in various public forums regarding reorganisation. Such a study is of significance because, in many ways, reorganisation remained an unfinished task in the immediate post-Independence period due to controversies and pressures emanating from the strong political movements of the period. Despite many changes over a period of 60 years, some of the ideas and solutions provided by Ambedkar on redrawing the map of India, it is argued here, could be of considerable relevance to the continuing, contentious and conflictual issue.

This volume emerged from 'Ambedkar and his Thoughts on Reorganisation of States' a research study under the TTI-IDRC (Think Tank Initiative, International Development Research Centre, Canada) project of the Indian Institute of Dalit Studies (IIDS), New Delhi. The authors are grateful to Professor Sukhadeo Thorat, who provided us with the opportunity to take up this study. This study has helped us enrich our understanding of the evolution of Indian federal democracy which is part of the larger project of nation-building in many ways. During this study we have been helped by many scholars, all of whom cannot be mentioned here. But, Dr Raja Sekhar Vundru's help of providing us with all the volumes of *Dr. Babasaheb Ambedkar's Writings and Speeches* deserves special mention.

We would like to thank Dr. Babasaheb Ambedkar Source Material Publication Committee, Government of Maharashtra, Mumbai—especially, Prof. Avinash Dolas (Member Secretary)—for permission to carry extracts from Ambedkar's original works. We have made the best of efforts to carry these extracts as they were published in the editions we referred to; along with errors of commission and omission, if any. We have therefore retained original inconsistencies across publications with regard to style of numbering, level heads, capitalisation, punctuation and spelling. In Part I of this volume, maps that were originally drawn by Ambedkar for 'Thoughts on Linguistic States' were redrawn by the Cartography team of Sangam Books. In this process, we chose to retain the erroneous spellings of the original in keeping with our attempt to faithfully reproduce the leader's work.

The first seven of eight chapters in Part II of this volume, i.e. Compendium, have been arranged chronologically. However, the last chapter, 'States and Minorities,' has been placed at the end although it is one of Ambedkar's earlier works. This is because of the strikingly unique and pertinent contribution this piece offers to the debate on states reorganisation—that of providing safeguards for the Scheduled Castes. All explanatory endnotes in Compendium have been included by us for the benefit of the reader. Footnotes in pages 119 and 120 are exact reproductions from the original work.

Finally, we would like to acknowledge the excellent handling of the manuscript by Roopa Sharma and her team, particularly Antony Arul Valan whose editing skills have helped improve the quality of the manuscript.

New Delhi
18 March 2014

Sudha Pai
Avinash Kumar

# Part I

# Tracing Ambedkar's Thoughts on States Reorganisation

# Introduction

*If you are going to settle these things with the help of your party, remember that your party is not perpetual. You can see the signs of waning even now before your eye.*

B. R. Ambedkar[1]

One of the most significant developments over the last two decades in India has been the increasing demand for reorganisation of the states created at Independence. Redrawing the map of India was a complex and protracted process in the 1950s. It involved a number of difficult steps beginning with Partition, the integration of princely states into the Indian Union and carving out of new states within a federal structure that reflected the desires of people of the various regions. As an important component of the project of nation-building in the immediate post-Independence period, the challenge also was to create a democratic and participative system of governance. In response to these needs, the Government of India constituted a three-man States Reorganisation Commission (SRC) to 'examine objectively and dispassionately the question of reorganisation of states of the Indian Union, so that the welfare of the people of each constituent unit as well as the nation as a whole is promoted' on 22 December 1953. The SRC was chaired by Syed Fazal Ali, a former Supreme Court judge, and the other two members were historian K. M. Panikkar and Rajya Sabha member H. N. Kunzru. The SRC submitted its report on 30 September 1955 and the map of India was redrawn. However, this redrawing remained an unfinished task.

Based on the continuing demands and changing political scenario, there have been at least three rounds of reorganisation subsequently. The first was as early as in the 1960s, with the creation of the states of Maharashtra and Gujarat in 1960, Nagaland in 1963, and Haryana and Punjab in 1966. The second major round was in the 1970s, when the North-East was split up and several new states were created. A third round began in 2000 with creation of three smaller states—Jharkhand, Uttaranchal (now, Uttarakhand) and Chhattisgarh—carved out of the large states in the northern Hindi-belt.[2] While the older demands of statehood were not yet addressed, several new demands such as Coorg in Karnataka, Gorkhaland in West Bengal, Bodoland in Assam have emerged (*TNN* 2009; Mallik 2005). As many as 30 such demands seem to be pending for consideration before the government (Majeed 2003). In a recent essay B. G. Verghese has argued,

> There is no reason to resist the demand for more states subject to their techno-economic and administrative viability. There is no wrong in envisaging India at 2040–2050 with a population of around 1,600 million organized in 60 states, with an average population of 25 million each, and some 1,500 districts. At the base, there could be 15,000 development blocks, each with a population of around 100,000 governed by structures of local self-government through gram sabhas (village councils), panchayat samitis (a grouping of village councils at the block level comprising about 100–120 villages) and zila parishads (an aggregation of panchayat samitis at the district level, i.e. district council). (Verghese 2011: xviii)

Principles and rationale based on which the states were reorganised in the 1950s and in subsequent rounds continue to be debated, but little consensus on the manner in which the contemporary problems can be sorted out seems to be emerging. This has made the problem more complex and contentious, and has led to a serious law and order problem in several states today.

Undoubtedly much change has taken place in the country since the 1950s, and is reflected in the demands for reconfigurating the map of India today. The demands being voiced to redraw boundaries—particularly for the division of the large states created at Independence into smaller states—are in a different socioeconomic and political milieu. At least three major changes can be identified in which they could be located. First, democratisation has led to the rise of 'new sub-regional elites' from among the middle and lower castes/classes in many states that are keen to obtain a greater share in political power and in the fruits of post-Independence development. Second, with the decline of the single dominant party system and rise of parties based on regional and lower caste/class/communal identities in a post-Congress period, the states have come to play a more central and dominant role within the federation. This has led to a loose federation and decentralisation of power from the Centre to these social groups who are in the forefront of the demand for smaller states in which they hope to wield power. Third, simultaneously globalisation has led to the establishment of a market economy and greater space for private capital which in a post-reform period is contributing to increasing regional inequalities between states.[3]

In light of these developments, this volume is an attempt to revisit the mid-1950s when states reorganisation took place, the principles on which this was undertaken, the views of various national leaders and the contentious debates in various public forums regarding reorganisation. Such an analysis could be useful and relevant for understanding and perhaps finding solutions for the present. More specifically, this volume is an attempt to critically analyse the speeches and writings of Dr Bhim Rao Ambedkar on the subject of states reorganisation in India. The significance of such an exercise is not merely to throw academic light on the writings of Ambedkar which is a useful project in itself. Rather, we argue that despite the seminal changes over a period of 60 years mentioned above, some of the ideas and solutions proffered by Ambedkar on redrawing the map of India could be of considerable relevance to the continuing and still contentious debate on this issue.

As our study will show, Ambedkar in his speeches and writings had discussed and given considerable weight to many issues being debated today. Unlike Nehru, he supported the demand for reorganisation of states along linguistic lines. Aware of the dangers of reorganisation purely on linguism, Ambedkar pointed to ways in which contemporary problems could be brought together with the linguistic principle for which the demand was overwhelming and which could not be ignored any further. He also attempted to link his ideas on reorganisation to nationalism and nation-building as evinced in his early book *Thoughts on Pakistan*.[4] Equally relevant, Ambedkar's views are presented in the language of democracy. He is concerned about the size of states in a federation and its impact on federal balance. He suggests 'checks and balances' to prevent the tyranny of linguistic and communal majorities on minorities, and also to prevent clash between the national and regional language, the need for a state to have sufficient revenue, the need for proper governance, etc.

Such a discussion would be meaningful because in many ways reorganisation remained an unfinished task in the immediate post-Independence period due to the controversies and pressures emanating from the strong political movements of the period. These problems remain unaddressed even today. Ambedkar studied the situation in detail and put forward ideas and solutions. With the privileging of the linguistic principle, however, his ideas were not considered by the Congress leaders of the time and were swept aside. Ambedkar's skilful analysis of the pros and cons of linguism and other concerns retain relevance even today. In fact, if we seriously consider some of the contemporary demands for reorganisation, we seem to be moving towards some of the solutions Ambedkar offered. Thus, our attempt in this study is to situate Ambedkar in our present-day endeavour to resolve contemporary demands of reorganisation. This is particularly true in the case of Andhra Pradesh and Maharashtra, two states on which Ambedkar focused and drew important lessons from for the country.

## Ambedkar in the Literature on States Reorganisation

While much has been written on Ambedkar's views on caste, identity, untouchability, Buddhism, and the larger context in which his sociopolitical views emerged (Rodrigues 2002; Jaffrelot 2004; Zelliot 1972, 1996; Omvedt 1994, 2003; Keer 1994/1964; Wilkinson and Thomas 1972; Gore 1993; Das 1980; Sangharakshita 1986); his views on the issue of reorganisation of states have not attracted serious scholarship. Similarly, while the controversy over reorganisation of states has attracted many Indian and foreign observers ever since the 1950s, barring few, almost all have ignored Ambedkar's views on the subject.

A few examples should make this clear. Joan Bondurant, who in her seminal study *Regionalism versus Provincialism: A Study in Problems of Indian National Unity* (1958) made an exhaustive analysis of the views of the nationalist leadership and other political parties, including the left parties, using original sources, wrote in detail on the process of the redrawing of the map of India including the movements for linguistic states between 1947 and 1955. But, Bondurant does not discuss the writings of Ambedkar. This is surprising because the monograph provides a day-to-day account of the events concerning reorganisation and the various views and opinions expressed by various contesting parties.

Marshall Windmiller (1954, 1956), writing on the issue of linguistic regionalism in India, first in *Pacific Affairs* and later in *Far Eastern Survey* (after the SRC submitted its report in 1956) devotes considerable attention to the differences of opinion and violent developments over whether Maharashtra was to be made a separate state and the position of Bombay city within it. Ambedkar was a member of the Bombay Legislature and he spoke and wrote extensively on the subject, but Windmiller does not mention Ambedkar, neither his speeches nor the recommendations he proffered.

The noteworthy exception among foreign scholars who dealt with Ambedkar's views on the subject is Selig S. Harrison (1960), who termed the period of post-states' reorganisation in 1956 as 'India's most dangerous decade'. Harrison's prophecy on Indian federalism proved false, but he understood Ambedkar's point (submitted before the Linguistic Provinces Commission in 1948) about the tyranny of linguistic and communal majorities on minorities in the smaller linguistic units and observed that behind the banner of language was the conflict between castes and their power relations. However, few years later, when Duncan B. Forrester (1970) wrote on the issue of sub-regionalism in India with special reference to Telangana, he once again missed Ambedkar's contribution on the subject.[5]

For Indian scholars the *Economic and Political Weekly* (earlier known as *The Economic Weekly*) provided space for academic discussion on the issue of reorganisation. Between 1953 and 1956 the journal devoted nearly 35 items to the issue of reorganisation (including editorials, letters to the editors, special articles, weekly notes and in other formats); but Ambedkar finds no mention.[6] The only exception is a passing reference to Ambedkar made in the review of *Reorganisation of Indian States* (Mukerji and Ramaswamy 1955) by N. A. Shah (1955).[7] Few years later, Krishna Kodesia's book *The Problem of Linguistic States in India* (1969) analyses in detail the opinions of several leaders, including Gandhi, Nehru, Rajagopalachari, Golwalkar, K. B. Menon, S. K. Sinha and B. C. Roy, on the process of reorganisation as well as several memorandums submitted by traders organisation and citizens committee from Bombay; but it does not provide Ambedkar's opinion on the subject.

Surprisingly, even after the revival of interest in the ideas of Ambedkar in the 1990s, scholars have seldom mentioned his contribution on the subject. More recently, Ramchandra Guha in his exhaustive study *India After Gandhi* (2007), devoting a special chapter on redrawing of the map of India after Independence, deals extensively with the position taken by Nehru, Gandhi and other leaders but is silent on Ambedkar. This despite the fact that Guha, on several occasions, describes Ambedkar as one of the most important leaders with rare intelligence and integrity, and has even invoked his views and insights to explain the present-day functioning of India's democracy (ibid.: 180–200).

A few recent noteworthy exceptions find Ambedkar's views on the subject praiseworthy. A. G. Noorani (2002) reviewing volume 30 of *Selected Works of Jawaharlal Nehru* (Prasad and Damodaran 2002) comments on views of both Nehru and Ambedkar on the report of the SRC. A few years later, Noorani (2010) devoted a special article on the views of Ambedkar on the subject. In reviewing *Selected Works*, Noorani points out that Nehru tried very bravely to preserve large bilingual states particularly the state of Bombay, which Nehru believed would prevent the linguistic chauvinism from sweeping the country. He holds that Nehru could well have relied on the weighty opinion of an advocate of Maharashtra State, Dr Ambedkar. He refers to 'Need for Checks and Balances', an article written by Ambedkar in *Times of India* in 1953—reproduced in Part II (Compendium) of this volume—in which Ambedkar does not oppose linguistic states, but is aware of the dangers of linguistic nationalism and puts forward a number of 'checks and balances' to ensure that a communal majority does not abuse its power in the garb of linguistic states to oppress the minorities. Further, Noorani (2002, 2010) refers to Ambedkar's Statement to the Linguistic Provinces Commission set up by the Congress in 1948 where he urges that the official language of each province should be the same as the official language of the Union to avoid the states from moving away from each other leading to balkanisation.[8]

Partha Chatterjee (2006) in his essay 'B. R. Ambedkar and the Troubled Times of Citizenship' links Ambedkar's views on caste and the meaning of citizenship for Scheduled Castes to his thinking on reorganisation of the states. Apart from taking up some of Ambedkar's well-known writings, Chatterjee discusses his lesser-known book *Pakistan or the Partition of India* (written in 1941 and published in 1945)—excerpts from which are reproduced in Compendium here—in which he grappled with the need to further the struggle for universal and equal citizenship within the nation, and to secure special representation for the depressed classes in the body politic.[9]

It is only in recent years, with the rising demands for formation of smaller states, that some studies have begun to give attention to the views of Ambedkar on states reorganisation (Sarangi 2006; Sarangi and Pai 2011; Vundru 2010; Kumar 2011; Tillin 2014). However, a complete picture of the views put forward by Dr Bhim Rao Ambedkar, one of the principal architects of the Constitution, who wrote and spoke extensively in various public forums on the subject of states reorganisation in the 1940s and 1950s, precisely when reorganisation was taking place, is still not available. It is with this purpose that we undertake this exercise to analyse the speeches and writings of Ambedkar on the subject of states reorganisation at one place. This takes into consideration that reorganisation is an ongoing process and thus remains part of the larger project of nation-building in India. Started in 1956—with the creation of states on linguistic lines based on the report of the SRC—it has moved, over the decades, to other aspects such as underdevelopment, backwardness, participation, governance and position of minorities among others, many of which were addressed by Ambedkar in his lifetime. In today's situation, when the debate on redrawing the borders and reorganising the state has been reopened, we find that many of the ideas of Ambedkar are of considerable relevance in the rethinking that is underway.

## Differing Visions and Ambedkar's Ideas

At Independence, there were differing and at times conflicting visions within the political leadership of the period regarding the basis on which the regions on the subcontinent were to be reorganised. At least three can be mentioned. Most significant was the Nehruvian or nationalist vision which was largely shared by the central Congress leadership which had incorporated the principle of redistribution of provinces to be done 'on a linguistic basis on the demand of the majority of the population of the area concerned, subject to financial and administrative considerations' (Rao 1967a: 74).[10] However, given the circumstances in the country at the time of Independence which favoured only a few territorial and functional arrangements of decentralisation, the Congress leadership decided to prioritise the unity, security and future economic development of the newly-formed state over linguism and discouraged the idea of reorganising the states on linguistic principles. This viewpoint was sharply and at times violently opposed in the provinces by the local leaders of the Congress and the opposition parties who, as the representatives of linguistic communities, were keen to reorganise states on linguistic basis. As dominant social groups, they hoped this would enable them to capture state power in the newly-formed states in the immediate post-Independence period. A third viewpoint—which is not considered in this volume—was that of the Communist parties which held that every section of the Indian people which had 'common historical tradition, common language, culture, psychological make-up and common economic life' should be recognised as a 'distinct nationality with the right to exist as an autonomous state within the free Indian Union or federation' and this could not be ignored in any scheme of reorganisation.[11]

While all three views mentioned above are well known, Ambedkar's views are not widely known. Unlike many of his contemporaries he was not affected by the emotional outpourings and conflicts on linguistic division in the 1950s. Distancing himself carefully from the situation, he analysed the issue of reorganisation in a dispassionate, scientific and systematic manner. This was possible because, in contrast to Nehru, Ambedkar was not in a position of authority where he had to make decisions regarding reorganisation. Hence, Ambedkar emerges as a spectator and perceptive commentator on this key issue. At the same time, Ambedkar does not appear to be dogmatic. He seems to be a pragmatist, with an open mind evidenced from the shift he made on the issue of size of states in his later writings—particularly in the case of Maharashtra, an aspect discussed in detail a little later. Ambedkar was non-partisan and considered the issue from the standpoint of all the minorities in the states who were placed in a difficult position.

## Drawing a Framework from Ambedkar's Thoughts

Our analysis of the writings and speeches of Ambedkar on states reorganisation and its relevance to present-day problems is based on a framework drawn from his own work. This method is adopted because, in response to the demands and events of the time, Ambedkar was able to evolve 'criteria' on which reorganisation could take place, and was able to justify his recommendations in a rational manner. His arguments are not based simply on emotions or issues of identity. They are based on the need for a democratic federal structure in a large and plural society, which he links to issues of nation, nationality and citizenship.

These criteria evolved over time, but were identified and developed particularly from Ambedkar's critique of the SRC for defining statehood primarily on linguistic and cultural basis, and carving out the states mainly on a single issue, i.e. language. This happened, Ambedkar argued, because the Congress had blindly adhered to the linguistic principle throughout the colonial period and thereby contributed to the demand for reorganisation along linguistic lines. Consequently, many political leaders particularly in different regions were keen to reorganise states on linguistic basis so that each language gained a homeland in the subcontinent. The SRC was expected to look into issues such as preservation and strengthening of the unity and security of India, linguistic and cultural homogeneity, financial and administrative efficiency and the successful working of the national Five-Year Plans. The Commission did attempt to strike a balance between a strong Centre, and economically and administratively viable democratic states. However, as political events unfolded at that time, the Commission eventually emphasised on the primacy of the linguistic factor for demarcating the boundaries of the states over many other essential aspects such as size, development, representation and protection of minorities, etc. Ambedkar, in his writings, had accorded substantial importance to these neglected issues, some of which form the basis of the demands for reorganisation today.

Recognising the fact that reorganisation was a complex and multidimensional subject, Ambedkar developed his ideas on six major interrelated themes which underlie our analysis in the volume: 1) Pros and cons of linguistic states, the central argument on which the rest of his arguments are constructed; 2) Protection to minorities; 3) Nationalism and nationality; 4) Viability, size of states and federal balance; 5) Checks and balances to the linguistic arrangement; and, 6) Official language and reorganisation. Based on these larger themes, Ambedkar, in order to deal with the complexities involved in the process of reorganisation, specified the following 'criteria' on which actual states could be carved out:

- **Viability** formed a pragmatic, multidimensional and overarching concept that included many aspects. While language and culture constitute important components in any scheme of reorganisation, particularly in a country divided into cultural regions, he felt they were not sufficient for the creation of a federal structure. The concept could be used to further evolve criteria for reorganisation.
- **Size** was a key aspect of the concept of viability on which Ambedkar developed his ideas over a period of time. In 1948, he felt that all Marathi-speaking districts—including Bombay city with its large revenue contribution—should be brought together to create one large province with no room for choice or self-determination; a solution he felt was valid for all regions in the country. However, by 1955, after having considered many solutions for Maharashtra and other parts of the country Ambedkar came to the conclusion that economic viability and size were closely related and it would be better to create smaller states.
- **Economic feasibility** was a related variable used by Ambedkar. He argued that it was better not to create small provinces without revenue enough to run the administration efficiently. He warned against the formation of provinces merely to 'satisfy the ambition of few persons who wish to emerge as its leaders', as such a move, he felt, 'might leave the population without food, clothing or shelter'.
- **Equality of all citizens** was important for Ambedkar as he believed that large states could lead to the dominance of a communal majority over a linguistic or socially-disadvantaged minority. He felt that in smaller states provision of equality and social justice for minorities, particularly the Scheduled Castes, would be more possible.
- **Federal balance** through all the states being of a more or less similar size was required to enable a democratic system to function in a large and culturally-diverse country such as India.
- **The divisive issue of language**, Ambedkar held, was a problem that was necessary to keep in check. He held that to ensure no conflict based on language between the national language and the official language of each state, and between the latter and the language of the majority community in that state, the language of each province should not be made its official language.

## Situating Ambedkar in Contemporary Demands for Reorganisation

Our analyses of Ambedkar's writings and speeches on states reorganisation in this volume suggest that, despite considerable change in post-Independence India, many of his ideas retain their relevance today. At Independence, the demand was for the creation of states based largely on the linguistic principle with each state providing a homeland for a language and its people. Today, the issue of language has not totally lost its importance but it is variables such as smaller size, faster economic development, a more responsive bureaucratic structure, increased participative political order and inclusive development of various regions and sub-regions within the existing states, that have gained more importance.[12] In this situation, the issue of states reorganisation has come to occupy centre stage and spawn both strident demands as well as a debate on the principles on which future changes should be carried out. It is in this context that some aspects of Ambedkar's views on states reorganisation retain their relevance and need to be seriously considered.

A central idea in Ambedkar's framework, discussed above, with considerable relevance for the present is that reorganisation cannot be carried out on the basis of any single principle. Our experience has shown that states reorganisation is a complex and multifaceted exercise requiring attention simultaneously to many different aspects. Among these aspects with the rising demand for smaller states—particularly the division of the large states created at Independence—the issue of size of states is a central concern today. Large and unwieldy states such as Uttar Pradesh and Madhya Pradesh have proved to be less efficient or poorly governed than smaller states such as Haryana or Himachal Pradesh. The latter have shown faster development, and are more responsive to the needs of the people. Small- and medium-sized states, it is felt, would help mass mobilisation and greater participation in development by bringing government closer to the people and providing greater participation. At the same time, the issue of size is not a single aspect but has many associated dimensions which Ambedkar had pointed out; some of which are being realised and considered today.

Economic backwardness of sub-regions within large states has also emerged as an important ground on which demands for smaller states are being made. This is evident from the demands for several new states such as Vidarbha, Saurashtra, Bodoland and Harit Pradesh, among others. Ambedkar had drawn attention to a number of backward regions—particularly Marathwada, which had remained neglected under the Nizam and had hardly any facilities such as roads, schools, irrigation, food, etc. He argued that the people of Marathwada should be allowed to look after their own interests and decide what they want. He pointed out that the proponents of a United Maharashtra did not know enough about Marathwada and would confine themselves to looking after Poona and its environs. This has proved true today in the case of many sub-regions. In the colonial period, investment in commercial agriculture and industry was in select areas—coastal regions, deltas, river valleys and mineral-rich regions suited to imperial interests—leaving the vast hinterland underdeveloped. This distorted pattern of unequal development among regions continued into the post-Independence period. The result has been the development of capitalism in enclaves in all the big states of India surrounded by poorer regions that remain backward with undernourished and non-literate populations. Baghelkhand, Poorvanchal, Vidarbha and the inner tribal regions of Odisha have typically formed the deprived underbelly in these states. At Independence it had been envisaged that due to exchange of labour and capital between these regions, there would all-round development. But the reality has been internal colonialism, the better-off region grabbing the lion's share of resources and opportunities (Sarangi and Pai 2011). Addressing this problem has become an urgent necessity today.

The issue of size is today closely related to the issue of economic feasibility. However, the smaller states envisaged can be created provide they are economically viable with sufficient resources to fulfil the needs and aspirations of the people. Ambedkar had taken up this issue; in 1938, he opposed the proposal for the creation of the state of Karnatak out of regions such as Bijapur or Bellary because they were famine-stricken and would not yield enough revenue to look after the needs of the people in it. Too small a state, he held, which cannot find the means to carry on its administration should be avoided, as 'people do not live on culture ... they live on the resources they possess' (Ambedkar 1953b/1997). Similarly, he pointed out that bringing together parts of a region into a state—as had happened in the case of Orissa in the 1950s—was not as important as providing food and other essential requirements for them.

Among several reasons put forward by Ambedkar for small states, prominent was his view on equality of citizens. He felt that a communal majority in a state should not abuse its power under the garb of a linguistic state. His apprehension of the possible domination of Jats in Punjab, Reddys in Andhra and Marathas in Maharashtra, particularly over the lower castes, have proved to be true. The solution he put forward was providing various checks or safeguards to minorities—such as vesting special powers in the hands of the governor—to ensure that their rights were not trampled upon by the majority. Had these safeguards been put in place, it might have helped lessen the sense of marginalisation, remove feelings of being a minority and it might have eventually resolved the demand by many—such as the Coorgis, Gorkhas and Bodos—for a separate state.

Concerning size, Ambedkar was also critical of the great difference in size and population among the states proposed by the SRC. He argued that greater equality in the size of states and the interrelationships among them were critical features of a stable, democratic, federal polity. He wanted to balance the prevailing multilinguism in the country and the emerging federal structure, an aspect which—it is acknowledged—needs close attention today while forming smaller states. A related aspect that Ambedkar pointed out was the North-South divide in India as the northern states were large and the southern states much smaller. While such perceptions—which are related to size, linguistic and cultural differences—were very real in the first few decades after Independence, they have not completely disappeared. He was correct in pointing out that linguistic states could become over time more homogeneous and more politically conscious, and could create problems over sensitive issues such as language. This was evident in the anti-Hindi language movement of the 1960s which has taken new dimensions today with some states such as Karnataka demanding that their own language be made the medium of instruction and government work in their state. The problem of national language in a situation where each state has its own regional language and would like to promote it has not been resolved.

These problems are also evident in the demand made by the southern states in the 1970s that delimitation of parliamentary constituencies be postponed as it would give the large northern states a disproportionate number of members in Parliament, giving regional parties from these regions more clout. Nor is there a balance in the federation as the upper house does not provide equal representation to every state leaving the small states in the south and increasingly those in the North-East, unhappy at low representation in Parliament. The fear that Uttar Pradesh and other northern states would play an important role because of their size and the large contingents of members they may send to the Parliament, have proved to be true. It has distorted the functioning of the Union of states creating both suspicion and resentment. The principles of equality of size and representation, as suggested by Ambedkar remain relevant today following the decline of the single dominant party system at the Centre and the important position that the states and regional parties have come to play in India.

Most importantly, bringing together all his thinking on the subject of states reorganisation, Ambedkar, in 1955, suggested a way in which the issue of size and language could be brought together to satisfy both the cultural aspirations of the people and the need to carve out economically viable states of a reasonable size. The solution he offered was not one state speaking one language, i.e. monolinguistic states. He put forward the idea of creating more than one state speaking the same language. Maharashtra, for example, could be divided into four states, namely Maharashtra City State, Eastern Maharashtra, Central Maharashtra and Western Maharashtra, all speaking Marathi; Uttar Pradesh into three Hindi-speaking states, and so on. This solution was not considered in the 1950s. But four decades later, the division of Bihar into two states in November 2000, proves that the trajectory being followed in the Hindi heartland today is what Ambedkar proffered. Both Uttar Pradesh (demands already being raised) and Madhya Pradesh could be further divided into smaller states which could help in faster economic development. It is a viable solution for states in many parts of the country keeping in mind the optimal size of each state.

## Addressing Telangana

The struggle for a separate Telangana state from the large composite state of Andhra Pradesh, exemplifies several of Ambedkar's principles. Andhra was the first state in independent India to be formed on the linguistic principle, in 1952. While its formation was celebrated as the victory of those who stood for linguistic and cultural identity, Ambedkar felt that no clear thinking had taken place and the decision was marked by hesitation, constant shifts, contradictions and vacillations. Andhra, for Ambedkar, remained the typical example of a state formed due to emotional demands and was not a pragmatic solution. It was an 'artificial' merger of two regions that had little in common. The Andhra region under the British had experienced a strong language movement and participated in the national movement leading to the rise of regional consciousness. In contrast, the Hyderabad region under the Nizam had remained backward with little consciousness and Urdu was the language of a section of the elite. The merger was made on conditional grounds by the leaders of the Congress party from the two regions with an assurance to the people of Telangana that their economic interests would be safeguarded in the larger state.[13] However, the Gentleman's Agreement and other safeguards, such as, power sharing, domicile rules for reservation in public employment (popularly known as Mulki Rules), education and distribution of expenses of the various regions, were not adhered to and could not satisfy the people of Telangana.

Ambedkar's opinion proved correct, in just over a decade. All factors considered important by him, particularly manageable size and economic development of all regions and all sections of the population, assumed importance leading to a strong movement for a separate state of Telangana.[14] Both, the violent agitation led by the Telangana Praja Samithi popularised as 'Jai Telangana Agitation' in 1969 and later agitations from time to time in recent years show this clearly (Reddy and Sharma 1979). Despite continuous efforts, by the state government and the Centre, to supress demand for a separate state, the movement did not die down.

Demands for reorganisation have emerged in many states, but unlike Telangana, the level of regional consciousness has not reached its optimal level in many of these places. This was because the creation of a regional political party, Telangana Rashtra Samithi (TRS) founded by K. Chandrasekhara Rao in 2001, transformed the increasing political consciousness since the colonial period—from being a sociocultural movement for uniting the people of the region to a political movement for autonomy. Over the years, it has built up a wide support base of all social groups of students and government employees, cutting across caste, religion and gender.

The Congress party passed a resolution in 2001 proposing the establishment of a second SRC to consider redrawing the map of India and carving out smaller states. But it conveniently chose to forget the promise as soon as it was voted to power (as a coalition United Progressive Alliance [UPA]) in the 2004 Lok Sabha elections. It raised the issue again a year before the Lok Sabha and Assembly elections in Andhra Pradesh in 2008, only to form an alliance with the TRS. But fearing antagonism from Congress leaders from coastal Andhra, it did not fulfil its promise to the TRS. The 11-day fast by Rao in late 2009 pushed UPA-II to agree to a resolution on the formation of Telangana. It set up of a Committee for Consultations on the Situation in Andhra Pradesh (popularly known as the Justice Sri Krishna Committee) to look into the issue of statehood for Telangana in February 2010.

The observations made by the Committee in its report submitted after eight months shows that the Telangana movement today has moved beyond traditional issues of language and culture to those of equitable development of smaller regions and rights of people living in them. The Telangana movement, the Committee observed, should be seen as:

> The desire for greater democracy and empowerment within a political unit ... a movement which is not necessarily primordial but is essentially modern – in the direction of a balanced and equitable modernization ... cutting across caste, religion, gender and other divisions, the Telangana movement brings a focus on the development of the region as a whole, a focus on rights and access to regional resources and further, it pitches for a rights-based development perspective whereby groups and communities put forth their agendas within a larger vision of equitable development .... A major factor feeding into the mass support for the movement is the tremendous educational progress in Telangana among all social groups and classes, which feeds into the desire for better jobs, better living standards and a greater say in decision-making in the state and the region. The fact that educational progress has not been matched by an equal progress in levels of economic well-being among all social groups, adds to the sense of dissatisfaction. (GoI 2010: 412–17)

The central government, fearing that granting statehood to Telangana might lead to a plethora of demands in other states, did not act on the Justice Sri Krishna Committee report. However, due to the mounting agitation for Telangana, it finally announced its decision to grant statehood to Telangana in October 2013. The Andhra Pradesh Reorganisation Bill 2014 was presented and passed by both houses of the Parliament during the last session of the Fifteenth Lok Sabha in February 2014. It received President's assent on 1 March 2014.

## Organisation of the Volume

An attempt has been made in this volume to place Ambedkar's writings and speeches in the context in which they were presented. His ideas on the issue of states reorganisation developed over a period of time. He began to speak and write on the issue as early as 1938 and continued to do so until his death in 1956, a period when the issue acquired tremendous political significance in the country. He wrote, as discussed above, on a variety of aspects of reorganisation. The 1940s and 1950s, when Ambedkar wrote his most important essays on reorganisation, were a volatile period in the history of the country when a number of contesting ideas were being put forward. Each of the pieces he wrote was in response to actual events and developments taking place in the country, particularly in the former Bombay Presidency. They can be described as political documents as they engaged closely with the politics of the time.

The following major tracts, reports, speeches and articles written by him on reorganisation of the states are analysed in this volume.

### Tracts and Reports

i. *Pakistan or the Partition of India*, 1941.
ii. 'States and Minorities: What are Their Rights and How to secure them in the Constitution of Free India—Memorandum on the Safeguards for the Scheduled Castes submitted to the Constituent Assembly on behalf of the All India Scheduled Castes Federation', 1947.
iii. 'Maharashtra as a Linguistic Province: Statement Submitted to the Linguistic Provinces Commission', 1948.
iv. 'Thoughts on Linguistic States', 1955.

### Speeches

i. In the Bombay Legislative Assembly on 4 April 1938.
ii. On the Andhra State Bill in the Rajya Sabha on 2 September 1953.
iii. On the States Reorganisation Bill in the Rajya Sabha on 1 May 1956.

### Articles

i. 'Need for Checks and Balances', *The Times of India*, 23 April 1953.

ii. 'Ambedkar's Recipe for Maharashtra: Voice of the People', *The Free Press Journal*, 31 May 1956.

For the purpose of analysis, the writings/speeches of Ambedkar on reorganisation have been divided into periods, parallel to the events of the time. His ideas are studied chronologically because on some key issues, closely watching and analysing political developments, his views underwent change. The first period consists of his early writings beginning 1938 up until 1947 when he began to develop his views on issues of identity, language, minorities, democracy and nationalism on the subcontinent. Ambedkar was very aware of the fact that the colonial structure which was the result of imperial conquest and interests could not serve a democratic India after Independence and there was need to redraw the map of the subcontinent. These ideas hence need to be read and analysed in that context. The period between 1948 and 1954 forms a hiatus when important events took place: Partition, agitation for linguistic states, formation of the state of Andhra and agitation for a unified state of Maharashtra, a state to which he belonged. Accordingly, from 1955 begins a new period when political leaders including Ambedkar began to grapple with the report of the SRC and find solutions out of the conflicting demands for federal reorganisation. Here, Ambedkar addresses seminal issues such as size, economic viability, federal balance, language, minorities, etc. He revisits many issues he had considered earlier in the light of new developments.

Based on this periodisation, we provide a thematic analysis of Ambedkar's ideas as they unfolded over time on the reorganisation of states. The volume is organised in two parts. The first part presents and analyses Ambedkar's ideas on various aspects of states reorganisation. Apart from Introduction, this part has three chapters. The first chapter discusses the early themes in his writings and speeches between 1938 and 1948, and the second chapter focuses on the period between 1948 and 1955. The third chapter puts forward the solutions that Ambedkar offers, from the mid-1950s onwards, along which the reorganisation of the country he argues could take place, discussing the six major themes mentioned above. The second part of the volume is a compendium of his speeches and writings on the subject during the period 1938–56; while tracts, reports and articles are in most cases fully reproduced, in the case of books only excerpts have been provided.

## Notes

1. While opposing the formation of large linguistic states in the Rajya Sabha during the discussion on States Reorganisation Bill, 2 May 1956. Unless stated otherwise, all quotations and reference to Ambedkar's writings have been taken from the relevant documents produced in the second part of this volume.
2. For more discussion on these three rounds, see Sarangi and Pai (2011).
3. For more on this, see Pai (2013).
4. Later renamed as *Pakistan or the Partition of India*, 1945.
5. Forrester (1970) concluded that this kind of sub-regional conflict was an aspect of the growing pains of modernisation and was symptomatic of a new force of sub-regionalism and could well spark off separatist movements in many parts of India such as Rayalaseema, Vidarbha, Marathwada and various other places.
6. This includes the well-known article by G. S. Bhargava, 'India is a Multi-lingual Nation—Not a Multi-national State' (1956). Bhargava very aptly analysed that the reasons of disorder in the country in general and that of Bombay in particular was not because of the acceptance and propagation of the linguistic principle by the Congress, but because of its rejection and manipulation by the party according to its own convenience. The SRC recommendations, according to Bhargava, though by and large accepted the linguistic principle for the states in the south; while proposing the formation of the new Madhya Pradesh and favouring the retention of unwieldy Uttar Pradesh as it is, the commission found respite in the question of administrative convenience. With respect to Bombay and Punjab, all the four principles were subordinated to expediency. Without adducing any reason, the demand for a separate Maharashtra State with the city of Bombay as capital was turned down. So too was the idea of a Punjabi State, which was not entertained at all. However, Bhargava in his analysis does not mention the writings of Ambedkar.
7. Authored by Krishna P. Mukerji and Suhasini Ramaswamy of the Bombay University it was published by Popular Book Depot, Bombay. For more details, see Shah (1955).
8. Noorani describes how Nehru was influenced by his rather emotional confidant V. K. Krishna Menon who viewed the recommendations of the SRC pertaining to the creation of separate states—particularly Kerala and Tamil Nadu—as inadvisable for economic, political, administrative, strategic and national security reasons. He looked upon the sectarian sub-nationalism as fascist, anti-national, and ultimately leading towards balkanisation. Menon's emotional statement, 'we will Balkanise India if we further dismember the State instead of creating larger units' such as 'Southern State, a Dakshin Pradesh, as a corollary to Uttar Pradesh, which could include the present Tamil Nadu, Travancore, Cochin, Malabar and possibly Kanara up to Kasaragode' was so much liked by Nehru that he circulated this note among his cabinet colleagues. And, as a reply to Menon, Nehru wrote: 'Nobody here likes the proposal for a Kerala State as suggested ... but, this apart, I am sure that it will be bad for Kerala and for its neighbouring States. But what are we to do? No other neighbouring State agrees to have Kerala; Kamaraj Nadar and the Madras Cabinet absolutely

refuse to have anything to do with it. So do the Karnataka people.' It was only in the later years that Nehru was constrained to tell Menon: 'I am afraid you do not quite appreciate the kind of forces we have to contend against in India at the present moment. When you suggest that States should become merely administrative divisions and far greater power should be concentrated in the Centre, you say something which is utterly beyond anyone's capacity to do at the present moment.'

9. Chatterjee describes how Ambedkar discusses both the Muslim and the Hindu case for a separate nation and then the alternatives available to the communities, if there was no partition. The most striking feature of the argument presented by Ambedkar, Chatterjee opines, was that he adopted a position of perfect neutrality, with no stake either in the Muslim or Hindu side. Ambedkar comes to the conclusion that partition would be better for both Muslims and Hindus. He showed that Hindu dominance could be a serious threat in a united India where more than a third of the population was Muslim. Following Partition, the Muslims in Hindustan would be a small and widely-scattered minority with little ground left for a party like the Hindu Mahasabha which would wither away. And as for the lower orders of Hindu society, they would make common cause with the Muslim minority to fight the Hindu high castes for their rights of citizenship and social dignity.
10. This can be traced back to the early 1920s when Congress Committees were formed, more or less, on the basis of linguistic area. However, this was officially incorporated into the Constitution of the Congress in May 1928 on the basis of recommendations of a committee set up under the chairmanship of Motilal Nehru to 'determine the principles of the Constitution for India' (the other seven members of the committee were Ali Imam, Tej Bahadur Sapru, M. S. Aney, Sardar Mangal Singh, Shuaib Quraisshi, Subhas Chandra Bose and G. R. Pradhan). The committee submitted its report, also known as Nehru Report on 10 August 1928. The resolution was reaffirmed in October 1937, July 1938, and again in the election manifesto of 1945–46. On 27 November 1947, Prime Minister Nehru on behalf of the Government of India accepted the principle underlying the demand for linguistic provinces in the Constituent Assembly. For more details on the Nehru Report, see Rao (1967a: 58–75); See also, Editorial (1953).
11. The Communist Party of India had accepted this resolution on the problem of nationalities and the future state structure of India at the Party Congress in 1943. For more details, see Mishra (1972).
12. For a more detailed discussion see Sarangi and Pai (2011).
13. The Constitution (Seventh Amendment) Act, 1956, inter alia, substituted a new Article 371, the relevant part of which reads: Article 371(1): 'Notwithstanding anything in this Constitution, the President may, by order made with respect to the State of Andhra Pradesh … provide for the constitution and functions of regional committees of the Legislative Assembly of the State, for the modifications to be made in the rules of business of the Government and in the rules of procedure of the Legislative Assembly of the State and for any special responsibility of the Governor in order to secure the proper functioning of the

regional committees.' The Public Employment (Requirement as to Residence) Act, 1957, was enacted inter alia to provide for employment opportunities for residents of Telangana area and soon a Regional Committee of the Legislative Assembly of the state was also constituted in 1958.

14. Andhra Pradesh, which is the fourth-largest state in India, unlike other big states has very large districts both in size and population. An all-India comparison of districts shows that Andhra Pradesh stands at the top on the list with nearly 12,000 sq km as the average size (more than double the average size of a district in the country) and 36,80,675 (approximately) as the average population (more than double the average population of a district in the country). Even the smallest of all districts in size (Srikakulam: 5837 sq km; ignoring Hyderabad which is just 227 sq km) and population (Vizianagaram: 22,45,103) is bigger than the all-India averages respectively. The other two states with more than double the average size of the districts of the country—Rajasthan (the largest state) and Jammu and Kashmir (the sixth-largest state)—however, do not face any such demand. The largeness of the districts of Andhra Pradesh in light of the sustained movement for Telangana over the last 60 years, certainly may have added its share to the rising discontent.

# 1

# Preparing the Ground

## Early Writings of Ambedkar on States Reorganisation

Dr Ambedkar's ideas on future territorial reorganisation of the Indian subcontinent—once Independence was achieved—began to be formed in the late colonial period. These ideas crystallised in response to British attempts to restructure the provinces and the demands made by the national movement. The provinces established by the British through conquest and for military and administrative convenience, had remained largely unchanged. But with rise of the national movement, feelings of regional awareness had begun to emerge within the provinces. This is evident in the violent opposition by the people in Bengal to the attempt of the colonial government to divide the province in 1905. With the support of the national movement, it ultimately led to annulment in 1909. In the 1920s with rising regional consciousness, the Indian National Congress (INC) under the leadership of Gandhi put forward the idea of reorganisation of the provinces along linguistic lines and divided its own provincial branches along linguistic lines thereby encouraging such feelings. A number of language movements in various provinces also encouraged the idea of reorganisation of the subcontinent along linguistic lines.

The British government on its part (through its Montague–Chelmsford Reforms which formed the basis of the Government of India Act 1919) had already rejected the linguistic reorganisation of provinces as impractical. However, a decade later, the British administration recognised the necessity for the creation of linguistic states (particularly Orissa) and asked the Simon Commission to report on the matter. The Commission reported in favour of the creation of linguistic states. This forced the government to set up a Boundary Commission under the chairmanship of Samuel O' Donnell to examine and report on administrative, financial and other consequences of setting up a separate administration and demarcate the boundaries of Orissa Province in September 1931. And finally, Orissa Province and Sind Province were created in 1936 and 1937 respectively.

The INC had been supporting the idea of linguistic states in many forums and movements. Sachchidananda Sinha, an INC member in the Imperial Council, had moved a resolution for the amalgamation of the Oriya-speaking tracts into a single unit within the existing province of Bihar and Orissa. In 1927, in a resolution supporting the redistribution of provinces on the linguistic basis, it referred to the right of self determination of the people speaking the same language and bound by the same tradition and culture. The Motilal Nehru Report of 1928 also examined this demand in detail and recommended to take into account factors such as administrative convenience and financial viability along with 'people's wishes and the linguistic unity of the area' concerned. It is against this backdrop that the early speeches and writings of Ambedkar on the question of reorganisation are examined in this chapter.

Ambedkar's ideas on the advantages and disadvantages of linguistic states began to be formed during the late 1930s. One of his earliest statements on reorganisation was a lengthy speech in the Bombay Legislative Assembly (BLA) in response to a resolution introduced by a member of the assembly in 1938, for the formation of a separate Kanarese-speaking state of Karnatak carved out of parts of the Madras and Bombay presidencies and some princely states. By this time, the Act of 1935 had been adopted and it was obvious that Independence would be granted very soon and the map of India would be redrawn. Ambedkar, on this occasion, had risen to oppose the resolution on the ground that the feeling of Indianness was still in its embryo and had just begun to ripen. Therefore, to allow other loyalties or feeling of culture or feeling of nationality—whether on the basis of religion or region or language such as Kanarese or Gujarati—to grow simultaneously, Ambedkar believed, was the greatest crime to commit. The second occasion was in 1941 through his book *Thoughts on Pakistan*, written in response to the resolution on the 'Two Nation Theory' by the Muslim League in its annual session held in Lahore (22 March–24 March 1940). This worried Ambedkar and he felt that it was necessary to ponder over the issue by connecting it with the larger debate on nation, nationality and citizenship. Ambedkar also explores the impact of the division of the Indian subcontinent along communal and linguistic lines.

The third occasion of Ambedkar's expression came after Independence in 1948 through his written statement to the Linguistic Provinces Commission. The Linguistic Provinces Commission, also known as the Dar Commission (after its Chairman) was set up on 21 February 1948 on the recommendation of Ambedkar in his capacity as Chairman of the Drafting Committee of the Constituent Assembly (appointed on 30 August 1947). The agitation for linguistic provinces—particularly Andhra—had increased during the period of transfer of power. The supporters held a conference in Delhi on 8 December 1946, a day before the inaugural meet of the Constituent Assembly.[1] Pattabhi Sitaramayya in his presidential address repeated the demand for linguistic provinces, called upon the Assembly to accept the same in principle and set up the machinery for redistribution. Later when the Assembly met for the first time, many members supporting the demand submitted four memorandums in the first three weeks. The Steering Committee (under the Chairmanship of Dr Rajendra Prasad) had earlier decided that the Assembly, was not competent to take up the issue;[2] but the Constituent Assembly under the increasing pressure of the agitators since the early months of 1947 could not resist it further (Rao 1967b: 613).[3] Soon after Independence, on 27 November 1947, Prime Minister Nehru made an announcement on behalf of the Government of India in the Constituent Assembly. He accepted the principle underlying the demand for linguistic provinces and mentioned specifically that Andhra could be made a separate unit in the First Schedule of the new Constitution as was done in the case of Sind and Orissa by the Government of India Act. 1935 (Rao 1967d: 439).[4]

Ambedkar, however, felt that mere listing of Andhra as a separate state in the First Schedule of the Constitution would not suffice as the issue of linguistic reorganisation needed to be examined together with that of other linguistic regions. He therefore, on 21 February 1948 recommended that a Commission be appointed immediately to enquire into and work out all relevant matters not only as regards Andhra but also other linguistic regions.[5] Accordingly, the Dar Commission was appointed on 17 June 1948 to 'examine and report on the formation of the new provinces of Andhra, Karnatak, Kerala and Maharashtra and on the administrative, financial and other consequences of the creation of such new provinces.'[6]

At Independence there were similarities in the views of Nehru and Ambedkar on the subject of reorganisation. While both were not opposed to the idea of linguistic reorganisation in principle, they were worried about the impact it would have on the fragile unity and security of India. Nehru was initially attracted to the idea of linguistic reorganisation, but Partition and the riots that followed immediately brought a change in his thinking. He realised that reorganisation based on language was problematic in the prevailing situation. There was need to concentrate upon the security and unity of the country, and a pressing need to look after defence, food, refugees, inflation, production, etc. Ambedkar however was more dispassionate and felt that objective criteria had to be drawn to decide whether a proposed linguistic state would be viable and states which satisfied that should be formed. At this stage both were agreeable to large states, an idea that Ambedkar was to change in the mid-1950s. However, there were major differences in the principles underlying, method of implementation and the desired outcomes between the ideas of Nehru and Ambedkar.

When the Dar Commission started looking into the issue, Ambedkar, not as Chairman of the Drafting Committee but as a person who understood Maharashtra in great detail and had been active in state politics since the 1920s, presented a written statement—'Maharashtra as a Linguistic Province'—to the Commission. This is a key document of his thoughts on reorganisation. Many of his later ideas about the merits and demerits of the proposal for linguistic provinces, particularly in reference to the formation of the state of Maharashtra, find genesis in this document. Here he had clearly stated that there was nothing new in the demand for linguistic provinces by Bombay, Madras and the Central Provinces, as six provinces—namely East Punjab, United Provinces, Bihar, West Bengal, Assam and Orissa—already existed as linguistic provinces. Thus, when the principle of linguistic provinces is accepted in the case of six provinces, three others asking for the same principle to be applied, cannot be asked to wait indefinitely. It is important to note that Ambedkar's position, since he spoke last on this issue in the Bombay Legislative Assembly in 1938, discussed above, had changed significantly.

However, the report of the Commission submitted on 10 December 1948—despite showing some desire for linguism—after discussing the advantages and disadvantages of such a step, warned against the formation of linguistic provinces as they would have a 'sub-national bias' and would militate against the welding of India into one nation. Further, the Commission held that it could be 'safely assumed that linguistic groups as sub-nations do not exist anywhere at present' and went on to argue that if 'the intentions were to bring sub-nations into existence, there could not be a better way of doing it' than by creating linguistic states. The Commission also held that the conditions to be considered for an area to be properly formed into a state were geographical contiguity, financial self-sufficiency, capacity for future development and the consent of the people affected. It found no reason in the formation of new provinces out of those referred to them and suggested that reorganisation for some of the existing states could be taken up in the future only after the Indian states had been integrated and Indian nationality well established (GoI 1948).[7]

Some of the themes that were present in Ambedkar's speech in the BLA and in his statement to the Linguistic Commission—'Maharashtra as a Linguistic Province'—are discussed below.

## Pros and Cons of Linguistic States

Speaking in the BLA in 1938, Ambedkar pointed out that though the power to create new states was not vested in the respective legislatures and could only be done by the governor-general; if at all the issue of linguistic reorganisation was to be discussed in the Assembly, it needed to be based on dispassionate and on well spelt out criteria of nation-building.

Ambedkar examined the idea of a separate Karnatak State on the basis of whether the areas to be separated had suffered by being part of the Bombay Presidency, in terms of obtaining adequate representation, holding office or finance. He also asked if breaking away and forming their own state would bring them any significant gain. He felt that the city of Bombay was neither wholly Marathi- nor wholly Gujarati- nor wholly Kanarese-speaking. On a purely population basis, considering the 81 seats which had gone to the Marathi-speaking people, Ambedkar argued, the Gujarati-speaking people (who were 16 per cent of the population) should have got 27 seats and the Kanarese-speaking people (who were 12 per cent of the population) should have got 21 seats. However, the seats given to them—31 and 28 respectively—were higher than their population percentage.

Similarly, regarding the distribution of the 16 offices in the two houses in the Bombay Presidency, according to Ambedkar, the Marathi-speaking people's quota was 9.3, the Gujarati-speaking people's quota was 3.6, and the quota of the Kanarese-speaking people was 3.1. However, the actual distribution of offices had been 6, 6 and 4 respectively. Thus, Ambedkar argued that the Kanarese-speaking people, had not been done any injustice either in the matter of seats or offices and had not suffered in any way by remaining within the Bombay Presidency.

Ambedkar also raised the important question of finance. He pointed out that the new province was not economically viable. He held that bringing together 'all the limbs'—i.e. parts of a region into a state, as had happened in Orissa—was not as important as to being able to provide food for them. It was better to not create small provinces without the revenue needed to run a local board. He warned that the formation of a province would satisfy the ambition of a few persons who wish to emerge as its leaders, but such a move might leave the population without food, clothing and shelter. He specifically added that many of the districts out of which Karnatak State was being proposed—such as Bijapur or Bellary—were famine-stricken and would not yield enough revenue to look after the needs of the people in it. Thus, Ambedkar was clear that reorganisation of provinces should not be carried out purely based on the emotive feelings of culture and linguistic identity, but on well thought out economic and political principles.

Although Ambedkar carried forward some of these ideas in his tract, 'Maharashtra as a Linguistic Province' (1948/1979), his opinion on the issue of linguism had changed significantly. He did not accept the claims forwarded by the supporters of linguistic provinces that Indian provinces had all the elements of a 'distinct nationality' and they should be 'allowed to grow to their fullest in nationhood', he agreed that the popular demand for linguistic states had to be recognised and examined as claims and counterclaims were being made. He strongly felt that there were distinct advantages in creating linguistic provinces in the country.

Ambedkar argued that democracy and linguistic provincialism

are complementary processes. Democracy works better in linguistic provinces rather than in mixed provinces; a linguistic province produces what democracy needs, namely social homogeneity, i.e. a common language and culture that can promote unity. In contrast, heterogeneity in a state with a democratic structure creates division into hostile groups and power is used to promote the interests of a particular group allowing it to dominate over the others. Greater social homogeneity leads to greater democracy as there are fewer social barriers and antipathy. Pointing to history, Ambedkar argues that wherever there are high levels of heterogeneity in the population the chances of hostility, discrimination, neglect, suppression and domination of one group over the other are greater (ibid.).

In sum, forcefully juxtaposing heterogeneous peoples into a common system of governance may create and promote hatred between them as they do not have feelings of belongingness to begin with. On the other hand, a state which is homogeneous in its population can work for the true ends of democracy, for there are no artificial barriers or social antipathies which lead to the misuse of political power. Pointing to the intense enmity between Maharashtrians and Gujaratis or Andhrites and Tamilians, Ambedkar held that separate linguistic states would remove those cultural tensions and strengthen democracy. He also pointed out that until then the presence of the Congress party and the leadership of Nehru had held them together, but as these features gradually disappear, the situation would not remain the same.

However, Ambedkar was well aware that the demand for linguistic provinces is an 'explosive force that carried with it all the force of blowing up the nation'. And therefore, he cautiously points out all the dangers that were inherent and those that could arise if the map of India was redrawn along linguistic lines (ibid.).

First, a linguistic state with its own language could in time develop into an 'independent nationality' and India could become a 'medieval' society consisting of warring states. Considering that separate federal and state governments would be created which would enjoy autonomy, Ambedkar felt that it could create as many nations as there were groups with pride in their language and culture leading to the central legislature becoming an arena of 'separate and solidified nations' with a mentality of political insubordination that would make the working of the central government impossible. Second, it would be fatal to the maintenance of the necessary administrative and judicial relations between the Centre and the provinces. If each province adopts its own language as the official language the central government will have to correspond in as many official languages as there are linguistic provinces.

As a solution to these problems, Ambedkar suggested, 'There is no danger in creating linguistic provinces. Danger lies in creating linguistic provinces with the language of each province as its official language.' The fear that linguistic states with their provincial language as official language may lead to 'the creation of Provincial nationalities' and ruin the idea of 'United India' can be averted if the Constitution of India mandated that the 'official language of every province shall be the same as the official language of the Central Government'. He found it necessary for sustaining the cultural unity. Under no circumstances, Ambedkar argued, should the linguistic provinces be allowed to make their provincial languages as official (languages).

## The Question of Maharashtra

It is against this backdrop that Ambedkar (1948/1979) argues whether Maharashtra should be made into a separate province. While agreeing that Maharashtra was united by language, Ambedkar applies three criteria or tests that a region must satisfy to be declared *viable* and thereby qualified to become a province: it must be of a certain size, it must have a certain volume of population and it must have a commensurate amount of revenue. In sum, a province must not only be self-supporting and (even if it agrees to live on a lower plane) it must have sufficient revenue to provide for a minimum standard of administration required for efficiency and the needs of social welfare. However, the issues of minorities and their position are not ignored in his discussion.

Regarding the issue of size, as shown in Table 1.1 here, Ambedkar presented the figures for the Maharashtra province in its two forms, viz. abridged: 12 districts of the Bombay Presidency and eight districts of Central Province and Berar, and unabridged: all the area occupied by the Marathi-speaking people as one single province. He made this classification in order to explain that even without the area and population of the Marathi-speaking people in various states, the proposed Maharashtra province would comprise an area of 84,151 square miles with a population of 1,54,33,400.

Table 1.1: Two Forms of Maharashtra

| | *Territory* | *Area in square miles* | *Total Population of the Territory* | *Total Marathi-speaking Population of the Territory* | *Percentage of Marathi-speaking Population to Total Population* |
|---|---|---|---|---|---|
| Abridged | 12 districts of the Bombay Presidency | 47,284 | 1,29,13,544 | 1,00,45,100 | 77.8 |
| | 8 Districts of CP and Berar | 36,865 | 70,20,694 | 53,88,300 | 76.7 |
| | Total | 84,151 | 1,99,34,238 | 1,54,33,400 | 77.4 |
| Unabridged | States within Bombay Presidency | 11,314 | 27,20,207 | 21,20,700 | 77.9 |
| | Marathi-speaking districts of Hyderabad State | 22,766 | 42,49,272 | 32,99,300 | 77.6 |
| | Goa | 1534 | 5,80,000 | 5,20,000 | 89.6 |
| | State of Bastar | 13,701 | 6,33,888 | 2,12,300 | 33.5 |
| | Total | 49,315 | 81,83,367 | 61,42,300 | – |
| | GRAND TOTAL | 1,33,466 | 2,81,17,605 | 2,15,85,700 | 76.8 |
| Comparison with USA | Delaware (the state with smallest area in USA) | 2057 | | | |
| | New York (the state with highest population in USA) | | 1,26,32,890 | | |

*Source*: Prepared by the authors based on two tables in Ambedkar (1948/1979).

Turning to the revenue side of the province, he points out that existing estimates showed that the total annual revenue at the existing rate of taxation which would accrue to the abridged Maharashtra province will be approximately Rs 25,61,51,000. Further, a comparison with other states being proposed in the Union of India showed that Maharashtra would be not merely viable but a strong province in terms of area, population and revenue.

Table 1.2: Comparison of Annual Revenues of Existing and Proposed Linguistic Provinces

| *Province* | *Area in square miles* | *Population* | *Annual Revenue* |
|---|---|---|---|
| Existing Linguistic Provinces | | | |
| United Provinces | 1,06,247 | 5,50,20,617 | 32,65,08,000 |
| Bihar | 69,745 | 3,63,40,151 | 16,26,78,000 |
| Orissa | 32,198 | 82,28,544 | 4,60,62,000 |
| New Linguistic Provinces | | | |
| Andhra | 70,000 | 1,90,00,000 | – |
| Karnatak | 25,000 | 45,00,000 | – |
| Kerala | 6000 | 35,00,000 | – |

*Source*: Ambedkar (1948/1979).

Based on these calculations, Ambedkar grapples with the controversy whether Maharashtra should be united into one province, or two sub-provinces: one province consisting of the Marathi-speaking districts of Bombay Presidency and the other of the Marathi-speaking districts of the colonial provinces of CP and Berar. At this point in 1948, he argues that all the Marathi-speaking districts should be united as the sub-divisions have no support from the public and arise merely out of the fear among some politicians in CP and Berar that their political careers would suffer vis-à-vis the tall leaders of Bombay Presidency. Thus, Ambedkar (1948/1979) argues that all areas which are contiguous and speak the same language must be brought together to create larger provinces, there should be no room for 'choice' or 'self-determination'. This, as we shall see, was an idea that Ambedkar was to change by 1955.

The most controversial issue in the reorganisation of Maharashtra was regarding the city of Bombay. Two proposals were being forwarded: the creation of linguistic states should be postponed or Bombay City should be made a separate state. The pressure for this came mainly from Gujarati businessmen / industrialists who had settled for long in the city. Ambedkar swiftly dismissed both the pleas—the first as 'escapism' and second as 'irrational'. Replying on the first plea, he said that the issues involved were so important that it should be faced squarely and decided immediately (ibid.).

Ambedkar holds that the second plea, which claims that Bombay was never part of Maharashtra or of the Maratha Empire, is invalid. He felt that the 'verdict of history' may not help decide this issue, but that 'Geography favoured Bombay's inclusion in Maharashtra'. He held that Bombay's situation on the coast close to Daman and Karwar has made it a part of Maharashtra. The Maratha Empire was a land-based power, and did not care to conquer Bombay and become a sea power. Ambedkar also refutes the question about the percentage of Marathi-speaking population of Bombay. He opines that 'if people from all parts of India were allowed to come to Bombay and settle there, why should the Maharashtrians suffer? The present state of the population cannot therefore be ground to lessen the claim of Maharashtrians on Bombay?'

Regarding the claims of Gujarati businessmen, who were long settled in Bombay, Ambedkar pointed out that they did not come to Bombay voluntarily. 'They were brought by the East India Company in 1671 as *Adatias* or go-betweens to help them in their trade', and they were granted exclusive trading rights—such as land for warehouses, liberty to trade in the ships of East India Company without paying customs, and many more. Thus, the monopoly of Gujarati businessmen on the trade in Bombay was 'not on the basis of free and equal competition with other traders', but on the basis of the favours granted by the Europeans to the Gujaratis. Ambedkar emphasised that Bombay was an 'emporium' and a port that served the whole country, not merely the Gujaratis. However, he states, this should not be the basis to deny Maharashtrians the right to Bombay who in turn should not discriminate against Gujarati businessmen who might be in a minority in Bombay. Such discrimination, Ambedkar points out, can take place in any state against business minorities which should be dealt with by the law and the courts. Besides, he also held that to argue that Maharashtrians would live off the surplus generated by Gujaratis was devoid of any substance. The surplus generated by trade and commerce in Bombay, he feels, will be spent on the rest of the province. It will help bear the expenditure of the government and contribute to the central pool from which the whole country will benefit. Ambedkar pointed out that such arguments could also be made with regard to Calcutta where, although a commercial and industrial hub, Bengalis are a minority. Calcutta, despite being part of the Bengal province, has been fruitful for both Bengal as well as the whole of eastern India.

Ambedkar also pointed that in deciding upon the issue of exclusion of Bombay from Maharashtra, it would also have to take into account the position of Calcutta, which, like Bombay, was the chief emporium of the whole of eastern part of India. Like the Maharashtrians in Bombay the Bengalis did not own the trade and industry of Calcutta. The position of the Bengalis vis-à-vis Calcutta was worse than the position of the Maharashtrians vis-à-vis Bombay. For, the Maharashtrians could at least claim that they have supplied labour if not capital for the trade and industry of Bombay, the Bengalis cannot even say this.

Dealing with the arguments that multilingual states would be better for the country and that reorganisation should be on 'rational' rather than linguistic lines, Ambedkar held that such arguments were 'too late' as the people of Maharashtra and the rest of the country have shown great desire for linguistic states. He in fact feels that those making these arguments are doing so to keep Bombay out of Maharashtra. Moreover, he is dismissive of the use of the ideas of Lord Acton who refers to 'inferior and superior races' and 'nationalities' living together, resulting in state and nation being made commensurate leading to the stronger races ruling over and even exterminating the inferior. He wonders which group is inferior—Maharashtrians or Gujaratis? States reorganisation, he points out, is for administrative purposes and in every area there will be a numerically dominant community hence the problem is not limited to Maharashtra but will have to be recognised and dealt with in every state. The remedy, he strongly feels, is not a 'mixed state' but a strong state which ensures that power is not captured by a 'communal majority' but is exercised in the name of the people as a whole.

Finally, Ambedkar also points out that the creation of Greater Bombay by adding some parts of Maharashtra may not be a self-sufficient province based on the present level of taxation. It cannot be compared to provinces such as Assam or Orissa; it would require much greater revenue to sustain and would not be worthwhile. Moreover, to force Maharashtrians to do so, merely to satisfy Gujarati sentiments and demand, would be unfair just as the suggestion that the problem should be settled by arbitration he finds absurd. Thus, he comes to the conclusion that Maharashtra and Bombay are 'not merely inter-dependent, they are really one and integral. Severance between the two would be fatal to both.'

## Protection of Minorities

Ambedkar's ideas on the protection of minorities developed during the long movement he led for the depressed classes beginning in the 1920s. While most leaders did not pay attention to this issue, Ambedkar discussed it in many of his writings and speeches as he was very concerned about the impact reorganisation would have on smaller disadvantaged groups, specially the Scheduled Castes (SCs). He was able to relate the issue of reorganisation to both the position of SCs in the states that were to be formed as well as to adequate representation for them arising out his experiences of the Poona Pact.[8]

One of the grounds on which Ambedkar opposed the demand for carving out the separate linguistic state of Karnatak out of Madras Presidency, in his speech in the BLA, was protection of the interests of the minorities in linguistic provinces. He stated that being a member of a minority group, he was bound to consider the issue of formation of a Karnatak State from the standpoint of that minority. He held that 'along with the process of dismemberment of these Provincial areas there is going to be a dismemberment of the minorities' and therefore, the minorities did not feel a sense of belonging to the separate state of Maharashtra, Karnatak or Madras.

Ambedkar pointed out that while he was very glad that several members of the BLA who spoke in favour of the resolution did give an assurance that the interests of the Muslims and the interests of the SCs would be looked after, dismemberment of the SC community cannot be allowed leaving them dependent on the promised generosity and kindness of the majority community. The SCs who form a microscopic community wanted rights, not generosity; even weightage would not help as they are just a few lakhs in the population. The new province would on the one hand divide the Kanarese and the Marathas, and internally it would be a province dominated by the Lingayats. Thus, Ambedkar opposed the formation of a separate province on the grounds that the SCs would, in the process, lose even the strength they had in the existing polyglot province. The formation of a separate state of Karnatak as proposed would neither provide any greater benefits to Kanarese than they enjoy in the present dispensation, nor would it provide better protection to the minorities (including SCs) against the tyranny of the majority.

The issue of minorities once again assumed greater significance when the Constituent Assembly began its proceedings to draft the Constitution for a new India. The Constituent Assembly had set up an Advisory Committee to look into the issues related to minorities. The Advisory Committee further set up a sub-Committee on Minorities and Fundamental Rights.[9] It was due to the efforts of Ambedkar that the term 'minority', here did not denote only the numerical status of the group but also the claim that the group suffered from some kind of disadvantage with respect to the rest.[10] Thus, for the purpose of the Sub-Committee, SCs too were included in the definition of minorities.[11]

It is in these two committees that Ambedkar took up the question of the position of the SCs in detail. By 1947, it had become evident to Ambedkar that the British would transfer power into the hands of the leadership of the INC and would not recognise the SCs as a separate group in the negotiations preceding the transfer of power. Hence, the primary role of the Scheduled Caste Federation of India (SCFI)—a political party formed by Ambedkar in the late colonial period to protect the interests of the SCs—was to demand two safeguards for the SCs in independent India: separate electorates and protective discrimination.[12]

Consequently, in 1947 at the request of the Working Committee of the SCFI, Ambedkar wrote 'States and Minorities' as a memorandum to submit before the advisory committee. Later it was published as a pamphlet for the public. In 'States and Minorities', Ambedkar added a third demand on behalf of the SCFI: safeguards for the SCs who would be living in the states formed in the new federal structure.[13] He drafted the memorandum in the form of Articles for a constitution for a 'United States of India' as it was to be presented to the Constituent

Assembly. He compiled detailed notes and tables about the population of SCs in all states and its numerical minority status in relation to other communities. At the heart of the memorandum was the effort to ensure justice for minorities. He made special provisions for representation of minorities in the Legislature and the Executive with safeguards against the arbitrary removal of representatives of minorities. To prevent tyranny of the majority it provided for the representatives of the majority in the Executive to be elected by the whole house by single transferable vote and the representatives of the different minorities in the cabinet to be elected by members of each minority community by single transferable vote. A member of the cabinet can resign but can be removed only by impeachment by the House on the ground of corruption or treason. Each state of the Union should have an Officer called the Superintendent of Minority Affairs whose position would be similar to the Auditor General who would provide an annual report on the condition of minorities which would be placed before the Union Legislature and state legislatures. The memorandum also declares 'social boycott' of any group or person, or threat of a boycott, as an offence. Defining the term it provides detailed rules to prevent it from taking place under any circumstance or place.

The memorandum also appeals for guaranteed representation to SCs in the Legislature, Executive and civil services in ratio to their number in the population. Weightage where it was necessary to reduce a huge communal majority to reasonable dimensions it was provided should come out of the share of the majority and not at the cost of another minority community. Weightage carved out of the share of the majority should be divided among all minority communities equally or in inverse proportion to their economic position, social status and educational advance. Regarding the method of election it argued for adult franchise together with abolition of the Poona Pact and the introduction of the system of separate electorates. A similar system would be there for local bodies also. In the case of the civil services the conditions of services should not abrogate any concessions given by the Government of India to SCs and on every Public Service Commission there should be at least one SC representative.

Most important, the Constitution of the United States of India would undertake to make the safeguards described, part of the Constitutional law of India. The memorandum held that the provisions for Scheduled

Castes should not be altered, amended or abrogated except in accordance with prescribed rules. An amendment must be initiated as a resolution in the Lower House of the Legislature, not before 25 years had elapsed since the making of the Constitution and six months notice has been given to the House by the mover. On the passing of such a resolution, the Legislature would be dissolved, a new election held, the original resolution moved afresh in the new House and shall be deemed to have been passed if a majority of two-thirds of the members as well as two-thirds of members of the SCs elected through separate electorates pass it. The memorandum also provides safeguards for SCs in the Indian states by making it a precedent condition for every state that wishes to be admitted into the Indian Union, to agree that it would abide by all the safeguards provided in the Constitution for SCs.

As a leader of the SCs, which constituted an important minority in the Indian states, and as a person who held some very definite and distinct views on the subject, Ambedkar was very hopeful that the Constituent Assembly would include him as a member of the States Committee—set up on 21 December 1946—where he could argue for the protection of the interests of the SCs in the newly-formed states. But this did not happen. Expressing his sentiments, Ambedkar wrote:

> It was my hope that the Constituent Assembly would elect me to the States Committee. Evidently, it has found men of superior calibre for the work. It may also be because I am one of those who are outside the tabernacle and therefore undesirable. I am not sorry to find myself left out. My only regret is that I have lost an opportunity to which I was looking forward for placing my views for the consideration of the Committee. I have therefore chosen to do the next best thing—namely, to incorporate them in this brochure along with the Rights of Citizens, of Minorities and of the Scheduled Castes so that a wider public may know what they are, may value them for what they are worth and may make such use of them as it may deem fit. (Ambedkar 1947/1979)

## Nation and Nationality

Before we move to an analysis of Ambedkar's views on linguistic reorganisation of the country after Independence, there is one other aspect he wrote about in the late colonial period which needs attention as it places his later work in a historical context. Soon after Ambedkar opposed the formation of a separate Karnatak State describing division of states on the single basis of language and identity as undesirable in the BLA in 1938, the Muslim League in its annual session held in Lahore (22 March–24 March 1940) passed a resolution based on the 'Two Nation Theory'. Rejecting the ideology of a united India, it demanded the creation of an independent Muslim state consisting of Punjab, North-West Frontier Provinces (NWFP), Sindh and Baluchistan in the north-west, and Bengal and Assam in the north-east. Reacting to this, Ambedkar felt it necessary to ponder over the issues raised by Muslim League by connecting them to a larger debate on nation, nationality and citizenship in his book *Thoughts on Pakistan* written in 1941.[14] Taking recourse to history to define nationality, Ambedkar said that it was 'imbedded in the democratic theory of the sovereignty of the will of a people'. It did not require to be supported by any 'list of grievances', the will of the people was enough to justify it. It was a 'social feeling' and a 'corporate sentiment of oneness' which was double-edged, those charged with it felt that they were kith and kin. 'It is a feeling of "consciousness of kind" which on the one hand binds together those who have it, so strongly that it over-rides all differences arising out of economic conflicts or social gradations and, on the other, severs them from those who are not of their kind. It is a longing not to belong to any other group.'

Ambedkar then proceeds in the book to discuss a number of other seminal issues such as, when does a community become a nationality, what constitutes a 'People', what are the principles of self-determination and under what circumstances do they apply, etc. However, for the purpose of this study, two issues that Ambedkar writes about are of great relevance: division of the subcontinent along communal lines and its division along linguistic lines. Ambedkar refutes the claim by the Muslim League that Muslims in India form a separate nation by arguing that in terms of language, custom and identity there is little difference between the two communities. He pointed out that the social life of many Muslim groups was honeycombed with Hindu customs. For instance, 'the Avans of the Punjab, though they are nearly all Muslims, retained Hindu names and kept their genealogies in the Brahmanic fashion.' (Ambedkar 1945/1990: 15) Similarly, Hindu surnames were found among Muslims. For instance, 'the surname Chaudhari was a Hindu surname but is common among the Musalmans of UP and the Northern India.' (ibid.)

> ... there is no difference of race between the Hindus and the Muslims. That the Punjabi Musalman and the Punjabi Hindu, the UP Musalman and the UP Hindu, the Bihar Musalman and the Bihar Hindu, the Bengal Musalman and the Bengal Hindu, the Madras Musalman and the Madras Hindu, and the Bombay Musalman and the Bombay Hindu were racially of one stock. Indeed there was more racial affinity between the Madras Musalman and the Madras Brahmin than there was between the Madras Brahmin and the Punjab Brahmin. In the second place, reliance was placed upon linguistic unity between Hindus and Muslims. It was said that the Musalmans had no common language of their own which could mark them off as a linguistic group separate from the Hindus. On the contrary, there was a complete linguistic unity between the two. In the Punjab, both Hindus and Muslims spoke Punjabi. In Sind, both spoke Sindhi. In Bengal, both spoke Bengali. In Maharashtra, both spoke Marathi. So was in every province. It was only in towns that the Musalmans spoke Urdu and the Hindus the language of the province. But outside, in the mofussil, there was complete linguistic unity between Hindus and Musalmans. Thirdly, it was pointed out that India was the land which the Hindus and Musalmans have now inhabited together for centuries. It was not exclusively the land of the Hindus, nor was it exclusively the land of the Mahomedans. (ibid.)

Where then, Ambedkar asks, does the demand for a separate state of Pakistan come from? Ambedkar holds that the communal division was a deliberate creation. He points out that before the Act of 1935, Hindus were in majority in all but three provinces, viz. Punjab, Bengal and the NWFP. Of these, the Muslim majority in the NWFP was not effective, because there was no responsible government in that province. Hence, there were only two provinces—the Punjab and Bengal—wherein the Muslims were in majority and the Hindus in minority. The British agreed to the demands made by the Muslims to separate Sind from Bombay and create a new, self-governing province and second, that the NWFP, which was already a separate province, should be raised to the status of a self-governing province. These four provinces with Muslims in majority and Hindus in minority functioning as autonomous and self-governing provinces were not created by the British authorities for administrative convenience. Ambedkar found an answer to what motive underlay this scheme of Muslim provinces in what he called a 'system of hostages'. Explaining it he argues:

> The Hindus say that the motive for the Muslim insistence, both on statutory majority and separate electorates, was to enable the Muslims in the Muslim Provinces to mobilize and make effective Muslim power in its exclusive form and to the fullest extent possible. ... to place in the hands of the Muslims of the Muslim Provinces an effective weapon to tyrannize their Hindu minorities, in case the Muslim minorities in the Hindu Provinces were tyrannized by their

> Hindu majorities. The scheme thus became a system of protection, in which blast was to be met by counter-blast, terror by terror and tyranny by tyranny. The plan is undoubtedly, a dreadful one, involving the maintenance of justice and peace by retaliation, and providing an opportunity for the punishment of an innocent minority, Hindus in Muslim Provinces and Muslims in Hindu Provinces, for the sins of their co-religionists in other Provinces. It is a scheme of communal peace through a system of communal hostages ... (Ambedkar 1945 / 1990: 15)

Thus, the communal scheme of deciding nationality, for Ambedkar, was not so sacrosanct and absolute a principle as to give it the character of a categorical imperative, over-riding every other consideration. Ambedkar had very clearly stated that 'separation was not quite so essential for the maintenance and preservation of a distinct nationality'. Self-determination for a nationality, Ambedkar observed, though might take the form of cultural independence, its future form must depend upon the territorial layout of the population.

> If a nationality lives in easily severable and contiguous areas, other things being equal, a case can be made out for territorial independence. But where owing to an inextricable intermingling, the nationalities are so mixed up that the areas they occupy are not easily severable; then all that they can be entitled to is cultural independence. Territorial separation in a case like this is impossible. They are doomed to live together. The only other alternative they have is to migrate. (Ambedkar 1945 / 1990: 15)

Ambedkar was equally critical of Gandhi and the INC for introducing the principle of linguistic division of India in the 1920s. This principle was incorporated into the Constitution of the INC in May 1928 on the basis of the recommendation of a committee set up under the Chairmanship of Motilal Nehru (popularly known as the Nehru Report) to 'determine the principles of the Constitution for India'. Following this, the Congress reorganised all its branches throughout the country along linguistic lines. According to this Constitution, India was to be divided into the following provinces with the language and headquarters as follows:

Table 1.3: Provinces with the Language and Headquarters as Proposed in the Congress Constitution, 1928

| *Province* | *Language* | *Headquarters* |
|---|---|---|
| Ajmere-Merwara | Hindustani | Ajmere |
| Andhra | Telegu | Madras |

(Table 1.3 contd.)

(Table 1.3 contd.)

| *Province* | *Language* | *Headquarters* |
|---|---|---|
| Assam | Assamese | Gauhati |
| Bihar | Hindustani | Patna |
| Bengal | Bengali | Calcutta |
| Bombay (City) | Marathi-Gujarati | Bombay |
| Delhi | Hindustani | Delhi |
| Gujarat | Gujarati | Ahmedabad |
| Kamatak | Kannada | Dharwar |
| Kerala | Malayalam | Calicut |
| Mahakosal | Hindustani | Jubbulpore |
| Maharashtra | Marathi | Poona |
| Nagpur | Marathi | Nagpur |
| NWFP | Pushtu | Peshawar |
| Punjab | Punjabi | Lahore |
| Sind | Sindhi | Karachi |
| Tamil Nadu | Tamil | Madras |
| United Provinces | Hindustani | Lucknow |
| Utkal | Oriya | Cuttack |
| Vidarbha (Berar) | Marathi | Akola |

*Source*: Ambedkar (1945 / 1990).

Ambedkar observes that in adopting this principle and subsequently distributing the provinces along linguistic lines, the Congress leaders did not pay due attention to the fact that every administrative unit must be capable of supporting a minimum standard of civilised life, for which it must have sufficient area, population and revenue. The sole determining factor was language. He points out:

> No thought was given to the possibility that it might introduce a disruptive force in the already loose structure of the Indian social life. The scheme was, no doubt, put forth with the sole object of winning the people to the Congress by appealing to their local patriotism. The idea of linguistic provinces has come to stay and the demand for giving effect to it has become so insistent and irresistible that the Congress, when it came into power, was forced to put it into effect. ... Be that as it may, the fact remains that separation on linguistic basis is now an accepted

> principle with the Congress. It is no use saying that the separation of Karnatak and Andhra is based on a linguistic difference and that the claim to separation of Pakistan is based on a cultural difference. This is a distinction without difference. Linguistic difference is simply another name for cultural difference. ... If there is nothing shocking in the separation of Karnatak and Andhra, what is there to shock in the demand for the separation of Pakistan? If it is disruptive in its effect, it is no more disruptive than the separation of Hindu provinces such as Karnatak from Maharashtra or Andhra from Madras. *Pakistan is merely another manifestation of a cultural unit demanding freedom for the growth of its own distinctive culture.* (Ambedkar 1945 / 1990: 14; emphasis added)

Thus, the late colonial period was a time when national leaders began to think about the form that democratic government, particularly its federal character, should assume in post-Independence India. As we have seen starting from late 1930s, Ambedkar had begun to think about the future reorganisation of the Indian subcontinent. The idea of reorganisation along linguistic lines had already been put forward and supported by the INC from the 1920s. However, as Independence neared, the nationalist leadership which had enthusiastically adopted the idea during the colonial period now began to show distance from the same. It was felt that essential tasks of nation-building such as dealing with partition of the country, and the need to integrate the princely states and create a democratic Constitution should be accorded priority. Reorganisation along linguistic lines at that point, it was felt, might lead to divisive tendencies that the newly-formed republic might find difficult to withstand. While Ambedkar shared their concerns about these problems and the need to resolve them, he begins a serious examination of the linguistic principle and its suitability for independent India, a preoccupation which continues till his death in 1956.

Unlike the nationalist leadership, Ambedkar did not have to deal with the numerous agitations taking place regarding reorganisation. He was able to dispassionately consider the advantages and disadvantages of linguistic reorganisation. At this early stage Ambedkar seems ambivalent and open on the issue, seen in his consideration of the pros and cons of forming linguistic states. But his early writings are important as they prepared the ground for his later, more considered views on the subject. There are already glimpses about his concern that reorganisation should not be undertaken on a single basis. Two key issues which he discussed in greater depth in his later work—and which are important features on which he bases his scheme of reorganisation—viability and size, are mentioned though not discussed in detail around this time. He also relates reorganisation to the issues of nationality and protection of minorities, which he felt the INC and the post-Independence leadership were ignoring. This open and broad-based view of the issue of reorganisation enabled Ambedkar to avoid a rigid stand and change his ideas over time in keeping with the events taking place and the decisions made by the national leadership. We turn now to events of the early 1950s which played an important role in Ambedkar's later writings on the issue of states reorganisation.

## Notes

1. A resolution of *Samyukta Maharashtra* (Unified Maharashtra) was passed at Belgaum on 12 May 1946 and a conference, 'Maharashtra Ekikaran Parishad' was organised in Bombay on 28 July 1946 (Rao 1967b: 613, 617–18).
2. The only possibility of redistribution it expressed was in the assurance that India would be made up of the princely states and the provinces, 'whether with their present boundaries or with such others as may be determined by the Constituent Assembly.' (Austin 1967: 241–54)
3. The Union Constitution Committee (of which Dr Ambedkar was a member) and the Provincial Committees, at their joint meetings held on 5 June and 11 June 1947, set up a joint sub-committee to look into the question of forming linguistic provinces. The Joint Sub-Committee with its 10 members—including Dr Ambedkar—met under the chairmanship of B. Pattabhi Sitaramayya on 12 June 1947 and unanimously decided that, 'As soon as the Dominion Status Constitution comes into operation (August 15, 1947), the Dominion Government for the areas concerned should appoint a commission under a Dominion Act, if necessary, to examine the question of creating the proposed new provinces of Andhra, Karnataka, Kerala and Maharashtra and any other proposed provinces that may be specified in the order of appointment. The commission should submit its report as early as possible, so that the new provinces, if any, which it may recommend may be enumerated in the new Constitution and suitable provision made therein on the lines of sections 46 and 289 of the Government of India Act, 1935.' (Rao 1967b: 617–18)
4. However, Nehru added, 'First things must come first, and the first thing is the security and stability of India.' This led to rethinking on the whole question of states reorganisation. Nehru's reluctance to impose divisions of language on the recent division of religion was shared by both Vallabhbhai Patel and Rajagopalachari, and therefore the government was going very slow to look into the matter. This was seen by many as the postponement of state's reorganisation by the Constituent Assembly. See Austin (1967). Also, see Bondurant (1958: 27).
5. Although the issue of linguistic provinces had no direct relation with the drafting of the Constitution—except for the terms of Article 3—it was,

nevertheless, raised frequently in the course of debates in the Constituent Assembly (Bondurant 1958: 27).

6. S. K. Dar, retired Judge of the Allahabad High Court, was appointed the Chairman. Two other members of the Commission were Panna Lall (a retired member of the Indian Civil Service) and Jagatnarain Lal (a member of the Constituent Assembly from Bihar) and B. C. Banerji who was the Secretary of the Commission.
7. The report concluded, 'The formation of provinces on exclusively or even mainly linguistic considerations is not in the larger interest of the Indian Nation and should not be taken in hand. ... In the formation of new provinces, whenever such a work is taken in hand, oneness of language may be one of the factors to be taken into consideration along with others; but it should not be the decisive or even the "main" factor ... if some new provinces come into being and produce more or less linguistic homogeneity they need not be objected to. ... We find that no new provinces out of those referred to us should be formed for the present.'
8. It was Ambedkar who—presenting before Simon Commission in Poona on 23 October 1928 and later representing the depressed classes in the Round Table Conference in London in the 1930s—convinced the British for a separate electorate for the SCs. Granted through Ramsay McDonald Award on 16 August 1932, the provision was soon critically altered (from the system of separate electorates, to reserved seats in joint or undifferentiated electorates) at the Poona Pact which followed Gandhi's fast-unto-death. This system was incorporated in the Government of India Act, 1935, and all the subsequent elections have since been following the same principle.
9. The Advisory Committee comprised of 57 members including Sardar Vallabhbhai Patel as its Chairman. The Advisory Committee submitted its report to the Constituent Assembly on 27 August 1947. Ambedkar was a member of both the Advisory Committee and Sub-Committee. See Rao (1967a, 1967b, 1967c, 1967d, 1968).
10. For more details, see Rao (2009: 118–63).
11. However, the minority status for the SCs had not come with any claim of cultural distinctness from the majority community. Rather, it was said that they were culturally a part of Hinduism, and hence they were only a 'political minority', where the term 'minority' connoted to not that of numerical disadvantage but entitlement to special treatment on account of social and economic 'backwardness'. The inclusion of SCs, however, was regarded unfavourable for the Hindu society by the nationalist school and it consistently sought to exclude the category from the ambit of minority.
12 For details, see Bandyopadhyay (2000).
13 When the Advisory Committee led by Sardar Patel in May 1948 decided to abolish reservations for minorities, including those for the SCs, it was Ambedkar who staged a walkout of the Constituent Assembly and did not attend the House until Congress agreed on the inclusion of certain provisions for the welfare of the untouchables which Ambedkar suggested on 16 November 1949. Congress moved a resolution to substitute the word 'minorities' by the words 'certain classes' and exclude the SCs from the ambit of minority permanently.

See Parkash (2002); Constituent Assembly Debates, vol. 5, p. 227. Also, see Wadhwa (1975: 4–8). On the issue of fundamental rights too, it was Ambedkar who—at a time when voting rights were restricted only to the rich, the landed and the tax payers—envisioned the power of universal adult franchise. He saw elections as a weapon in the hands of the most oppressed sections of society for demanding politico-legal equality. Thus, while demanding reserved seats for SCs, Ambedkar insisted on pushing for universal adult franchise. In his strong defence of universal adult franchise, Ambedkar laid to rest even the argument of illiteracy: 'My feeling is that every man is intelligent enough to understand exactly what he wants. Literacy has not much bearing on this point; a man may be illiterate, none the less he may be very intelligent.' Ambedkar's idea was found to be so radical that Sardar Patel expressed apprehensions that the Indian states may not agree to it and would even view it as encroaching upon their rights. See Rao (1967b). Also, see Vundru (2012).

14. The book published by Thackeray and Company in Bombay in 1941 as a long tract consisting of about 272 pages, 15 chapters, 14 appendices and three maps was republished in 1945 under a new title, *Pakistan or the Partition of India* with a new introduction by Ambedkar. Its original manuscript was a report submitted to the Executive Council of the Indian Labour Party (ILP) in August 1940 (It was later printed for distribution without any change). Following the Lahore Resolution on Pakistan by the Muslim League, the Executive Council of the ILP met to consider what attitude it should adopt towards this project of Pakistan. The Executive Council, though was attracted to the scheme of Pakistan in as much as it meant the creation of ethnic states as a solution of the communal problem, did not, however, feel competent to pronounce at that stage a decided opinion on the issue of Pakistan. It, therefore, resolved to appoint a committee to study the question and make a report on it. The committee consisted of Ambedkar (as the Chairman), M. V. Donde, S. C. Joshi, R. R. Bhole, D. G. Jadhav and A. V. Chitre, all belonging to the ILP. D. V. Pradhan (Member, Bombay Municipal Corporation) acted as Secretary to the committee. The committee prepared a report on Pakistan which was submitted to the Executive Council, which then resolved that the report should be published. Ambedkar mentions in the introduction that it was a reply to the resolution on Pakistan by the Muslim League asking for Partition of India which had brought varied reactions from the populace and intelligentsia. As it was a controversial subject and because Ambedkar held that it was not a demand that would go away with time or be resolved, he felt the need to deal with it in detail as essential. For more details, see Ambedkar (1945/1990).

# 2

# Lessons from Andhra State

## Events, Debates and Formation of States Reorganisation Commission

The period between 1948 and 1954 formed a hiatus when several important events took place: incorporation of the state of Hyderabad into the Union of India, agitation and formation of Andhra State, agitation for a unified state of Maharashtra, and formation of the three-man SRC—which was set up by the Government of India in response to the conflicting demands for reorganisation by regional political leaders, on 22 December 1953. The SRC submitted a report of 267 pages after travelling over 38,000 miles, interviewing over 9,000 persons and examining approximately 2,000 'well-considered memoranda' on 30 September 1955. During this period, Ambedkar, as a member of the Constituent Assembly and later as a Member of Parliament and the first Law Minister of independent India, was politically involved in the process of redrawing the map of India along federal lines.[1] A brief narration of the events and debates during this time is provided in this chapter to place Ambedkar's intervention and his later writings in proper context.

## Formation of Andhra State

The report of the Dar Commission created great discontent among a section of Congressmen, particularly leaders in the provinces. Hence, at the Jaipur session of the Congress in 1948, it was decided that another Committee, whose terms of reference would include a reconsideration of the report of the Dar Commission, would be set up. This new committee was popularly known as JVP[2] Committee. Though it conceded that the linguistic principle was proposed and actively supported by the Congress in the past—in its report submitted on 1 April 1949—the Committee concluded that, 'We should prefer to postpone the formation of new provinces for a few years so that we might concentrate during this period on other matters of vital importance and not allow ourselves to be distracted by the question.' (JVP 1949: 1) It argued that redistribution be considered only 'after careful thought being given to each separate state' and the question of a separate state of Andhra should be seen in isolation from others as 'there appeared to be a large measure of consent behind it and the largest compact area likely to form part of this linguistic province is situated in one province.' The Committee, therefore, recommended that 'measures may be taken to implement it.' It also laid down some conditions for approaching the question of linguistic division of the country (ibid.: 14–15).[3]

The Committee also expressed the opinion that a Maharashtra Province could be formed subject to conditions similar to those laid down for Andhra and to the constitution of 'a separate unit of Greater Bombay'. With regard to Karnatak and Kerala, the Committee stated that the new provinces could be formed in conjunction with certain states—Travancore and Cochin in the case of Kerala, and Mysore and Hyderabad in the case of Karnatak—which would form substantial parts of the new provinces. 'This can be brought about not by a merger of the present provincial areas into the states, but by the reverse process and must entail virtual disappearance of these states.' (ibid.: 9) Regarding North India, the Committee recommended that adjustments of provincial boundaries could not be considered although some rectifications of boundaries might 'ultimately' be necessary. However, no agreement could be reached with regard to the areas to be included in Andhra and so the central government declared it as impractical. In the case of Karnatak and Kerala there was disappointment in these regions as no steps were considered. The Congress Working Committee adopted the report of the JVP Committee in April 1949, and it remained the position of the party as seen in its election manifesto of 1951.

With confusion prevailing over the issue, the Drafting Committee of the Constituent Assembly could not mention Andhra as a separate province in Schedule I of Article 3. This 'resistance of Oligarchy', as Austin (1967) describes, disturbed Ambedkar and he took a significant step which has made the process of reorganisation more open and easy for the states in post-Independence India. He suggested that for reorganisation of territories of states falling in Part I, all that should be necessary before receiving the assent of the President was 'consultation' and not 'consent'. He moved an amendment in the Draft Constitution on 17 November 1948 in order to bring changes in the two restrictions: (1) that there must be, before the initiation of any action, representation made to the President by a majority of the representatives of the territory in the Legislature of the state, or a resolution on their behalf passed by the Legislature of any state whose boundaries or name will be affected by the proposal contained in the Bill; and (2) that there shall be consent—imposed by the Assembly on Article 3. Ambedkar felt that if there was 'a small minority which felt very strongly that its position will not be safeguarded unless the boundary of the State was changed,' all that was necessary was consultation and not consent. He also added that since 'the position of the provinces is different from the position of the States … the Government need not be bound to require the consent of the provinces to change their boundaries; while in the case of the Indian States it is appropriate, in view of the fact that sovereignty remains with them … their consent should be obtained.'[4] Despite opposition from some sections, the Assembly adopted both these amendments and accepted in principle that Parliament may form a new state by combining two states or by the separation of a territory from a state, may increase or diminish the area of any state, and may alter its boundaries or name on the recommendation of the President after s/he has 'ascertained' the views of the Legislature(s) of the state(s) concerned. It would not require the complex mechanism of Constitutional Amendment (Austin 1967).

However, the demands for the creation of a separate state of Andhra could not be avoided for long. The disappointed proponents of linguistic states during the summer of 1951 started expressing their anger acutely in the form of a series of fasts, petitions, street marches, and organised popular campaigns for a separate state of Andhra.[5] The agitation was so strong that the issue of linguistic states became a very important issue in the first general election in Madras, Maharashtra, Kerala and Karnataka. With marked divisions in these states within the Congress party itself, it was forced to take a troubled stand:

> A demand for a re-distribution of provinces on a linguistic basis has been persistently made in the south and west of India. … While linguistic reasons

> have undoubtedly a certain cultural and other importance, there are other factors also such as economic, administrative and financial, which have to be taken into consideration. (Bondurant 1958: 32)

As a result of this, the election proved to be disastrous for Congress. The Communists in Andhra, who supported the idea of linguistic states, won significant victories. Out of the 62 Communist members elected in the Madras Legislative Assembly, 41 were from Andhra. Congress could win only 40 out of the 140 seats of the Madras Assembly from Andhra.[6] Thus, when the Communists presented a resolution in the Lok Sabha for the immediate creation of linguistic states in July 1952, Prime Minister Nehru spoke against this move. He however, declared his support for a separate state of Andhra provided that the criteria proposed by the JVP committee regarding Madras city and Rayalseema were accepted (Bondurant 1958: 32).

By the end of 1952 the agitation for a separate Andhra State for the Telugu-speaking people of the Madras Presidency had reached a dramatic climax. On 19 October 1952 Potti Sriramulu, a Gandhian, began a 'fast-unto-death' to demand the creation of separate Andhra State in Madras.[7] But the government took no action until he laid down his life on 15 December 1952. Sriramulu's death led to a series of violent protests and processions by the people in the Andhra region. Hence, on 19 December Nehru announced that his government had decided to form a state of Andhra consisting of only the Telugu-speaking areas of the present Madras State excluding Madras city.[8]

Ambedkar (1953a/1979) termed this announcement of creation of Andhra State as 'a *pindadan* to the departed soul of Mr. Sriramulu by the Prime Minister'.[9] He even suspected 'whether such action on the part of the Government would have been tolerated in any other country'. The government however, moved the Andhra State Bill in the Lok Sabha and got it passed on 27 August 1953. It was then introduced in the Rajya Sabha on 1 September 1953. Ambedkar once again made an important intervention when he rose to speak on this occasion in the Rajya Sabha on 2 September 1953. He drew the attention of the House to the contradictions and vacillations in the position of the Centre with regard to the reorganisation of the states in Independent India.

In his speech, Ambedkar explained how the ruling party (INC) ever since it adopted the principle of linguism in 1920 has been making constant shifts on the issue and had remained hesitant in charting out a clear-cut policy with regard to adoption of the linguistic reorganisation for the country, especially after Independence. In contrast to those who were celebrating the creation of Andhra as the victory for linguistic and cultural identity, Ambedkar took the opportunity to point out that the conditions under which the Andhra State was formed would not only encourage regionalism among other linguistic groups, but also give the impression that New Delhi was more responsive to violence than peaceful negotiations. Ambedkar also raised the issue of financial viability of the proposed Andhra State. He pointed out that the new province would not be economically viable as it would begin with a deficit of Rs 5 crore. This meant that those who supported its formation hadn't considered its economic viability and stability, and were rather driven by the logic of language and culture. It would be difficult to find ways to increase the revenue or reduce the expenditure in a new state.

The state of Andhra finally came into existence on 1 October 1953 with the Act of Parliament (the Andhra State Act of 1953) receiving President's assent on 14 September.[10] However, constituting India's first state on linguistic basis after Independence was not an easy task. The question of capital and the finances for the new state remained unsettled. After being forced to leave Madras, the new state had to accept Kurnool, a destination decided by the central government, as the state capital.[11] There also arose a number of conflicting demands. The Telugu-speaking regions of the state of Hyderabad, known as Telangana, which accounted for more than 50 per cent of the area of the state, was still not part of the newly-created Telugu-speaking Andhra State.[12] Therefore, following the formation of the Andhra State—during the parliamentary debates during 1953–55—sentiments in favour of unification of all the Telugu-speaking areas had started being expressed by members of Parliament representing the erstwhile state of Hyderabad and the new Andhra State. Those in favour of unification had started visualising Hyderabad as the state capital. But there were many who were opposed to the unification and had started demanding a separate state of Telangana. Demands were also raised to divide the state of Hyderabad on the basis of linguistic and cultural affinity.[13]

These conflicting demands, however, were not confined to Andhra alone. In the Marathi-speaking areas a number of Congressmen demanding unification of the Marathi-speaking areas of Bombay, Madhya Pradesh (MP) and Hyderabad with Bombay as the capital, signed the Nagpur Pact. Members of the MP Assembly in October 1953 supported a separate state of Mahavidarbha, to be made up of eight Marathi-speaking districts of MP and Hyderabad. Demands were also raised to keep Bombay as a separate city. Simultaneously, there were demands for a separate state of Karnatak which would include parts of the proposed state of Maharashtra. Demands were also made for a Punjabi-speaking state by the Sikhs and a separate state of Kerala. There was both appreciation of the creation of the new state as well as trenchant criticism of the handling of the situation by the government which had led to a situation where it seemed linguistic reorganisation was now merely a matter of time (Thirumali 2013: 36–37).

## Formation of the States Reorganisation Commission

The SRC faced the complex and difficult task of re-drawing the boundaries of states with varying degrees of local autonomy made up of different language and cultural groups, classified in the Indian Constitution in three different categories—Part A, Part B and Part C. The Commission was given the task of preserving and strengthening of the unity and security of India while at the same time making recommendations regarding the political subdivisions of India that would simultaneously satisfy the demands of linguistic minorities and strengthen their ties to each other within the constitutional framework. In this task it faced the problem that a linguistic state of Andhra had already been created and this reinforced the feeling that the reorganisation would be along linguistic lines.[14] In its report, the SRC clearly stated,

> After a full consideration of the problem in all its aspects we have come to the conclusion that it is neither possible not desirable to reorganize states on the basis of the single test of either language or culture, but a balanced approach to the whole problem is necessary in the interest of national unity. All the Committees and Commissions which have previously gone into the matter such as the Dhar Commission and J.V.P. Committee have rightly expressed themselves against a monistic approach to the problem. (GoI 1955)

The basic recommendation of the SRC was the creation of 16 states and three centrally-administered territories. On the demand for the disintegration of the Hyderabad State into linguistic and cultural affinity, the SRC, in recommendation no. 4 of the report (GoI 1955: 257), says:

i. The Kannada-speaking districts of Raichur and Gulbarga be transferred to the then Mysore State (the proposed Karnataka State),
ii. The Marathwada districts should also be detached from Hyderabad State,
iii. the residuary state of Hyderabad, might unite with Andhra if the former state's legislature favoured this move by a two-third majority after the 1961 elections.

The Commission, based on its observation during its visit to assess public opinion in Hyderabad, Warangal, Karimnagar and Nalgonda districts of the Telangana region, was in favour of keeping the Telugu-speaking areas of Hyderabad as a separate state. It found that the political opinion in the state of Hyderabad had yet not 'crystalised'. Indicating its disfavour for the idea of linguistic states, the SRC observed:

> It has to be remembered that linguistic and other group loyalties have deep roots in the soil and history of India. The culture-based regionalism, centering round the idea of linguistic homogeneity represents to the average Indian values easily intelligible to him. Indian nationalism, on the other hand, has still to develop into a positive concept. It must acquire a deeper content before it becomes ideologically adequate to withstand the gravitational pull of the traditional narrower loyalties. In these circumstances, further emphasis on narrow loyalties by equating linguistic regions with political and administrative frontiers, must diminish the broader sense of the unity of the country. (ibid.: 43)

The preliminary discussion on the SRC report was held in almost all the states in November 1955 and was introduced in the Lok Sabha and the Rajya Sabha in December the same year. The government, however, while announcing its views on most of the matters of the report on 16 January 1956, categorically rejected many of its recommendations and made clear that it did not consider the report to be the final word.[15]

During the debate on the SRC report, Nehru held, 'I recognize that the language of the people is a vital matter for their development ... but there is a distinction between developing the language to the fullest extent and this passion for building up a wall around a linguistic area and calling it a border ... that in order to make them and their language grow, a barrier must be erected between them and others.' (quoted in Nag 1993: 1532) He wanted '[h]ealthy nationalism to counter these foolish and tribal attitudes as also provincialism,' and claimed that the provinces were created only with 'administrative objectives' (Brecher 1959: 257). He found virtues in the provinces as they existed; in the composite culture of Hyderabad where people spoke different languages and the cosmopolitanism of Bombay which he felt would be 'vandalistic to throw away'.[16] There was also a feeling that apart from some regions such as Punjab, Bengal and Madras, other regions particularly those lying in the Hindi heartland were not clearly defined. He was not sure whether linguism as the basis of a federal structure would be acceptable to all regions.

In the winter of 1955, during violent agitations for division along linguistic lines when Parliament had just begun to discuss the SRC report, Nehru made one last attempt to put forward his idea of large multilingual states. On 31 December 1955, he proposed a plan under which India would be divided into four or five large divisions or Zones in each of which there would be an advisory Zonal Council, based on the idea of Panch Mahapradesh Shila. The Common Zonal Council for four to five states would initially be advisory, with the Centre associated with it. Later, it could develop into something more substantial. Nehru emphasised that in this way the emphasis would be on common economic problems within the zones, it could 'develop the habit of cooperative working' (Bondurant 1958: 55). The proposal was met with far greater enthusiasm than what the government had hoped for. The members of Parliament who were worried over the divisive tendencies in reorganisation along linguistic lines seized upon the proposal as the solution. Rajagopalachari vigorously pressed for a Dakshina Pradesh, a large state in the south, while others called for zonal Parliaments.[17] The merger proposal was initially greeted with great enthusiasm as it was felt that 'it was revolt of reason against the narrow provincialism of the day ...'. Many newspaper editorials and leaders also hailed it as a proposal that would enable the country to rise above narrow parochial tendencies, ensure unity and security and concentrate on rapid economic development.[18] The proposal to merge Bengal and Bihar and create a large bilingual eastern state/zone was supported in January 1956 by the chief ministers of both states (Bondurant 1958: 56).[19] Eventually five large zonal councils were established—North, South, East, West and

Central—vide Part III of the States Re-organisation Act, 1956, to help the states included in them to cooperate in economic development of the entire region.

Thus, given the complex situation, the SRC failed to avoid the already existing contradictions. Despite the statement that the creation of linguistic states would impede national unity, the Commission did make important concessions to the linguistic principle by recommending new linguistic states for the Malayalees, the Tamils and the Kannadigas, and the continuation of other states (such as Uttar Pradesh, Bengal and Orissa) which already existed as fairly homogenous linguistic units. It postponed its decision with regard to three matters, viz. Punjab, Bellary and Telangana, and for the Marathi speakers the Commission recommended against the creation of a linguistic state. This proved to be a signal for more agitation and violence, culminating in riots and bloodshed at Bombay. Between September 1955 when the SRC report was submitted and November 1956 when the reorganisation of states was undertaken there were a number of agitations, often violent, that made conflicting demands in parts of the country that the government found extremely hard to resolve.[20]

## Agitations for Maharashtra: Conflicting Demands

The agitation for a state of Maharashtra, following the creation of a separate Andhra State, was a powerful, articulate and well-organised demand for a separate state. And Ambedkar wrote extensively and eventually based his thinking regarding the other states on the example of Maharashtra. Therefore, it is necessary to examine in some detail the Commission's proposals for the state of Maharashtra and the events following its report. The Commission had recommended the distribution of Marathi-speaking people over three states—12 Marathi-speaking districts in Bombay, eight in Madhya Pradesh and five in Hyderabad. According to Census reports (1954: 58), Maharashtrians constituted 44 per cent, Gujaratis 32 per cent, Kannada speakers 12 per cent of the total population of Bombay State. The rest were immigrants speaking other languages. The greatest difficulty was with regard to the problem of Bombay City. Of the total Marathi-speaking population, more than

50 per cent were in the Bombay State. It was therefore Bombay that became the rallying point for Samyukta Maharashtra Movement.[21]

The SRC had recommended that: (1) Kutch and Saurashtra (Gujarati states) and the five Marathi districts of Hyderabad be added to the existing state of Bombay, and (2) four Kannada districts in the south be separated and added to the new Karnatak State. The recommendation of the SRC concerning Bombay State and Bombay City thus pitted the state leadership of the Congress party against the central leadership.

Regarding Vidarbha, the SRC recommended formation of a separate state as it was a revenue surplus area. It also pointed out that Maharashtra without Greater Bombay was likely to be a deficit area on revenue account. The Commission also noted that there was some reluctance in the Vidarbha region on joining Maharashtra on the suspicion that its resources would not be spent within its own area on suitable development schemes and projects. The Commission also pointed out that the land and tenancy laws in the Vidarbha region would have to be modelled on those of the Bombay State and a period of transition would lead to many problems for that region. The Gujaratis seemed quite satisfied with SRC report, as they were not only assured about their status quo position in Bombay City, but also in the state as a whole.

The SRC had made an attempt to balance the two communities, the Maharashtrians and the Gujaratis, in the new state. It recommended Vidarbha as a separate state (which otherwise would have upset this balance in favour of the Maharashtrians). But the SRC could not avoid the wrath of the Maharashtrians who, thinking on similar lines, saw the exclusion of Vidarbha from their proposed composite state as a favour to the Gujarati community. This was anticipated by the central government and therefore, the prime minister appealed to Maharashtrians to keep calm before the SRC was to submit its report. Even the SRC report, which was made public on 10 October 1955, some observers believe, 'had been leaked to the press before that date, so that its recommendations concerning Bombay came as no surprise' (Windmiller 1956: 132). Taking further preventive steps, the Bombay government had also issued orders 'prohibiting processions and demonstrations for a two-week period' on 28 September 1955, and reinforced heavy security both in Poona and Bombay. (ibid.)

Although recent in origin then, the situation regarding the redrawing of boundaries for the proposed state of Maharashtra was much more complex than that for the state of Andhra. Unlike the Telugu-speaking people who had accepted the Centre's proposal to leave the city of Madras and accept Kurnool as its capital, the Marathi-speaking people never gave up their demand for the inclusion of Bombay City in Samyukta Maharashtra and even refused to accept Bombay as a bilingual state. Thus, notwithstanding the SRC report, the Congress high command on 9 November 1955 put forward another new proposal, dividing the existing state into three separate units: (1) Samyukta Maharashtra with Vidarbha and Marathwada, (2) Gujarat with Saurashtra and Kutch, and (3) Bombay City. The third unit, Bombay City, was given the option to join either Maharashtra or Gujarat at the end of five years. But the leaders of Maharashtra, instead of accepting the proposal of Congress high command, opted to stick their neck out for the recommendation of the SRC making Maharashtra a bilingual state including Vidarbha. They also made a counter-provision that Gujarat could 'opt out' of Maharashtra, if it wished so after a period of five years (ibid.: 133).[22] However, no agreement could be reached between the state and the central leadership.

Throughout the last part of 1955 well-organised demonstrations were staged by proponents of Samyukta Maharashtra who demanded the merger of Bombay City into a new Maharashtra State. In late-November 1955 over a hundred Maharashtrian members of the BLA resigned in protest over Chief Minister Morarji Desai's acceptance of the new proposal though they were later persuaded to withdraw their resignations. By mid-January 1956 riots in Bombay City had resulted in firing with considerable bloodshed (ibid.).[23]

Meanwhile on 6 March 1956, Minister for Home Affairs Govind Ballabh Pant introduced the States Reorganisation Bill, affecting 12 out of 17 Part A and B States, in the Lok Sabha. This carried the plan for a centrally-administered Bombay City. The Lok Sabha referred the Bill to a Joint Select Committee for study. The Bombay Legislature approved the States Reorganisation Bill on 7 April 1956 but with numerous Congressmen remaining absent, some 20 voting against and over 70 abstaining. It was doubted if the three-way solution for Bombay would have enough support to prevent further agitations.

To show its firmness behind the plan for a centrally-administered Bombay City, the central leadership decided to hold the All India Congress Committee meeting in Bombay in June. But Maharashtrian agitators were equally adamant and they expressed their dissent by rioting outside the meeting place and stoning the cars of Congress officials. Responding to the events, Nehru held that the government would not yield to violence and intimidation and the three-state formula would stand and be the official one. At this occasion, Nehru's statement that in five years 'the citizens of this great city should be the arbiters of its destiny' further increased the intensity of violent protest and resulted in a severe loss of life in Bombay. He had added, 'It might be well asked why the future of Bombay should not be decided here and now. My answer would be that for the moment the city of Bombay has disqualified itself to decide so.' As for the effect the Congress party's position on Bombay might have on the upcoming elections in Maharashtra, he added, 'Let the elections go to hell. I am tired of listening to talks of pleasing this party and that party. To base one's actions and policies on election prospects is the mentality of weak-minded men.' (quoted in Windmiller 1956)[24]

The plan actually remained the official decision of the central government throughout the deliberations of the Joint Select Committee in Parliament during the first part of 1956. But there were dissenting notes in this committee by Congress members from the state of Bombay who, in all fora, made it clear that they would oppose this policy. The Joint Select Committee's report to Parliament, presented in late-July was greeted with protests by Maharashtrians, right in front of the Parliament building. Giving yet another blow to the government, Finance Minister C. D. Deshmukh, resigned from the Cabinet and charged the prime minister of mishandling the situation of Bombay and working in an 'unconstitutional' way (Windmiller 1956). This made the situation look more tensed.

Finally, Home Minister G. B. Pant moved an official amendment to the States Reorganisation Bill on 7 August providing for the creation of a bigger bilingual Bombay State consisting of Bombay City, Maharashtra, Saurashtra, Gujarat, Kutch, Vidarbha and Marathwada, and it passed through Lower House by 241 to 40 votes and was unanimously passed in Upper House. The Congress Parliamentary Party, which had already met on 6 August, adopted a resolution supporting the proposal.[25]

Regarding the Telugu-speaking state, the central leadership, despite Nehru's reluctance, decided in February 1956 contrary to a categorical recommendation of the SRC to merge the residuary Hyderabad State with Andhra and create a unified Vishalandhra. With nothing in their favour, the protagonists of Telangana had to console themselves only with the safeguards that they deemed necessary in the interest of the people of Telangana, formulated in the form of an agreement between the leaders of two regions in what is popularly known as 'Gentlemen's Agreement'.[26] Subsequently, the States Reorganisation Bill was moved in the Rajya Sabha on 30 April 1956 as the Lok Sabha unanimously had agreed to a joint sitting of the Houses for the consideration of the Bill.[27] It was finally passed by the Lok Sabha on 21 November 1956 and the Rajya Sabha on 27 November 1956.

Thus, the immediate post-Independence period was marked by debates, conflicts and even violent movements regarding the issue of reorganisation of the states. It was a period of ferment when different views were expressed by leaders belonging to different political parties and regions. While the INC had supported the principle of linguistic reorganisation in the colonial period, at Independence the nationalist leadership led by Nehru felt that the issue could be postponed until more pressing and serious matters such as Partition, integration of the states, the growing food crisis, etc. were resolved. When the demand for linguistic states became very strong, SRC was established but it was too late and the government had to bow to public opinion.

Much of this was centred in the Deccan plateau where, unlike in the deep south and the north, linguistic boundaries were not clear. These conflicts affected two major regions, Andhra and Maharashtra and the manner in which they were to be organised in the new federal structure. The creation of the state of Andhra opened the door for demands by other states for linguistic reorganisation and set the trend for the future. The state of Andhra was formed with the merger of two different sub-regions with a sizeable section remaining opposed to it and yearning for an independent identity for the Telangana region. In the later years, this dissatisfaction gained further momentum and became the most pressing demand for statehood in the country. In the case of Maharashtra also, it continued as an interim solution. The issue remained alive even after the SRC, affecting the campaign for the second general elections in 1956 only to weaken the Congress further in the regions. The 'permanent solution' as Bondurant remarks, remained open.[28] Separate states of Maharashtra and Gujarat had to be formed later.

Ambedkar's later writings and speeches were greatly influenced by the highly volatile political backdrop discussed above. Recognising the urgency of the matter, Ambedkar conveyed his views on the report of the SRC to the prime minister by sending him a telegram, whereby he categorically objected to several recommendations of the SRC, but most particularly two recommendations on which he had been expressing his views. First, he suggested that several of the recommendations of the Commission were not only of great danger to the central government, but also to minorities and SCs. According to Ambedkar, 'There will be no protection to Scheduled Castes under aegis of a State in which overwhelming majority is opposed to recognition of Scheduled Castes as human beings ... fear consequences might be very serious. Scheduled Castes are now without any political safeguard'. Fearing that the SCs' 'desperation may take to any kind of violence', he requested the prime minister to pay serious attention to this question.[29] Second, he held that formation of linguistic states, although essential, should not be decided by any sort of hooliganism. It must be solved by reasoning, discussion and building consensus.

Ambedkar continued to think and write about these issues. But, more importantly, from 1955 onwards he began to critically consider and evaluate the report of the SRC. As it became clear, given the tremendous public demand, that the government would have to consider forming linguistic states, Ambedkar began to seriously reconsider some of his own earlier ideas and to formulate a scheme whereby both the issue of language and other features he considered essential, could be put together to create a viable and democratic, federal structure for India. We turn now to these ideas which constitute the later writings of Ambedkar on states reorganisation and discuss them in detail in the next chapter.

## Notes

1. With the partition of the country and consequently of Bengal, Ambedkar had ceased to be a member of the Constituent Assembly. But the Congress party which had earlier opposed his entry into the Constituent Assembly came forward and sponsored his entry into the Assembly. Rajendra Prasad, Chairman of the Constituent Assembly, on 30 June 1947 wrote to B. G. Kher, Prime Minister of Bombay, directing him to have Ambedkar elected from Maharashtra immediately. Accordingly, Ambedkar was re-elected in July 1947 from Bombay as a member of the Constituent Assembly. Soon after that, Prime Minister Nehru invited him to join the Cabinet he formed on 15 August 1947 on the eve of Independence. Ambedkar accepted the invitation and became India's first Law Minister. On 29 August 1947, the Assembly

unanimously elected Ambedkar as Chairman of the Drafting Committee which was assigned the task of framing the draft of the Indian Constitution.

2. It derived its name from the names of tall Congress leaders Jawaharlal Nehru, Vallabhbhai Patel and Pattabhi Sitaramayya.
3. The conditions were: (a) When the Congress had given the seal of its approval to the general principle of linguistic provinces it was not faced with the practical application of the principle and hence it has not considered all the implications and consequences that arose from this practical application; (b) The primary consideration must be the security, unity and economic prosperity of India, and every separatist and disruptive tendency should be rigorously discouraged; (c) Language was not only a binding force, but also a separating one; and (d) The old Congress policy of having linguistic provinces could only be applied after careful thought had been given to each separate case and creating which could jeopardise the political and economic stability of the country.
4. *Constituent Assembly of India Debates (Proceedings)*, vol. 7, Wednesday, 17 November 1948.
5. In the monsoon of 1951, a Congressman-turned-swami named Sitaram (Gollapudi Seetaram) went on a hunger strike demanding the immediate creation of an Andhra State. He gave it up after five weeks on 20 September 1951 only in response to an appeal by Sarvodaya leader, Vinoba Bhave. See *Hindu* (2006).
6. In the Madras Legislative Assembly too, the Congress could secure only 152 seats. Non-Congress members in the Legislature, numbering 164, formed themselves into a United Democratic Front (UDF) and elected T. Prakasam as their leader. However, the governor nominated C. Rajagopalachari to the Legislative Council and invited him to form the ministry.
7. Born in Madras in 1901, Sriramulu studied Sanitary Engineering and was employed in the Railways. In 1930, he resigned from his post to join the Salt Satyagraha led by Gandhi. Later, he spent some time at the Sabarmati Ashram. It was here that Sriramulu won the affection and the approbation of Gandhi and, influenced by his ideals, he had gone on his first fast-unto-death to demand the opening of all temples in Madras Province to Harijans on 25 November 1946. In an effort to protect the interests of the Telugu people in the Madras Presidency, he had gone on a lengthy fast earlier as well, but had stopped it when Prime Minister Jawaharlal Nehru promised to support the creation of an Andhra State.
8. The 11 districts were Srikakulam, Visakhapatnam, East Godavari, West Godavari, Krishna, Guntur, Nellore, Chittoor, Cuddapah, Anantapur and Kurnool, and the three taluks of the Bellary District were Rayadurg, Adoni and Alur (Bondurant 1958).
9. *Pindadaan* (literally, offering to a departed soul) is a ceremony in the Hindu religious tradition performed after a person's death by his family members.
10. The new state of Andhra consisted of the districts of Srikakulam, Visakhapatnam, East Godavari, West Godavari, Krishna, Guntur, Nellore, Chittoor, Cuddapah, Anantapur and Kurnool, and the taluks of Rayadurg, Adoni and Alur of the Bellary District (excluding Madras City).

11. This was done in accordance with the Sri Bagh Pact of 15 November 1937, between the leaders of coastal Andhra and Rayalaseema (the two Telugu-speaking regions of the then Madras Presidency) during the separate Andhra movement. It was agreed that 'the location of the University, the Headquarters and the High Court may advantageously be in different places so as not to concentrate all civil importance at the same Centre. Accordingly, it is agreed that while the University may continue to be where it is, the High Court and the metropolis be located in suitable places in the coastal districts and the Rayalaseema, the choice being given to Rayalaseema.' For details of the Sri Bagh Pact, see Appendix 1.1 of the Srikrishna Committee Report (GoI 2010: 33–34).
12. The state of Hyderabad, earlier under Nizams, was incorporated into the Union of India on 13 September 1948. The Telugu-speaking districts in the state were Mahabubnagar, Nalgonda, Warangal, Karimnagar, Adilabad, Nizamabad, Khammam, Medak and the city of Hyderabad (including Ranga Reddy District).
13. For details on people and events supporting or opposing unification of all Telugu-speaking districts, see Thirumali (2013). Also see the report submitted by the Committee for Consultations on the Situation in Andhra Pradesh, 2010.
14. For details, see Bondurant (1958: 47).
15. To know the day-to-day happenings covering the events of the period, see Bondurant (1958).
16. See Gopal and Iyengar (2003: 261).
17. In a note to Nehru on 28 September 1955, Krishna Menon too had suggested the creation of 'a Southern State, a Dakshina Pradesh, as a corollary to Uttar Pradesh, which could include the present Tamil Nadu, Travancore, Cochin, Malabar and possibly Kanara upto Kasargode'. See Noorani (2002).
18. For details, see Bondurant (1958: 56).
19. The CWC supported it strongly as a 'significant example of that positive approach to the problem of Indian unity' made in its 9 November 1955 Resolution which took 'national unity and solidarity' as the 'overriding considerations to be borne in mind in determining the constitutional structure of India'. It was also felt that such proposals would turn the minds of people from narrow provincial rivalries to a larger integration and to Indian unity. But opposition surfaced very soon and the proposal could not be carried forward. In Bengal and Bihar Congressmen were divided between party and provincial loyalties. There were also differences over the boundary between the two which the SRC had found very difficult to resolve. Eventually it could not be sustained specially due to the opposition of the Socialist and Communist party which, argued that there were nationalities on the subcontinent and felt the move was directed towards weakening the autonomy of the newly-formed linguistic states and rendering them powerless. Also, they felt that the demand for linguistic reorganisation had reached a momentum and could not be set aside. Right-wing parties saw in it a proposal to form a unitary state eventually. As agitations began, it became obvious that many Congressmen

who had hoped that such a step would tilt the scales in favour of bilingual states—in which less scope for separatist and fissiparous forces to emerge—also were not enthusiastic. Following a by-election in May 1956 in Bengal, in which the Congress candidate Ashoke Sen did not perform well, the idea was withdrawn.

20. For details, see Bondurant (1958: 47).
21. Windmiller (1956) observed that the enthusiasm for the creation of Samyukta Maharashtra was strongest in the Marathi districts of Bombay but did not find as much support in Vidarbha (the Marathi districts of Madhya Pradesh) or Marathwada (the Marathi districts of Hyderabad). A resolution of Samyukta Maharashtra was passed at Belgaum under the leadership of G. T. Madkholkar, D. V. Potdar, Shankarrao Deo, Keshavrao Jhede and S. S. Navre on 12 May 1946, and a conference, 'Maharashtra Ekikaran Parishad', was organised by S. K. Patil and presided by Shankarrao Deo in Bombay on 28 July 1946. Veteran Congressman, Shankarrao Deo was made the president of the Samyukta Maharashtra Parishad and the celebrated Cambridge-trained economist D. R. Gadgil was made its secretary and chief theoretician. Also see Guha (2007: 180–200).
22. Also see Annamalai (n.d.).
23. Also see Bombay Legislative Council Debates, 1956, vol. 34.
24. For a more interesting account of the day-to-day events in Bombay, see the series of news reports published by *DNA*, Mumbai, in May 2010. Some of these are Tare (2010), Kolhatkar (2010), Gangan (2010) and Khapre (2010). Also see Guha (2007).
25. See http://www.hindu.com/2006/08/08/stories/2006080803330700.htm (accessed 12 May 2012).
26. The meeting was held at Hyderabad House, New Delhi, on 20 February 1956. The members signatory to the agreement were B. Gopala Reddy (Chief Minister of Andhra), N. Sanjeeva Reddy (Deputy Chief Minister of Andhra), G. Latchanna (Minister in the Andhra Cabinet and Leader of the Krishikar Lok Party, a constituent of the United Congress Front which contested the 1955 Andhra elections and formed the Ministry), A. Satyanarayana Raju (President, Andhra Provincial Congress Committee), B. Ramakrishna Rao (Chief Minister, Hyderabad), Dr M. Chenna Reddy (Minister, Hyderabad), K. V. Ranga Reddy (Minister, Hyderabad) and J. V. Narsingh Rao (President, Hyderabad Provincial Congress Committee). For more details on this agreement, see Srikrishna Report (GoI 2010).
27. Though the Bill had some financial provisions—and according to the norms practised and the rules framed for the regulation of business in the Lok Sabha, such Bills ordinarily, were to be referred only to a Select Committee consisting of the members of the Lok Sabha—taking in view its unique importance, the Lok Sabha suspended the relevant rule and agreed that this Bill should be considered by the representatives of both Houses. The motion was adopted in the Rajya Sabha with the names of Chandulal P. Parikh, Biswanath Das, K. Madhava Menon, Capt. Awadhesh Pratap Singh, Dr Anup Singh, A. Satyanarayana Raju, M. D. Tumpalliwar, K. S. Hegde, Tarkeshwar Pande, T. R. Deogirikar, Dr P. Subbarayah, J. V. K. Vaubharao, V. K. Dhage, Kishen

Chand, Surendra Mahanty, Kakasaheb Kalelkar and Govind Ballabh Pant (the Mover) as members of the Select Committee on 3 May 1956.

28. For details, see Bondurant (1958: 76–77).
29. Ambedkar's telegram to Jawaharlal Nehru regarding formation of linguistic states, dated 17 January 1956. See Khairmode (2003: 56–57).

# 3

# Offering Solutions

## Later Writings of Ambedkar on States Reorganisation

The submission of the SRC report in 1955 marks a turning point in the debate on states reorganisation in the immediate post-Independence period. Although the report clearly stated that the states should not be reorganised on a single variable, i.e. language, and discussed other criteria as well, eventually given the political situation of the period, much of its recommendations were based on the linguistic principle. Also, the formation of the state of Andhra in 1952, which was a major concession by the Nehruvian government to the strong movements in the country for the formation of linguistic states, rendered it necessary for the government to proceed along this path. Thus, from 1955 onwards Ambedkar began to seriously interrogate the recommendations made by the SRC and develop some of the key principles that he had been discussing earlier. His 'Thoughts on Linguistic States', which was written after the submission of the SRC report, is a major work on reorganisation that brings together all the ideas which he had gradually developed through various writings since the late 1930s on the subject.

This chapter discusses Ambedkar's ideas on reorganisation of states through his speeches and writings after the formation of the Andhra State, which departs in many ways from his earlier ones. Ambedkar points out that while earlier opinions were formed on the basis of fragmentary data, it was only after the SRC report that he could visualise a complete picture. Based on this larger data, Ambedkar proffers a detailed critique of the principles underlying reorganisation of the states provided by the SRC in its report and some important alternative solutions. This is done by developing his ideas on some key principles on which, he argues, a federal structure could be created. While in his 'Statement Submitted to the Linguistic Committee' in 1948 much of Ambedkar's work had focused on Maharashtra, in his 'Thoughts on Linguistic States' he attempts to apply some of these basic principles to the country as a whole. He also provides some 'checks and balances' that he argues, if applied, would ensure a stronger federation and better reorganisation of states in the subcontinent. In this later work, recognising that he had modified his position on many issues, Ambedkar felt he had opted for 'responsibility over consistency'. This chapter discusses the key principles for the reorganisation of states in the federation and its application as developed by Ambedkar. Since Ambedkar wrote extensively on Maharashtra, his views on it are examined separately.

## Key Principles for the States in the Federation

Before discussing the formation of individual states, Ambedkar first proposes and analyses some key principles on which he argues the federation should be constructed. He does not exclude the principle of linguistic reorganisation, but tries to bring the two sets of ideas together in a manner which he felt might satisfy the demand for linguistic reorganisation as well as the needs of the federation. The key principles he proposes are viability, optimal size, federal balance, language of the states created and political majority. He then proceeds to apply these to major states in the country. While the principles had been broached earlier by Ambedkar, he now begins to consider these as collectively essential for a federation, particularly the Indian federation given its size and complexity.

Ambedkar recognised the centrality of the key issue of viability of a federation and within it the viability of each of the states that would be created. He relates this to many other issues but primarily to the size of each state and the resulting federal balance of the federation. Describing the federation that would be formed as an indissoluble union of the 'United States of India' he points to two types of states that would be created within it—the provinces and the centrally-administered areas. And then, Ambedkar answers to how one defines *viability*. Maintaining his earlier position, Ambedkar affirms that for a province to exist, it should not merely be self-supporting, but must qualify certain tests such as size, volume of population and a commensurate amount of revenue. He strongly feels that all states should have sufficient revenue to provide for a minimum standard of efficient administration and fulfil the needs of social welfare of its people. Explaining the manner in which states would be admitted into the Indian Union, Ambedkar (1947/1979) had said,

> A State shall not be deemed to be a Qualified State unless it is proved that it is of a standard size prescribed by the Union Legislature and is endowed with natural resources capable of supporting a descent standard of living for its people and can, by reason of its revenues and population function as an autonomous State, protect itself against external aggression, maintain Law and Order against internal disturbance and guarantee to its subjects minimum standards of administration and welfare which are expected from a modern State.

The question of size of the states was important for Ambedkar not only from the point of language and administrative efficiency, which were the only aspects that the SRC had considered. He pointed out that *equality* of size of states in a federation, and the *interrelationships* among states were extremely important aspects in a democratic polity. Based on these arguments, he was critical of the manner in which the SRC had recommended the division of the map of India. Ambedkar describes the exercise undertaken by the SRC as based on 'linguism and nothing else' or as 'linguism as excelsis', i.e. the Commission had taken into consideration only language and no other factor. Examining the area and population of the proposed states, he describes the result as 'fantastic'. He points out that the Commission seemed to think that the size of a state and equality in the size of the states constituting a federation was not important. This was, he said, a 'most terrible error cost' which if not rectified in time would lead to a great deal of trouble.

Ambedkar pointed out that the size and population of the states as proposed by the SRC (see Table 3.1), varied disproportionately. There were eight states with a population between 10 and 20 millions (Rajasthan, Punjab, Orissa, Kerala, Karnataka, Vidarbha, Hyderabad and Andhra); four with a population between 20 and 40 millions (Madhya Pradesh, Bengal, Madras and Bihar); one with over 40 million (Bombay); and one with over 60 million (Uttar Pradesh). He also pointed out that the Commission's decision to ignore the views of one of its members, K. M. Pannikar, was a great mistake. Pannikar, in his dissenting note to the Commission had argued that too great a disparity in size among states (particularly Uttar Pradesh) could lead to suspicion and resentment among states and generate forces likely to be divisive of the federation.

Table 3.1: New States Proposed by the SRC

| *Name of the State* | *Area (square mile)* | *Population (millions)* |
|---|---|---|
| Madras | 50,170 | 30.0 |
| Kerala | 14,980 | 13.6 |
| Karnatak | 72,730 | 19.0 |
| Hyderabad | 45,300 | 11.3 |
| Andhra | 64,950 | 20.9 |
| Bombay | 1,51,360 | 40.2 |
| Vidarbha | 36,880 | 7.6 |
| Madhya Pradesh | 1,71,200 | 26.1 |
| Rajasthan | 1,32,300 | 16.0 |
| Punjab | 58,140 | 17.2 |
| Uttar Pradesh | 1,13,410 | 63.2 |
| Bihar | 66,520 | 38.2 |
| West Bengal | 34,590 | 26.5 |
| Assam | 89,040 | 9.7 |
| Orissa | 60,140 | 14.6 |
| Jammu and Kashmir | 92,780 | 4.4 |

*Source*: Compiled by the authors from GoI (1955).

A second fault Ambedkar finds in the SRC recommendation is what he terms 'hidden' but 'very real'. The SRC, by creating big states, he feared, had introduced a new political problem of North versus South (see Map 3.1). He held that this scheme of dividing India in the name of linguistic states was not 'innocuous' but 'full of poison' and argued strongly for its reversal.

Table 3.2: Region-wise Comparison of States as Proposed by SRC

| *Southern States* | | *Central States* | | *Northern States* | |
|---|---|---|---|---|---|
| *Name* | *Population (in crores)* | *Name* | *Population (in crores)* | *Name* | *Population (in crores)* |
| Madras | 3.00 | Maharashtra | 3.31 | Uttar Pradesh | 6.32 |
| Kerala | 1.36 | Gujarat | 1.13 | Bihar | 3.85. |
| Karnataka | 1.90 | Saurashtra | 0.4 | Madhya Pradesh | |
| Andhra | 1.09 | Kutch | 0.5 | Rajasthan | 2.61 |
| Hyderabad | 1.13 | | | Punjab | 1.72 |

*Source*: Ambedkar (1955/1979).

Moreover, there were important differences between the two areas in terms of language and culture, as a result of which there was mutual suspicion and very little understanding, and Ambedkar warns of signs of a break-up. Ambedkar further argues that in the Indian Constitution, unlike in the US, the two Houses are not coequal in authority. In the US, the Senate is a powerful house and its consent is needed for money Bills. This makes a great difference to the disparity in the population. Also, he points out that in the Soviet Union and in Prussia, in the interest of the Union and to maintain the balance, weightage was given to the smaller units.

Ambedkar also refers to a statement by Rajagopalachari on the recommendations of the SRC in *Times of India*, on 27 November 1955, where Rajagopalachari had expressed his opinion in favour of large southern states 'for preserving the political significance of that part of the country. To cut the South up into Tamil, Malayalam and other small States will result only in complete insignificance of everybody and, in the net result, India as a whole will be the poorer.' Further, Ambedkar pointed out that Rajagopalachari had privately been more frank and explicit to him on the issue during a discussion on the drafting of the Constitution when the latter was Head of State. Rajagopalachari had held that one federation for the whole of India will not work, even with equal representation from all areas. Ambedkar reported that Rajagopalachari's fear was that the prime minister and President, in such

MAP 3.1: India – North vs South

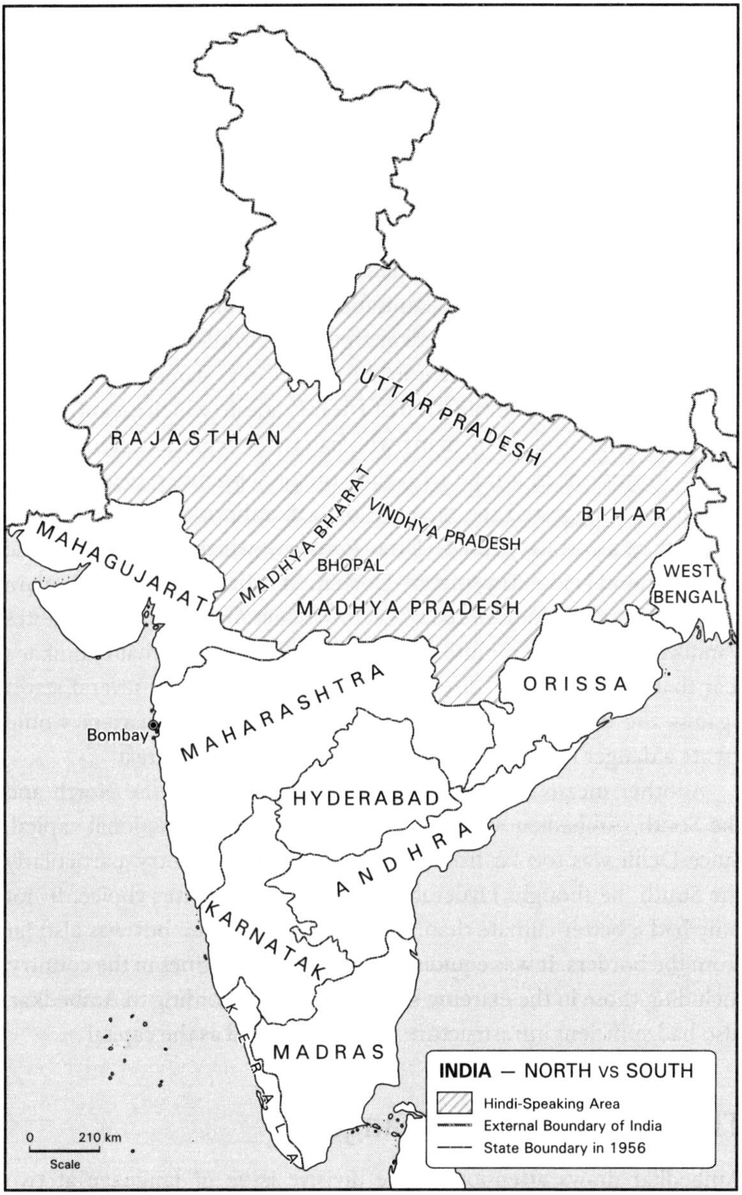


*Source*: Prepared by the authors based on a map in Ambedkar (1955/1979).

a federation, will always be from the Hindi-speaking area. The latter had even suggested that Ambedkar consider having two federations—North and South.

Ambedkar points out that these 'real' thoughts of Rajagopalachari, which he did not openly voice, showed what Congressmen from the South were feeling. He warns that India could also experience a war between the North and the South as in the USA as cultural differences were in his opinion 'very combustible' and it was necessary to take steps to prevent this from happening. The recommendation of the Commission would lead to consolidation of the North into large states such as Uttar Pradesh, and balkanisation of the South into a number of smaller Dravidian states. Ambedkar argues that to allow one state to have such preponderating influence in the Centre was dangerous. Already apprehensions of the domination of Uttar Pradesh (which meant, of the North) had been voiced by many who had made representations before the Commission. In a note to Nehru on 28 September 1955, Krishna Menon had suggested the creation of 'a Southern State, a Dakshina Pradesh, as a corollary to UP [Uttar Pradesh], which could include the present Tamil Nadu, Travancore, Cochin, Malabar and possibly Kanara upto Kasargode' (Noorani 2002). On this aspect Ambedkar again quotes Pannikar's dissenting minute. Therefore, Ambedkar felt that Pannikar's fear that the feelings of distrust and resentment felt by several states against the dominance of Uttar Pradesh in all-India matters would create a danger to the unity of India, was not out of context.

Another means of removing the tension between the North and the South, Ambedkar suggested, was to relocate the national capital. Since Delhi was too far from many parts of the country, particularly the South, he thought Hyderabad would make a better choice. It not only had a better climate than the extremes of Delhi, but was also far from the borders. It was equidistant from all major cities in the country, including those in the extreme south. The city, according to Ambedkar, also had sufficient infrastructure to be nominated as the capital.

## The Divisive Issue of Language

Ambedkar draws attention to the divisive issue of language at two levels. First, he had already warned in his 'Statement Submitted to the Linguistic Commission' (1948/1979) that the danger was not in creating linguistic provinces but with according the language of each province official status. Linguistic states with their regional language as official language could lead to many nations. However, this never came as close as the contentious claim of the government that 'linguistic States would break up the unity of India'. During his speech in the Rajya Sabha on the Andhra State Bill, Ambedkar (1953b/1997) pointed out that of the 27 states existing in the country, 23 were linguistic states and only four were multilingual. However, he added:

> These 23 linguistic States have not been able to disrupt the unity of India. ... We have, by God's grace achieved not only independence but also unity, and it is our bounden duty, no matter to what party we belong, to see that this independence and this unity is retained. But, to say, in the face of this fact with 23 linguistic states, that linguistic States would break up the unity of India is to say something which is puerile. They *(read the government)* must produce some very weighty arguments in support of their contention that they cannot pursue a policy of creating linguistic States. (ibid.)

He felt that the Commissions, including SRC, had ignored important issues under the veil of the argument of the unity of the country. The SRC's silence on the important issue of division between the North and the South over the issue of the national language, Ambedkar felt, was one such example. He reminded the House, how the Congress party itself was deeply divided during the consideration of Article 115 of the Draft Constitution of India which dealt with the issue of adopting Hindi as the national language. The Article generated considerable 'heat and opposition' in the Constituent Assembly and when put to vote, resulted in a tie (78:78) with equal votes both for and against Hindi. It could sail through the House, in the second voting, by just a margin of one vote (78 against 77). Ambedkar used this example to reveal how much the South disliked the North; a dislike, which he felt, could grow into hatred if the North remained consolidated and the South was disintegrated and if the North continued to exercise a disproportionate influence on the politics of India.

Based on this discussion of the anomalies and problems involved in reorganisation of the states, Ambedkar, in 1956, raises a seminal question: Is it necessary to follow the principle that the SRC recommended, 'One State for One Language'? The Commission had taken the view that the creation of one single state for all people speaking one language was the rule to be observed. Ambedkar held that this was a dangerous step as it had created states with great disparity of size and it would be impossible for the small states to bear the weight of the big states. Regarding size, too, Ambedkar held that it was not easy to fix the optimal size of each state and argued that most of the southern states would become 'mixed' states.

Ambedkar had addressed this question earlier in an article (1953a/1979) in *Times of India*. He argued that all people speaking one language need not be consolidated under the jurisdiction of a single state. 'There could be more than one state with the same language.' The formula of 'One State, One Language', he pointed out, was not to be confused with that of 'One Language, One State'. The latter meant that all people speaking one language would be brought under one government, irrespective of area, population and dissimilarity of conditions among the people. 'One State, One Language', he pointed out, was the universal feature of almost every state, be it Germany, England or the USA. Taking Austria as a case, Ambedkar tried to explain how departure from this rule has created dangers for state's existence. Therefore, with so many languages in India, he felt, a unilingual state would be more stable than a multilingual state. A state has to be 'built on fellow-feeling,' a 'corporate sentiment of oneness' which brings all together. Moreover, a unilingual state would be more stable than a multilingual state, which he felt was also borne out by an examination of other states such as Germany, France or Italy, which are homogeneous states with a single language.

Ambedkar explains the importance of the idea of 'One State, One Language' by illustrating with clarity the reasons why the speakers of different languages start 'hating' each other. He argued that it is not because of any 'natural antipathy' between them, but because of bringing them together in 'juxtaposition'. Explaining it he further adds:

> Why do Tamils hate Andhras and Andhras hate Tamils? Why do Andhras in Hyderabad hate Maharashtrians and Maharashtrians hate Andhras? Why do Gujaratis hate Maharashtrians and Maharashtrians hate Gujaratis? The answer is very simple. It is not because there is any natural antipathy between the two. The hatred is due to the fact that they are put in juxtaposition and forced to take part in a common cycle of participation, such as Government. There is no other answer. (Ambedkar 1953a/1979)

He rather, felt that people speaking one language if divided into many states based on the some 'check and balances' of criterion—such as requirements of efficient administration, needs of the different areas, sentiments of the different areas, and proportion between the majority and the minority—would not only lessen the importance of regional feelings and differences and work as a solvent to racial and cultural conflicts, but also remove the existing disparity in size.

Based on this principle Ambedkar was not only critical of the retention of a mixed state of Bombay as advocated by the SRC, but also proposed to divide the three states of Uttar Pradesh, Bihar and Madhya Pradesh into smaller units. This division would not conflict with the

MAP 3.2: Division of Uttar Pradesh

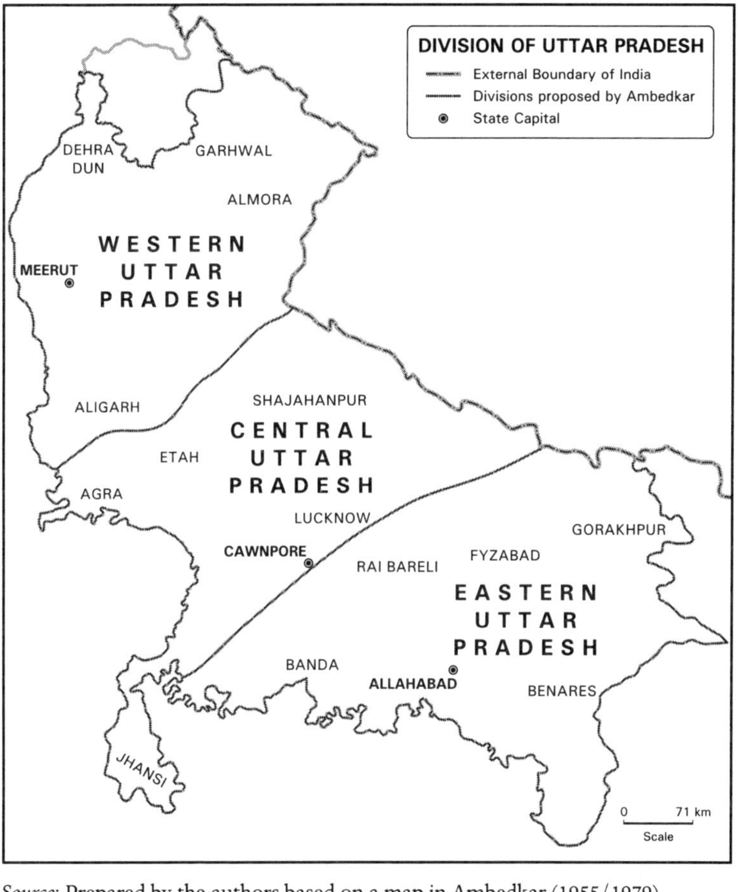


*Source*: Prepared by the authors based on a map in Ambedkar (1955/1979).

underlying principles of a linguistic state as each resulting state would be a linguistic state. He pointed out that G. B. Pant, Congress leader from Uttar Pradesh, had said in Parliament that he had no objection to the division of Uttar Pradesh into three states. Each of these three states should have a population of approximately two crore, which should be regarded as the standard size of population for a state to administer effectively. Ambedkar also provided the boundary lines of the three states in an accompanying map (see Map 3.2) as well as their capitals, viz. Meerut, Cawnpore and Allahabad.

MAP 3.3: Division of Bihar

*Source*: Prepared by the authors based on a map in Ambedkar (1955/1979).

Similarly in the case of Bihar Ambedkar proposed that it should be divided it into two states (see Map 3.3) with each state having a population of a little over one and half crores, which he points out is not a small population for one government to administer. Together with providing their boundary lines in Map 3.3 their capitals would be Patna and Ranchi which are situated quite in the centre of the two states.

Regarding Madhya Pradesh (MP), he pointed out that two possibilities were available—the Old and the New MP. Old MP, created by colonial authorities, consisted of the Central Provinces and Berar, and some princely states out of the eastern states. It had a population of 2.5 crore, its Legislature had 223 members and it consisted of 22 districts. New MP, as planned by the SRC, would consist of:

1. Fourteen districts of Old MP,
2. Whole of Bhopal,
3. Whole of Vindhya Pradesh,
4. Madhya Bharat, except Sunel enclave of Mandasaur district and
5. Sironj subdivision of Kola district of Rajasthan.

Having considered both these entities, Ambedkar recommended that the latter proposed by the SRC could be divided into two states: Northern MP and Southern MP (see Map 3.4). He held that they should not be allowed to be formed as one state which he described as a 'monster' and which even Nehru had expressed surprise at.

The state of Northern MP could consist of the following areas:

1. Whole of Vindhya Pradesh and
2. Whole state of Bhopal.

The state of Southern MP could consist of:

1. Whole state of Indore and
2. Fourteen districts of Mahakosal

MAP 3.4: Division of Madhya Pradesh

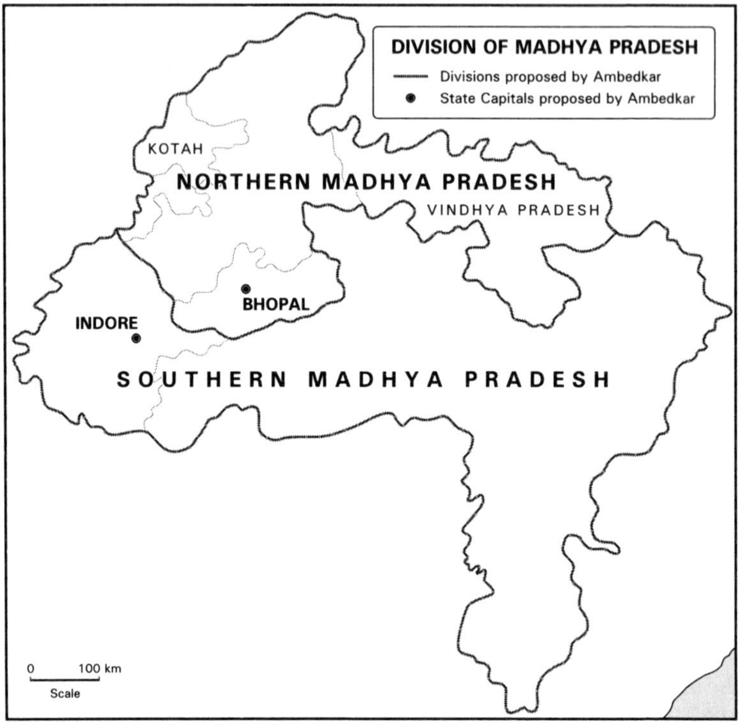


*Source*: Prepared by the authors based on a map in Ambedkar (1955/1979).

## Political Majority vs Communal Majority

Any federal arrangement, Ambedkar felt, should ensure that the ruler was a political majority and not a communal majority. Here the social composition of the state—i.e. the distribution of religious and caste groups in different linguistic areas—was important, an aspect about which he feels little information was available. Ambedkar felt that this was an aspect that needed to be urgently examined as in many states, castes are so distributed that in any given area one or two castes are dominant and others are subservient to it. This subservience arises from their smaller numbers and economic dependence on the dominant castes, as the latter own not only most of the land in the villages, but also businesses, jobs, etc. in the urban areas. This could happen, Ambedkar argued, for example, in Punjab where Jats, in Andhra Pradesh where Kammas and Reddys, in Karnataka where Lingayats and Vokkaligas, and in Maharashtra where Marathas are dominant.

Writing extensively about the problem of communal majorities in the 1953 article in *Times of India*, Ambedkar pointed out:

> Take the Punjab of PEPSU. The Jats dominate the whole area. The untouchables live in subordinate dependence on them. Take Andhra—there are two or three major communities spread over the linguistic area. They are either the Reddis or the Kammas and the Kappus. They hold all the land, all the offices, all the business. The untouchables live in subordinate dependence on them. Take Maharashtra. The Marathas are a huge majority in every village in Maharashtra. The Brahmins, the Gujars, the Kolis and the untouchables live in subordinate co-operation. ... In a linguistic State what would remain for the smaller communities to look to? Can they hope to be elected to the Legislature? Can they hope to maintain a place in the State service? Can they expect any attention to their economic betterment? In these circumstances, the creation of a linguistic State means the handing over of Swaraj to a communal majority. ... Those who cannot understand this aspect of the problem would understand it better if instead of speaking in terms of linguistic State we spoke of a Jat State, a Reddy State or a Maratha State. (Ambedkar 1953a/1979)

Ambedkar felt that, unlike many other nations, where linguistic states were a common phenomenon, linguism in India was loaded with communalism. They were rather synonyms. Creating a linguistic province in India meant handing over 'the strings of administration to one single community which happens to be the majority community', which instead of adopting a responsible behaviour, gets 'charged with a feeling of its own sacred existence' and begins to practice 'the worst kind of communalism which otherwise is called discrimination'. This only creates 'injustice' and 'ill-feeling'.

Ambedkar wanted to ensure that a communal majority should not abuse its power under the garb of a linguistic state. He also pointed out that this kind of communal setup also had important repercussions on the system of single-member constituencies adopted under the Constitution. Since voting is always community based, the candidate of the majority community would win due to support of sheer numbers and not competence. Moreover, there isn't only one hierarchical system; each caste has all the exclusiveness and pride which a nation has, leading to a collection of 'major and minor nations' on the subcontinent. Thus, with the creation of linguistic states in such situation, Ambedkar opined 'rivalries would be sharpened, and minorities would be crushed'.

In the case of the creation of Andhra State, Ambedkar felt that the government had not paid heed to the demographic composition of the state which could lead to conflict and violence. Speaking on the occasion of the Andhra State Bill in the Rajya Sabha on 2 September 1953, he said that in the new state Reddys and Kammas—upper-caste Hindu communities who are numerically large and spread across the state—controlled most of the land, were local officers, and would suppress and dominate the SCs who are landless, poor and vulnerable to caste-based atrocities.

As a remedy to this, Ambedkar suggested two safeguards. One, avoid making large states. He felt that, 'the larger the State the smaller the proportion of the minority to the majority ... a small stone of a consolidated majority placed on the chest of the minority may be borne, but it would be crushed by the weight of a huge mountain. Therefore creation of smaller States is a safeguard to the minorities.' However, this came with a warning that too small a state which cannot find the means to carry on its administration should be avoided. Two, adopt mechanisms to protect minorities against the tyranny of majority rule by dominant communities, as practised in several democracies. He particularly provided the examples of Canada and Britain. In Canada, where Roman Catholics and Protestants are bound within a single federation, the former have a right to appeal to the Governor-General who can investigate into any wrong they feel has been done to them. Similarly in Britain, despite England and Scotland being united, a Special Secretary for Scotland exists to look after the interests of the Scottish people; two committees exist in the British Parliament that safeguard the rights of Wales and Scotland, and members of these regions are selected in all committees so that they have a say in all the policies made by the government.

No such safeguards, Ambedkar pointed out, had been provided to the regions which were put together to form Andhra. The coastal region was the dominant region in the state and no safeguards were provided for the Rayalaseema region. This problem was not limited to Andhra, he cautioned. If Bihar and Bengal were to form a single state, Bengalis who are found in large parts of eastern India, would have an unfair advantage. Ambedkar argued that in such states the governor could be vested with certain special powers to protect the minorities against the tyranny of the majority. Minority groups should have the power to appeal to the governor to set aside any act of injustice that may be done to that group. Also, the state should establish committees of members belonging to the different linguistic sections which would have the right to hear grievances and right to ask the ministry to look after the special needs of each group. He held that, 'People do not live on culture. People do not live on Language. They live on the resources they possess.'

## The Solution for Maharashtra

Ambedkar's proposal regarding Maharashtra is worthy of separate treatment as this was a major area of controversy. He had been attempting to address the issue for a long time. He points out that following the report of the SRC, by the end of 1955, there were four proposals in the field:

1. To retain the Bombay State as it is, i.e. to retain it as a mixed state consisting of Maharashtra, Gujarat and Bombay.
2. To disrupt the existing state and to separate Maharashtra and Gujarat and make them into two separate states.
3. To make United Maharashtra with Bombay as one state.
4. To separate Bombay from Maharashtra and make it a separate city state.

Ambedkar proposes that Bombay as a 'mixed State' should be done away with. While in 1948 he was an advocate of a unified state of Maharashtra, now in keeping with his idea of 'One State, One Language' he wanted to divide Maharashtra into four states (see Map 3.5),

1. Maharashtra City State which would consist of
   a. City of Bombay
   b. Such area of Maharashtra as would enable it to be a good and strong city state.
2. Western Maharashtra
   a. Thana
   b. Kolaba
   c. Ratnagiri
   d. Poona
   e. North Satara

- f. South Satara
- g. Kolhapur
  and
- h. Marathi-speaking territories given over to Karnataka.

3. Central Maharashtra
   - a. Dang
   - b. East Khandesh
   - c. West Khandesh
   - d. Nasik
   - e. Ahmednagar
   - f. Aurangabad
   - g. Nanded
   - h. Parbhani
   - i. Beed
   - j. Usmanabad
   - k. Sholapur City and the Marathi-speaking area of Sholapur District
     and
   - l. Marathi-speaking territories given over to Telangana.
4. Eastern Maharashtra
   - a. Buldhana
   - b. Yeotmal
   - c. Akola
   - d. Arnraoti
   - e. Wardha
   - f. Chanda
   - g. Nagpur
   - h. Bhandara
     and
   - i. Marathi-speaking territories given to the Hindi states.

Ambedkar then proceeds to provide the reasons for the solution he is providing for Maharashtra. It is useful to consider it in detail as many of his arguments find resonance today, not only for Maharashtra but also for all big states such as Andhra Pradesh or Uttar Pradesh consisting of many regions that were unified to form a single state on the basis of language.

MAP 3.5: Division of Maharashtra

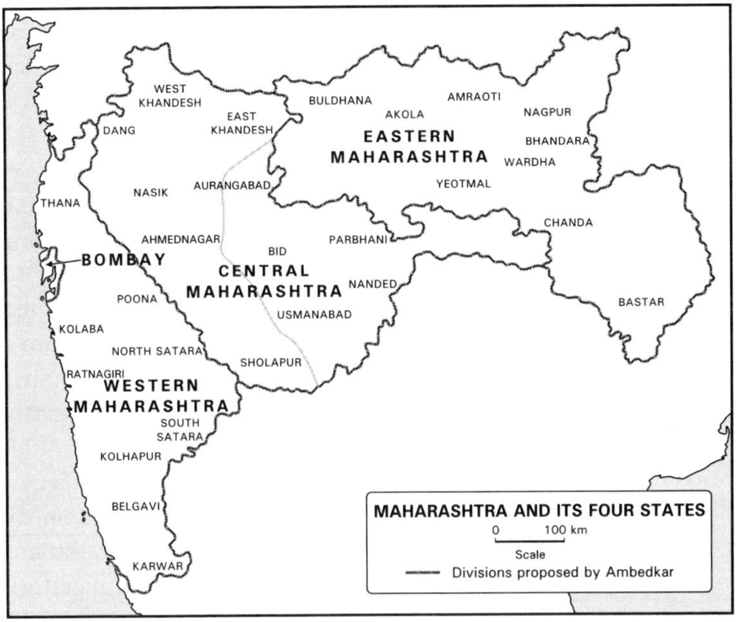


*Source*: Prepared by the authors based on a map in Ambedkar (1955/1979).

Ambedkar first demolishes all the arguments for a mixed state that would bring the Marathi- and Gujarati-speaking populations together. Evaluating the experience of Maharashtrians under the existing mixed state, he points out that they have 'suffered terribly on many counts'. He notes that Maharashtrians have not been provided adequate space in the governance of the mixed state. In the Bombay Legislature, the number of Gujarati members is only 106 while the number of Maharashtrians is 149. However, the number of Gujarati and Maharashtrian ministers in the cabinet is the same and only among the deputy ministers does the latter have a majority of one. Second, the allocation of subjects is skewed both among the ministers and deputy ministers, with the Gujarati ministers having twice as many as their Maharashtrian counterparts. He cites the example of Morarji Desai who had been allocated 105 subjects while Hirey who was the Maharashtrian choice for chief minister had been allocated only 49.

Moving to distribution of expenditure per capita on development in the Gujarat and Maharashtra region, he finds that the amount spent on the former was consistently higher. Ambedkar describes this as discrimination and grave injustice leading to subordination which no Maharashtrian should tolerate. He feels that his arguments have 'blown off' the idea of a mixed state.

Regarding the issue of the position of the city of Bombay on which Gujaratis and Maharashtrians were sharply divided, with the latter wanting it to be part of Maharashtra and the former wanting it to be a separate state, two alternatives were put forward: not to break-up the bilingual state of Bombay into two linguistic units, and second, put forward by the CWC, to make the city of Bombay into a separate state. As stated earlier in this volume, Ambedkar examines the arguments for removing Bombay from the rest of Maharashtra and finds them unjustified. He finds the argument that the Marathi-speaking population does not form a majority of the total population city of Bombay, suffering from a number of weaknesses. First, Bombay is geographically a part of Maharashtra, even if Maharashtrians are in a minority in the city; second, Bombay has a large migratory population—including Gujaratis—that comes from various parts of India to find employment in this port city of opportunity as there is no local law restricting citizenship. Despite this influx, which has been going on for over 200 years, the Maharashtrian population has remained at 48 per cent. He pointed out the original inhabitants of Bombay were the Koli fishermen and it was acquired by the Portuguese and later the British.

Ambedkar also feels that Bombay—like Calcutta or Madras—is a composite city that has been built not by capital belonging to Gujarati businessmen as was claimed, but by European capital over a period of time together with the labour of the Maharashtrian population. Gujaratis form only about 10 per cent of the population and would get very few seats in the Legislature though they have sunk much capital in the city. He admits that withdrawal of Gujarati capital could affect employment until Maharashtra develops. But he feels that Gujarati money cannot stand up to Maharashtrian self-respect and pride. Also, Bombay City cannot exist alone and would become 'Mohenjodaro' or City of the Dead, as its lifelines lie in the hinterlands which supply the required labour, electricity and water. Ambedkar strongly feels that another reason why Bombay City should be made a separate state is the need to protect the minorities and the SCs living in villages, who are constantly subjected to tyranny, oppression and even murders by the members of the majority communities. In a mixed state they will face the oppression of the large majority. He points out that leaders of the SCs who have reached the safety of urban areas have forgotten the tyranny of the villages in the interior.

Rather than making Bombay a separate city state, Ambedkar holds that division of Maharashtra into four Marathi-speaking states as described earlier, would resolve the problem. He feels that the real objection to the creation of Bombay as a separate state arises from the fact that the name 'Bombay' does not carry within it the sense that it is part of Maharashtra. It was with this idea that he proposed the new name 'Maharashtra City State' that would 'carry on its face the word Maharashtra' and would also ease the tension between Maharashtrians and Gujaratis. He finds many advantages in the proposed 'Maharashtra City State'. It would be a surplus state as its revenue was considerable, arising from taxes on property and electricity. However, he advocates a proper division of revenues to help all the four states to be formed. While property tax in the city state would have to be spent for its own development—as Bombay does not produce electricity—revenue accruing from its taxation should be shared among the four proposed states of Maharashtra. This would also ease the financial strain that the three Maharashtra states were likely to suffer due to the separation of Bombay.

Having dealt with Bombay, Ambedkar provides arguments for the division of the rest of Maharashtra into three states. The distribution of population, area and revenue of the three states was arranged as shown in Map 3.5 and Table 3.5. Eastern Maharashtra, he holds, is already a separate state with a well-established administration, revenue and judicial system separated from the 'trammels' of the Hindi-speaking people. He further proposes the division of the Maharashtra part of Bombay and Marathwada into two equal states. This required the transfer of six districts from Maharashtra part of the Bombay State to Marathwada.

Table 3.3: The Population Area and Revenue of the Three Maharashtra States

| *Name of State* | *Total Population of the Territory* | *Area in square miles* | *Total Revenue* | *Total Expenditure* |
|---|---|---|---|---|
| Western Maharashtra | 1,26,77,316 | 30,028 | 26,24,20,441 | not known |
| Central Maharashtra | 1,24,09,044 | 55,482 | 21,63,80,095 | not known |
| Eastern Maharashtra | 80,27,130 | 39,004 | 9,41,11,012 | not known |
| Total | 3,31,13,490 | 1,24,514 | 57,29,11,548 | not known |

*Source*: Ambedkar (1955/1979).

Ambedkar then proceeds to present the advantages of such an arrangement. He points out that his proposal is not new; from very ancient times Maharashtra had been known as *Trai Maharashtrika*, or as divided into three states. He points out that it was mentioned in the *Mahavamsa* and Pali literature in reference to the missionaries sent by Ashok to different parts of the world for the purpose of propagating Buddhism. Ambedkar argues that Bombay was then not known, and goes on to state that it would have been the fourth part of Maharashtra otherwise. The existence of three states speaking Marathi would help develop the language and fulfil other cultural needs as well.

Coming to the present, Ambedkar felt that the present Maharashtra state shall be divided into four states as governing United Maharashtra with more than 33 million Marathi-speaking people spread across 1,74,514 square miles through a single government was simply not feasible. He rhetorically points out:

> The Maharashtrians are not planning to declare war on U.P. and therefore they need not have a common front. Even from the point of view of Marathas why should there be this consolidation? What affiliation has a Maratha of Satara got with the Maratha of Aurangabad? What affiliation has a Maratha of Nasik got with the Maratha of Ratnagiri? What care and interest a Maratha of Satara is going to bestow upon the problems of the Maratha of Aurangabad? What care and interest a Maratha of Nasik is going to bestow upon the problems of the Maratha of Ratnagiri? (Ambedkar 1955/1979)

Most important, Ambedkar categorically pointed out that if the four regions were not separated, the existing extreme inequalities between them would continue. With the example of Marathwada, which had suffered neglect under the rule of the Nizam of Hyderabad, Ambedkar raised the issue of inequalities in the field of industry, income, education and agriculture between Eastern and Western Maharashtra on the one hand and Central Maharashtra on the other. He also pointed out that all Maratha ministers in the then Bombay Cabinet were from Satara District or Nasik District, and none from the Konkan. Ambedkar strongly felt that if they remained together there was little guarantee that the better off areas would look after the interests of the poorer regions. All the benefits will be cornered by the people of better off areas in a United Maharashtra. On the contrary, the division of Maharashtra, Ambedkar argued, would give each region a government of its own consisting of local persons and the chief ministers would be Maharashtrians, unlike the then Chief Minister Morarji Desai, who was a non-Maharashtrian. The existence of separate governments would also mean that Maharashtrians—whom he describes as a politically-backward community—would receive training to become ministers and carry on self-government. For Ambedkar, United Maharashtra was like a 'big banyan tree under which no other plant can flourish'.

Finally, Ambedkar points out that there is need to reclaim 'lost territory' which was Marathi-speaking but had been given by the SRC to other states. The areas which Ambedkar was referring to were (1) Belgaum Taluka with the City of Belgaum; (2) Khanapur Taluka; (3) Chikori Taluka including Nipani; (4) Supa Taluka; (5) Karwar Taluka; (6) Nilanga Taluka in Bidar; (7) Ahamadpur Taluka in Bidar; (8) Udgir Taluka in Bidar; and (9) Rajgir Taluka in Adilabad. Some parts of Vidarbha were also given to the neighbouring Hindi-speaking state. According to Ambedkar, Maharashtrians constituted a large part of the population in these areas. He viewed this arrangement by the SRC as 'clipping the wings of Maharashtra by handing over Marathi-speaking people to non Marathi speaking States' particularly Karnatak. He calls this 'political vandalism' and holds that the wrong done by the Commission to Maharashtra had to be remedied.

The ideas written by Ambedkar in 'Thoughts on Linguistic States' were reiterated by him in a final speech he made on states reorganisation in the Rajya Sabha on 2 May 1956. Here, yet again, he strongly opposed the creation of 'monolithic monstrous states' with huge area and population, such as UP and Bihar which he holds would be ungovernable states. He was particularly concerned about Maharashtra and Uttar Pradesh, and points out that G. B. Pant had earlier agreed to the division of Uttar Pradesh but was then keeping quiet in the house. Ambedkar also argues that the issue of size has important political consequences which have not been realised. The most important being the need to maintain a balance among states within the federation, states which are too large or too small should be avoided. He points out that, in the US, the size of states varies but it does not matter as all states have equal powers; the Lower and Upper Houses have the same powers and all the states have equal representation in the Upper House without reference to population. Ambedkar points out that, in India the states are not equal and do not have the same number of members in the Upper House, and also noted that the Rajya Sabha does not have any power so far as finance is concerned. For the same reason, Ambedkar once again pleads that Hyderabad should be made a second capital as it was closer to the southern states while Delhi was very far away. It had beautiful and useful buildings and other necessities that a capital required. Ambedkar warned members that any political settlement that was made by the ruling party without taking the Opposition along would lead to problems and would be uprooted when the Opposition came to power. In sum, Ambedkar felt that the federation was badly built; there are 'many holes in this federation and it may crack … we have no union. We have no unity and any time this whole thing may crack.' (Ambedkar 1956a/1997) The unity was artificial and not well conceived as it rested only on language.

Ambedkar once again voices his concern that the SCs and minorities would be without any political safeguard and vulnerable to oppression by the majority in the large states that were being envisaged. Rather than attachment to language and culture, ministers of a state, he feels, should be trained to take responsibility for the administrative and economic needs of a region. Explaining the case of a college which he himself had established in Marathwada, he felt that it needed special attention for development. This, he argues, was possible only under a separate autonomous body and not under the Poona University within the large state of Maharashtra.

Ambedkar was also very critical of the city of Bombay, one of the premier cities in the country, being kept separate from any state in the proposed Bill. He felt that if Calcutta and Madras could be kept with Western Bengal and Madras State respectively, there was no reason for Bombay to be kept outside Maharashtra.

However, owing to his illness, he had to leave the house after he made his speech. Following his speech in the Rajya Sabha, Ambedkar found that there were some criticisms of his proposals on Bombay City. He found that both Maharashtrians and Gujaratis were worried about obtaining adequate representation in the city; particularly, the Gujaratis who felt they would not get more than two to four seats in a house of 100. Consequently, both groups were unhappy. Hence in an article titled 'Voice of the People' (Ambedkar 1956b/2002), he recommended that Bombay could be divided into two states. One could consist of six Marathi-speaking districts and parts of three other districts—viz. Surat, Belgaum and Karwar—which had Marathi speakers. This would give the Maharashtrians a compact cultural unit of 19,800 square miles and a total population of 90,67,413 in which they could obtain a majority. However, he continued to remain strongly against the formation of a monstrous united state of Maharashtra. He also felt that the capital of such a state should not be either Nagpur or Poona as was being suggested. Rather, he suggests that Aurangabad should be the capital and calls upon the Congress party to make this decision at the earliest.

When Parliament finally passed the States Reorganisation (Amendment) Bill, 1956, Ambedkar had gone to participate in the Fourth World Buddhist Conference at Kathmandu. He soon breathed his last on 6 December 1956. In fact, both Vishalandhra and the separate states of Maharashtra and Gujarat were formed after Ambedkar's death.

Thus, the mid-1950s was a period when, following the submission of the SRC report, many solutions were put forward and debated for redrawing the map of the Indian subcontinent. Our analysis of Ambedkar's writings in this period shows that he stands out among the political leaders of the time as a thinker who proffered solutions through his writings and speeches only after a systematic study of the recommendations of the SRC, the feasibility of the demands of various political groups, the attempts made by the government to resolve these conflicting demands and also the rapidly-changing political situation.

Setting politics aside, he carefully studied the issues involved over a period of time and was not averse to shifting his position as seen in the fresh solutions he offers for reorganisation in 1955.

In 'Thoughts on Linguistic States,' which represents the maturing of Ambedkar's ideas on the subject over two decades, he agreed that in a country of diverse cultural regions, states should be formed on linguistic lines. It would create cultural homogeneity and unity among the population. But he co-joined the principle of linguism to a number of well thought out key federal principles which, he argued, would support and strengthen the federation, if implemented. Unity that rested only on language, Ambedkar felt, will always remain artificial. A number of safeguards were also provided to prevent the formation of a cultural majority, to safeguard all minorities and to remove divisions over language with other states and the Centre. These ideas were carefully applied to individual states such as Uttar Pradesh, Madhya Pradesh and Rajasthan to prevent the formation of states that were too large and unwieldy so as to ensure viability and equality of size within the federation. The issue of the North-South divide and the need of a capital city acceptable to all regions also bothered Ambedkar. Finally, he gave much thought to Maharashtra, a state he knew well, and tried hard to find a solution that would both address the economic problems faced by this region as well as satisfy different sections of the population.

# In Lieu of a Conclusion

The recent formation of the state of Telangana out of the larger state of Andhra Pradesh shows that reorganisation of India's federal structure is an ongoing task, a part of the larger project of nation-building. Andhra Pradesh was one of the states Ambedkar was concerned about when it was formed in 1953. Critical of the manner in which it was formed he felt that Nehru, instead of creating states after due consideration of their socio-economic feasibility and needs, had bowed to pressure. Speaking on the debate when the Bill for the formation of Andhra was introduced in Parliament, he pointed out that the INC had no clear policy with regard to reorganisation and such a step would create the impression that the central government was open to pressure and lead to haphazard reorganisation of the Indian subcontinent. The conflictual manner in which the recent division of Andhra Pradesh into two smaller states—Seemandhra and Telangana—took place makes it necessary to briefly consider the future trajectory that such a reconfiguration project may take. Clearly, there are differences over the principles on which states should be divided together with the role of the Centre in this process, both of which could create problems as more demands emerge. The formation of states in the 1960s and 1970s largely represented the completion of unfinished tasks from the late colonial period. The more recent formation of three states in 2000, and now of Telangana, is a product of changes that have taken place in post-Independence India. This makes it necessary to briefly discuss the continuing relevance of Ambedkar's ideas, the changes that have taken place since the 1950s and the principles on which future reorganisation could take place.

Reorganising state boundaries in most constitutional democracies is a difficult task, involving a complex process. At Independence, India opted for a federation where changing the existing boundaries of the state or creating new units was relatively easier. Article 3 of the Indian Constitution confers the power of creating new states upon the Parliament, either on the basis of a Presidential recommendation or a resolution passed by the State Assembly concerned. In the case of the former, the President, however, has to send the proposed Bill (drafted by the Centre) to the Legislature of the concerned state(s) for expressing their views within a period as may be specified in the reference or within a further period as the President may allow. The State Assembly after discussion may either forward it to the Centre or may choose not respond to the President's proposal within the time specified. In either of these situations, the central government can present the Bill in Parliament and send it to the President for final assent after it is passed in both the Houses. It does not require the complex mechanism of constitutional amendment. As discussed in Chapter Two, it was Ambedkar who played a significant role in making the process of reorganisation more open and easy for the states in post-Independence India. He had suggested that for reorganisation of states (falling in Part I of the first schedule), all that was needed from the State Assembly was consultation. Ambedkar felt that if there was 'a small minority which felt very strongly that its position will not be safeguarded unless the boundary of the State were changed ... all that was necessary is consultation. Consent is not required.' (CAD 1948)

The response of the Andhra Pradesh State Assembly to the recent attempt by the Centre to reorganise the state into two separate units has made this attempt by Ambedkar very relevant to the present-day context. The struggle for statehood for Telangana, as discussed in Chapter One, has a long history. However, when the Union Cabinet—in order to address the prolonged movement for Telangana—decided to grant statehood to the region in October 2013, it led to violent opposition from the Seemandhra region, not just by the Opposition, but also by the ruling Congress' MLAs, members of Parliament and cabinet ministers. Several of them submitted resignations, some even from the Congress party, which is in power both at the Centre and in the state. The chief minister of Andhra Pradesh, Kiran Reddy, sat in protest at Jantar Mantar against his own party's decision. When the Andhra Pradesh Reorganisation Bill, 2013, was sent to the Andhra Pradesh State Assembly in January 2014, he further ensured that it was not passed by the House by personally introducing a resolution to reject the Bill. The

Bill was rejected through a voice vote under Rule 77 of the Assembly amidst chaos. Moreover, when the Centre went ahead with its decision to grant separate statehood to Telangana and managed to pass the Bill in Parliament in February 2014, the chief minister not only resigned from his post, but also floated his own party.

With the passage of the Bill in Parliament, following which it received President's assent on 1 March 2014, statehood for Telangana has become a reality,[1] but the implications of the opening up of this pandora's box is not related to just these two units. It relates to the larger issue of recasting the federal structure of the country, keeping in mind the mounting demands for division of several larger states created in 1956. Several states have already began raising the same questions, namely those of rights of regions and sub-regions to look after their own needs and aspirations through greater participation and better governance. In Uttar Pradesh there is demand in some areas for further division into four units, in Maharashtra into three or four units, in Orissa into two units separating the coast and the hinterlands, and in Bengal for separation of the hill areas populated by the Gorkhas. The boundaries between Maharashtra, Madhya Pradesh, Andhra Pradesh and Karnataka have been artificial with complaints of linguistic minorities left in each large state. This can be effectively met if many small states speaking the same language covering the central plateau region are carved out. These demands are part of the larger process of nation-building in which minorities, smaller groups and sub-regions that were not politically conscious at Independence now feel neglected as part of large states. There is also the need for a new federal structure in which the Centre and the states are on a more equal footing, enabling them to work in a more cooperative manner.

Concerns are also being raised regarding the future of the separate state of Telangana in this era of liberalisation, and if the emergence of a growing private sector within a market economy would benefit the people of this region. In economic terms the two regions have become intertwined in ways which makes separation a delicate task. It will be difficult for the poorly-educated and disadvantaged groups in the underdeveloped regions to obtain employment particularly in the dynamic sectors of the economy. Well-educated and better-off 'outsiders' might benefit leaving the people of the new state behind. Private businesses have already started moving out fearing that they would have to cater to demands for local employment (Sarangi and Pai 2011). It is widely being felt that the process has been slow, ad-hoc and piecemeal. Important issues such as sharing of river waters, electricity and other resources have not been worked out by the central government in a proper manner.

It is in this larger context that the ideas of Ambedkar discussed in this volume assume greater importance today. The mid-1950s was a period when, following the submission of the SRC report, many solutions were put forward and debated for redrawing the map of the Indian subcontinent. Our analysis of Ambedkar's writings in this period shows that he carefully studied the issues involved in the reorganisation of states over a period of time. Understanding the importance of the issue and the rapidly changing sociopolitical situation, he even shifted his position as seen in the fresh solutions he offers for reorganisation in 1955.

The demands for reconfiguring the map of India today arise in a much changed context, but the fault lines remain just as they existed in the 1950s. Ambedkar had pointed out many of these factors very clearly. Invoking Thomas Paine during his speech on the State Reorganisation Bill in the Rajya Sabha on 2 May 1956, Ambedkar had reminded the house, 'whatever is wrongly settled is never permanently settled; it has to be resettled'. The creation of Telangana proves him correct; the demand for a separate state never died down because it was based on the issue of sub-regional identity within the larger Vishalandhra. The demands for the creation of Gorkhaland and Bodoland—which are being opposed by sections within the larger states of West Bengal and Assam, of which they are presently a part—are also related to the same issue. The creation of the three new states in 2000—Jharkhand, Uttarakhand and Chhattisgarh, carved out respectively from Bihar, Uttar Pradesh and Madhya Pradesh—have all been shaped more or less along the lines suggested by Ambedkar. Similarly, the demands based on economic backwardness being made for carving out smaller states from large states such as Uttar Pradesh and Maharashtra, as the discussion in this volume shows, were raised by Ambedkar on several occasions. Speaking particularly about Maharashtra, Ambedkar had strongly felt that if all parts of Maharashtra remained together under the disguise of linguism, all the benefits would be cornered by the people of better-off areas in United Maharashtra. The division of Maharashtra, on the contrary, he suggested, would give each region a government of its own that would take better care of the people of the region.

At the same time, many changes have taken place since 1956 when the federal map of India was redrawn, and those will have to be considered when future reorganisation is undertaken. The country has experienced democratisation, which has raised political awareness and identity consciousness among a much larger section of the population who are today demanding statehood. Regionalisation of politics leading to emergence of new social groups has given the states a more prominent position within the Indian Union giving them the confidence to challenge the Centre. Federalisation of democratic structures and practices has strengthened the bargaining power of various states which have also followed their own distinctive 'political culture' and socioeconomic pattern of development. The large states of the Hindi region, which had no common identity at Independence apart from the Hindi language, have gradually acquired a common identity through caste-based movements. This rise of new sub-regional elites came along with the demand for formation of new, smaller states. This was further strengthened by the formation of coalition governments at the Centre in the last two decades.

Consequently, linguistic-cultural minorities in some of the larger states—such as Bodos in Assam, Coorgis in Karnataka and Gorkhas in West Bengal—have demanded formation of smaller states which could provide space for recognition of their languages and cultural identities. Yet, there is marked shift in recent decades, from the early years of 1950–60s, in the reasons underlying the demand for smaller states from language and culture to better governance, economic viability, a more accountable bureaucratic state apparatus, increased participative political order and better indices of development of various regions and sub-regions within the existing states. As many as 30 such demands seem to be pending for consideration before the government. A number of these demands reveal some of the inherent tensions between the Centre and the states with the latter asking for more autonomy in the spheres of culture, economy and polity.

With the growing intensity of such demands it is being felt that constitution of a second States Reorganisation Commission that would redraw the map of India and create many smaller states is inevitable. While this decision would strengthen the federal system, it is important to realise that such a task is more complex and difficult today. Historical experiences, culture and social structure of various regions in India are different and these differences have increased over time. A major divide is the Hindi-speaking and non-Hindi-speaking regions, but there are also differences within these regions and with other parts of the country. It is more difficult to divide states in southern and western India which have strong regional and linguistic identities developed over a long time. Similarly, demands for new states in the Hindi heartland in post-Independence India need to be understood in a distinct, situational context. They are the consequence of the political dynamics of a multi-level federal structure in the context of the decline of Congress dominance, rise of lower castes and emergence of Hindu nationalism. Thus, the same solutions may not work at the same time in all regions. The central intervention in the federal architecture is growing difficult day by day, and it requires close attention. Second, mere reduction in size by itself does not seem to resolve problems. While small states such as Kerala, Punjab or Himachal Pradesh seem to be performing well, this may not apply in all cases. The long-term histories of regional political regimes and political economies remain important in shaping the conditions for economic growth in specific areas.

Thus, an important lesson that Ambedkar had emphasised would be useful: rationalisation of boundaries, and scientific and proper use of economic resources shall be kept in place along with the idea of linguism. Boundaries are only administrative divisions and should not stop planning and better use of resources. In this process the idea, put forward by Ambedkar, of many small states constituting a 'United States of India' could play a useful role.

*Revisiting 1956* wishes to impress that there cannot be a conclusion for a discussion on Ambedkar's thoughts; that his thoughts on issues pertinent today have to resurface and be discussed. To facilitate this, we follow this part with a compendium of Ambedkar's works in large excerpts so that scholars and readers would find literature pertaining to states reorganisation from the massive corpus in a single place. As it paves way for the compendium, we hope that this essay broadens the debate on reorganisation by bringing to light Ambedkar's ideas in their continuing and pervading relevance today.

## Note

1. The new state of Telangana will consist of 10 of the 23 districts of undivided Andhra Pradesh. Hyderabad, which was the bone of contention between the two regions making division difficult, has been made the joint capital of both regions for a period of 10 years. The governor will be in charge of law and order in the area. The Centre will soon constitute an expert committee to study various alternatives regarding the new capital for the successor state of Andhra Pradesh and make appropriate recommendations in a period not exceeding six months from the date of enactment of the Andhra Pradesh Reorganisation Act, 2014. The Centre will also provide financial assistance to build the new capital. Both states will also continue to enjoy special status under Article 371 D of the Constitution, which was adopted in 1973 to provide equitable opportunity for all regions of Andhra Pradesh.

# Part II

## Speeches and Writings, 1938–56

*Compendium*

# I

# On Separate Karnatak Province

B. R. Ambedkar first articulated his opinion on the issue of linguistic provinces at the Bombay Legislative Assembly (BLA) when V. N. Jog presented a resolution for separate Karnataka Province on 4 April 1938. Ambedkar initially reminded the house about its inability to take up the issue on grounds that the resolution dealt with a problem which was not primarily the concern of that provincial government alone as it also affected certain areas which were then part of the Madras Presidency. The power of initiation for such matters, under Section 290, was given to the secretary of state. However, when the speaker of the House decided to discuss the issue in the House, Ambedkar chose to oppose the resolution.

He opposed the resolution for a separate Karnataka Assembly preferring Indian nationality over any particular culture, whether it was Hindu, Muslims, Kanarese or Gujarati. Ambedkar very categorically announced that being a representative of the Scheduled Castes (SCs) probably gave him an advantage over other members of the House, as they took no pride in being Maharashtrians or Gujaratis or Karnatakis. His views were dispassionate.

Ambedkar held that the idea of unifying all people of Karnatak was unrealistic, as a large portion of the Kanarese-speaking people were included within the boundaries of other Indian states. Thus getting the Kanarese-speaking people out from the jurisdiction and sovereignty of the Indian states in order to make them a part of the autonomous Kanarese-speaking province was not possible. He then also examined whether the Kanarese-speaking people were suffering in the matter of administration in the polyglot province. However, he came to the conclusion that no injustice was being done with the Kanarese-speaking people either in the matter of seats or in the matter of offices.

Looking at the issue from the standpoint of the minorities, Ambedkar opined that the dismemberment of the provincial areas would also lead to the dismemberment of the minorities. He pointed out that the Scheduled Castes of the proposed Karnatak State, with just two seats got their strength from the 13 members from other parts of the Bombay Presidency to look after them.

Ambedkar also touched upon the matter of finance and found that merely separating Karnatak from the Bombay Presidency was not going to make the situation any better for all the Kanarese-speaking people. The separation of the province might satisfy the ambitions of a few who want to figure as the heads of the province but the rest of the population who need to be fed, clothed and housed will not get any benefit out of this move of the leaders. He opined that there was an urgent need to genuinely look as to where the revenues to govern the state would emerge from.

***

Reproduced below are excerpts from *Dr. Babasaheb Ambedkar Writings and Speeches*, ed. Vasant Moon, vol. 2, 188–96 (Bombay: Government of Maharashtra, 1982).

## "SPEECH DELIVERED IN THE BOMBAY LEGISLATIVE ASSEMBLY ON APRIL 4, 1938

I rise to oppose the resolution moved by my honourable friend Mr. Jog. The subject of this resolution is undoubtedly a matter of great moment. I wonder how many members of this House will be prepared to consider this resolution, without importing into the discussion any sentiment or feeling. I think I, as representing the Scheduled Classes, probably have an advantage over other members of the House. If I may say so, I do not say figuratively but as a matter of most genuine feeling, that we representing the Scheduled Castes take no pride either in being Maharashtrians or Gujaratis or Karnatakis. For reasons which I need not enter into on this particular occasion, there are very many reasons why we think that this is not our land. However, I am using the argument in order to show to the House that by circumstances, I am capable of taking a dispassionate view, at any rate I am making a very serious attempt to take a dispassionate view, of the situation that has been presented to us by this resolution. Sir, it would be necessary and desirable for members of this House to bear in mind one fact which I think is of supreme importance. This Presidency of Bombay was, before the Act came into operation, composed of four different units—Gujarat, Maharashtra, Karnatak and Sind. This joint family has not been of recent origin. Karnatak, Maharashtra and Gujarat have been together for the last 115 years. Sind was with us for nearly 90 years. Sind has been separated. It is a matter of past which we need not dig up now. I mention this fact that we have been living together for the last 115 years only to emphasise the fact that those who want that this unity be sundered, that these three parts which are together be now separated, must consider this matter in a much more serious way and not on grounds which are purely sentimental.

The first thing I propose to consider is this. Our friend who has moved this resolution has given expression to the view that the proposition is only a part of the larger whole, the ideal being the unification of all Karnatak people, that this resolution is merely a step in that direction. Now, Sir, the question that I would like to ask on this aspect is this. Is it likely that this ideal, if my honourable friends will allow me to say this dream, could be realised, the ideal of all the Kanarese speaking people coming together? I have no doubt that this is a dream which can never come true, and the reason for my saying so is this. In a book which has been circulated, at any rate I have been fortunate in securing a copy of it, and which is called "A case for the unification of Karnatak"—I take it that it is a publication of the association which is responsible for this move—I find a statement on page 22 from which it is quite clear that a portion of the Kanarese-speaking people are included within the boundaries of Indian States. Having regard to this fact, the question I would like to ask my honourable friends who are supporting this motion is this: Is it possible to get out from the jurisdiction and sovereignty of the Indian States the Kanarese-speaking people so that they can become part of the autonomous Kanarese-speaking Province? I agree and grant that it is possible for the authorities who are responsible for the administration of British India to persuade the Madras Presidency or other administrations which are subject to British law to part with such territories which consist of Kanarese-speaking people, so that all of them will be consolidated together under one common administration. But I fail to understand how it would be possible for anybody to get Kanarese-speaking people who are now living in Indian States, as it is, to have their allegiance transferred from the States to any British Indian Province. The only conceivable situation in which I think that issue can be successfully thought out would be the transfer of some territory from British India to the Indian States in exchange for the territory occupied by the Kanarese-speaking people. Now, I wonder whether any body of people who are living under the Constitution given by the Government of India Act would be prepared to go within the jurisdiction of the Indian States, so that the Indian States may agree to transfer the Kanarese-speaking people from their domain. I see no prospect and, therefore, I ask those of the honourable members who are in charge of this resolution to consider if my submission is correct, namely, that it would be only possible for them to fully realise their ideal, namely, to have all the Kanarese-speaking people included in one common autonomous Government: Is it worth-while for them to separate a few Kanarese-speaking people occupying a few districts in British India and constitute it into an autonomous Province? If I may say so what is the use of taking a step, if we know before hand that the step is not going to lead to the ultimate goal?

Therefore, I will now turn to the second consideration. If it is not possible to realise the ideal of unifying all the Kanarese-speaking people by bringing them under one common autonomous rule, the question that arises in my judgement is this: Has there been any handicap, has there been any difficulty, in the matter of Kanarese-speaking people recouping or having all the advantages which justice can give them in this what I may call, the polyglot administration? I personally do not see that the Kanarese-speaking people are suffering any handicap in the matter of administration in this polyglot province.

...

I have examined this question from two different points of view. First of all, I take the question of the distribution of offices under the new Government. Have they suffered in that way? Have they obtained less than what was due to them? The second thing that I take by way of test is this: Have they obtained less representation in this House than what they are entitled to?... I take these figures, and, in taking these figures, I am leaving out of consideration composite territories, such as, for instance, the City of Bombay, which is really neither wholly Marathi-speaking nor wholly Gujarati, nor wholly Kanarese. I am leaving such areas aside; I am also leaving out of consideration the seats that are assigned to special interests, and I find these figures. So far as population is concerned, the Marathi-speaking population numbers 9,868,795—in Marathi-speaking, of course I include everybody, Hindus, Mussalmans and Scheduled Castes; I am only taking the linguistic basis—the Gujarati-speaking population number, 3,422,139; and the Kanarese-speaking people number 3,266,223. Now, the position regarding seats in this House is this. On a purely population basis, taking that the 81 seats which have gone to the Marathi-speaking people as the standard, as the norm, by which to judge, I find that the Gujarati-speaking people should have got 27 seats. The Kanarese-speaking population, according to the book that is circulated, is 12 per cent of the total, and on that basis, they were entitled to 21 seats. How many seats have been obtained by them in fact? The Gujarati-speaking people have obtained 31 seats, when, as a matter of fact, they were entitled only to 27 seats. The Kanarese-speaking people have received 28 seats, when, as a matter of fact, they were entitled only to 21.

Now, coming to the offices, taking the two Houses together there are 16 places. Now, on the basis of the ideal number of seats which each section was entitled to on the basis of its actual population, the Marathi-speaking people were entitled to 19.6, the Gujarati-speaking people were entitled to 3.3, and the Kanarese-speaking people were entitled to 3.1. Taking the distribution of offices on the basis of the actual number of seats obtained, irrespective of the question whether that was the right quota or not, the Marathi-speaking people's quota was 9.3, the Gujarati-speaking people's quota was 3.6, and the quota of the Kanarese-speaking people was 3.1. As a matter of fact, what has been the distribution of offices? Six have gone to the Marathi-speaking people; 6 have gone to the Gujarati-speaking people, and 4 have gone to the Kanarese-speaking people.

...

I take no pride in being a Maharashtrian, but the fact remains—and when I use it, I do want to caution the House that I am not citing it by way of complaint, that is not my object; I am citing it merely to point out a fact—the fact remains that the minority people, namely, the Gujarati-speaking and the Kanarese-speaking people, have not been done any injustice either in the matter of seats or in the matter of offices. Before this matter was discussed in this House, I told my honourable friend Mr. Jog quite plainly that if he proved to my knowledge and to my conviction that the Karnatak people suffered in any way—either they did not receive adequate and just representation in this House or that they did not receive sufficient representation in the Cabinet—they could always depend upon my support. I am always prepared to do this. But ... taking these figures—I have devoted the greatest care to the study of this subject; these are figures quoted from official data—speaking for myself at any rate, I do not see that the Karnatak people have suffered in any way by their remaining within the presidency of Bombay.

Now ... coming to the other argument, the question, which, I think is important, and which not only I on this side but those friends who are responsible for this resolution are bound to consider, is the financial question. Is it possible for this newly constituted Kanarese-speaking province to maintain financially the standard of expenditure which is accepted in modem times by every civilised Government? That, I think, is a very important question. Friends on the other side who have spoken in support of the resolution have drawn the attention of the House to a complaint that in the past Karnatak has suffered enormously by negligence on the part of the Government of this province.[1]

...

With regard to this question of finance, what I should like to say is this. In the book which has been circulated, we have been given certain figures. In Appendix B we are told that the total expenditure of the new Kanarese-speaking province would be about 2 crores, and the total revenue would be 2.57 lakhs. Now, I do not know how far the figures given in this appendix include what are called the overhead expenses of carrying on the administration of a province. What I find here are merely sums under certain heads of revenue and expenditure. I do not find anywhere here the expenditure that would be necessary to be incurred on paying a salary to a Governor; to his private staff; to the Secretaries; to the Ministers, to a Director of Public Instruction, who would be necessary; to an Inspector-General of Police; to a health officer—all those superior officers who are necessary for keeping the administration on the run.[2]

...

Assuming now for a moment that this is going to be the budget, and as framed here there is to be a surplus of some 5 or odd lakhs, the question that I would like to ask is this: Is this revenue going to be sufficient for providing all that a modern administration must provide? If my honourable friend were to acquaint himself as to what the revenue of the Bombay Municipality is, he will find that the revenue of the new Province will not be even half the revenue of the Bombay Municipality. The revenue of the Bombay Municipality is Rs. 4 crores, and even with the 4 crores the Bombay Municipality is not able to do all that a modern Government should. I really ask—and I am very serious in saying this—whether this is no consideration which ought to prevail. My learned friend has quoted in the course of this debate a speech delivered by the Prime Minister of Orissa where he has stated that he was very glad that all the limbs have been brought together. I wonder what my honourable friend would say if I stated to him that it is not quite so important to bring limbs together as to provide food for them. This is a question which has to be considered ... I do say and I say that with, all the emphasis, it is a most heart-rending thing in this country to see these people cut up into small bodies with revenue no more than that of an ordinary local board. The separation of the Province might satisfy the ambitions of a few people who want to figure as the heads of the Province but what about the rest of the population who need to be fed, who need to be clothed, and who need to be housed? None of us can tolerate this kind of thing. I do say that with all emphasis ... after all, what are these districts? Two of these districts are famine-stricken. The whole of Bijapur is a famine-stricken district. The whole of Bellary also I am told is famine-stricken. What revenue does he expect to get from the famine-stricken area? Merely by separating from the Bombay Presidency is that going to be a milch cow?

Then there is another question to which I advert and it is this: I being a member of a minority, I am bound to consider these things from the standpoint of the minority. I am very glad that several members who spoke in favour of the resolution did give us an assurance that the interests of the Muhammadans and the interests of the Harijans will be looked after. But I do want to say that, along with dismemberment of these Provincial areas there is going to be a dismemberment of the minorities. I cannot forget the fact that in the Karnatak we have only two seats. I am sure that those members of the Scheduled Classes who come from the Karnatak must be feeling that their strength lies in the fact that there are 13 members from other parts of the Presidency to look after them. What is to happen to them? I am sure, for instance, the Muhammadan community has got about 8 seats from the Karnatak.[3]

...

We cannot allow this kind of dismemberment. It is very good for the members of the majority community to say that they will be generous and they will be kind. We cannot depend upon their generosity and upon their kindness. We want rights and rights cannot be given in a generous, way. To a community which after all on a purely population basis forms only a microscopic minority, even supposing they were prepared to give weightage, what weightage could they give to a population which is about a few lakhs? This is one of the points on which I oppose this resolution. This dismemberment I am not prepared to accept. Our strength lies in a polyglot administration. I do not want to say, but I have my fears that if Karnatak is created as a separate Province, it would be a Province of all the Lingayats against everybody else. I am not mincing matters, but if, for instance, there was separation there would be a combination of the Marathas against the Kanarese. We don't want this kind of thing—and there cannot be a common front which we at present enjoy.

Then there is one other thing I would like to draw the attention of the House to—and with this I want to close—and that is I know there are people probably who would not agree with me but that is my conviction that the British, whatever they may have done in the course of history, whatever they may have failed to do—and there are many things which they have failed to do, which their self-interest probably did not permit them to do—have done two things which I am generous enough to admit as being two monuments of their rule in this country which will survive even when they go away. The one thing that they have done for us is a common code of law. You can travel from Kashmir down to South India and know that murder is the same thing whether you commit it in Kashmir, Punjab and the North-West Frontier Province, or whether you commit it in Rajah-mundry in Madras. You know what Transfer of Property means; you know what evidence means wherever you go ... I say such a thing we did not have. The other thing that the British have done is that they have given us a common Central Government. Such a thing we did not have before. The importance of this fact of having a common Central Government is not probably realised by all. But I think it is a very crucial fact. If today we are on the way of building a common nation, a spirit of nationality, a feeling that we are all one, it is due to the fact that we have a common Government; it is due to the fact that we realise that we are citizens of a common Government.

...

I would plead with the members of this House that they should do nothing whereby they would impair these two advantages which we have secured. Personally myself, I say openly that I do not believe that there is any place in this country for any particular culture, whether it is Hindu culture, or a Muhammadan culture, or a Kanarese culture or a Gujarati culture. There are things we cannot deny, but they are not to be cultivated as advantages, they are to be treated as disadvantages as something which divides our loyalty and takes away from us our common goal. That common goal is the building up of a feeling that we are all Indians. I do not like what some people say, that we are Indians first and Hindus afterwards or Muslims afterwards. I am not satisfied with that; I frankly say that I am not satisfied with that. I do not want that our loyalty as Indians should be in the slightest way affected by any competitive loyalty whether that loyalty arises out of our religion, out of our culture or out of our language. I want all people to be Indian first, Indian last and nothing else but Indians and therefore, I say that this is a resolution which directly runs counter to this ideal ... this is an ideal which we ought to cherish very zealously. I can quite understand that in a country like America, in a country like Germany, in a country like Europe, where the feeling of oneness is solidified, where there is no need to make anybody feel that he is not a German to tolerate anything that is of a separatistic character, but where the feeling that we are Indians is still in its embryo, is only beginning to ripen, to allow other loyalties, feeling of culture, feelings of nationality to grow simultaneously—I say deliberately—is the greatest crime that we can commit and I, for myself, will not be a party to it and I strongly, very strongly, oppose this resolution.”

## Notes

1. The Honourable Speaker of the Assembly at this point reminded Ambedkar about the time-limit.
2. V. N. Jog, the member who presented this resolution, at this moment told the House that one could find those figures in Appendix B in the other book.
3. Sir Ali Mahomed Khan Dehlavi corrected it by saying 'Only four'.

## II

# Maharashtra as a Linguistic Province

With the election of the Constituent Assembly in 1946, the agitation for linguistic provinces—particularly for Andhra—increased. The supporters demanded that the Constituent Assembly accept the principle of linguistic provinces and set up a machinery for redistribution. Prime Minister Nehru made an announcement on behalf of the Government of India in the Constituent Assembly on 27 November 1947 accepting the principle underlying the demand for linguistic provinces. He also declared the inclusion of Andhra as a separate unit in the First Schedule of the new Constitution as was done in the case of Sind and Orissa by the Government of India Act, 1935.

Ambedkar, then a member of the Constituent Assembly and the Chairman of the Drafting Committee of the Constitution (appointed on 30 August 1947), however, felt that the mere listing of Andhra as a separate state in the First Schedule of the Constitution would not suffice, as the issue needed to be examined together with that of other linguistic regions. On 21 February 1948, he therefore recommended that a Commission be appointed immediately to enquire into and work out all relevant matters not only on Andhra but also with regard to the other linguistic regions. Accordingly the Linguistic Provinces Commission, also known as Dar Commission (after its Chairman) was appointed on 17 June 1948 to 'examine and report on the formation of the new provinces of Andhra, Karnatak, Kerala and Maharashtra and on the administrative, financial and other consequences of the creation of such new provinces.'

When the Dar Commission started looking into the issue in 1948, Ambedkar presented it with a written statement—'Maharashtra as a Linguistic Province'. This is a key document of his thoughts on reorganisation. Much of his later ideas about the merits and problems of the proposal for linguistic provinces, find genesis in this document. Ambedkar stated here that there was nothing new in the demand made by Bombay, Madras and the Central Provinces for new states based on linguism as six provinces—namely East Punjab, United Provinces, Bihar, West Bengal, Assam and Orissa—already existed as linguistic provinces. Thus, when the principle of linguistic provinces was accepted in the case of a few provinces, the other provinces asking for the same cannot be asked to wait indefinitely.

Ambedkar's opinion had significantly changed since his last speech on the issue in the BLA, where he opposed the move for a separate Karnatak

State. Now he was strongly of the opinion that a linguistic province produces what democracy needs, namely, social homogeneity. Its absence creates a dangerous situation especially where a state is raised on a democratic structure. Democracy with in a heterogeneous population divided into groups which are hostile and anti-social towards one another, is bound to witness 'cases of discrimination, neglect, partiality, suppression of the interests of one group at the hands of another which happens to capture political power'. The reason, Ambedkar feels, lies in the exercise of power which, instead of being used impartially and for the benefit of all, is used for the aggrandisement of one group and to the detriment of another. On the other hand, a state with homogeneous population can work for the true ends of democracy, 'for there are no artificial barriers or social antipathies which lead to the misuse of political power. For a democracy to function properly, the subjects of the state must be so distributed as to form a single homogeneous group.' Given the democratic form that the Indian Constitution had chosen for its people, it was essential that, each province 'must be homogeneous in its population to make democracy in the province successful'.

However, he then pointed out some cautions for making a linguistic province: (1) there is no categorical imperative in the scheme of linguistic provinces which compels us to make the language of the province its official language; (2) though not all provinces may add up ending as a separate state like Pakistan, there is nothing wrong if the loosening of the ties in one direction is accompanied by their being tightened up in another direction; and (3) the imposition of an all-India official language on a linguistic province which may happen to be different from the language of the province should not be considered as coming in the way of maintaining provincial culture.

He then goes into examining the specific question of Maharashtra province and verifies its viability with certain tests such as size, volume of population and a commensurate amount of revenue. Amebdkar, like his earlier speech at the BLA, felt that for a province to exist, it should not merely be self-supporting, but must have sufficient revenue to provide for a minimum standard of administration required by efficiency and the needs of social welfare.

Ambedkar then goes on to discuss about the controversies over Bombay. After verifying the claims of all the parties, he categorically comes to the conclusion that Maharashtra and Bombay are not merely interdependent, but 'one and integral'. He refutes the suggestion that the problem of Bombay should be settled by arbitration.

***

Reproduced below are excerpts from *Dr. Babasaheb Ambedkar Writings and Speeches*, ed. Vasant Moon, vol. 1, 99–128 (Bombay: Government of Maharashtra, 1979).

## "MAHARASHTRA AS A LINGUISTIC PROVINCE: STATEMENT SUBMITTED TO THE LINGUISTIC PROVINCES COMMISSION

### THE PROBLEM OF LINGUISTIC PROVINCES

The question of Linguistic Provinces has not only led to a great deal of controversy born out of party prejudices and party interests but it has led to a difference of opinion as to the merits thereof. The points of controversy relate to claims and counter-claims as between contiguous Provinces to territories as well as to the terms of their inclusion. I shall deal with them at a later stage in so far as they relate to the creation of the Maharashtra Province. I shall first take up the question of the merits of the proposal for Linguistic Provinces.

### Purposes behind the demand for Linguistic Provinces

What is the purpose which lies behind the demand for Linguistic Provinces? The generality of those who advocate the creation of Linguistic Provinces do so because they believe that the Provinces have different languages and cultures. They should therefore have the fullest scope to develop their languages and their cultures. In other words, the Provinces have all the elements of a distinct nationality and they should be allowed the freedom to grow to their fullest in nationhood.

### Difficulties arising out of Linguistic Provinces

In discussing the question of creating such Linguistic Provinces it would be very short-sighted to omit from one's consideration the fact that the structure of Government of India of the future is to be cast in a dual form: (a) a Central Government and (b) a number of Provincial Governments inextricably inter-linked and inter-woven in the discharge of their respective Legislative, Executive and Administrative functions. Before one could agree to the creation of Linguistic Provinces, one must, therefore, consider the effects which Linguistic Provinces would have on the working of the Central Government.

Among the many effects that may be envisaged, the following are obvious:

(1) Linguistic Provinces will result in creating as many nations as there are groups with pride in their race, language arid literature. The Central Legislature will be a League of Nations and the Central Executive may become a meeting of separate and solidified nations filled with the consciousness of their being separate in culture and therefore in interests. They may develop the mentality of political insubordination, i.e., refusal to obey the majority

or of staging walk-outs. The development of such a mentality is not to be altogether discounted. If such a mentality grows it may easily make the working of the Central Government impossible.

(2) The creation of Linguistic Provinces would be fatal to the maintenance of the necessary administrative relations between the Centre and the Provinces. If each Province adopts its own language as its official language the Central Government will have to correspond in as many official languages as there are Linguistic Provinces. This must be accepted as an impossible task. How great a deadlock Linguistic Provinces will create in the working of the Governmental machine can be better understood by studying the effects of Linguistic Provinces on the Judiciary. In the new set-up, each Province will have a High Court with a series of subordinate courts below it. At the apex of these High Courts will be the Supreme Court with the right to hear appeals against the decisions of the High Courts. On the basis of Linguistic Provinces, Courts of each Province including its High Court will conduct their proceedings in the language of the Province. What is the Supreme Court to do when its jurisdiction is invoked for rectifying a wrong done by the High Court? The Supreme Court will have to close down. For, if it is to function—every judge of the Supreme Court—I am omitting for the moment the lawyers practising therein—must know the language of every Province—which it is impossible to provide for.

No one can contemplate such a situation with equanimity. It may lead to a break-up of India. Instead of remaining united, India may end in becoming Europe — faced with the prospect of chaos and disorder.

## Advantages from Linguistic Provinces

While it is true that the proposal of Linguistic Provinces creates a problem which goes to the very root of the matter—inasmuch as it affects the unity of India—there can be no doubt that the reconstruction of Provinces on linguistic basis has certain definite political advantages.

The main advantage of the scheme of Linguistic Provinces which appeals to me quite strongly is that Linguistic Provinces would make democracy work better than it would in mixed Provinces. A Linguistic Province produces what democracy needs, namely, social homogeneity. Now the homogeneity of a people depends upon their having a belief in a common origin, in the possession of a common language and literature, in their pride in a common historic tradition, community of social customs, etc. is a proposition which no student of sociology can dispute. The absence of a social homogeneity in a State creates a dangerous situation especially where such a State is raised on a democratic structure. History shows that democracy cannot work in a State where the population is not homogeneous. In a heterogeneous population divided into groups which are hostile and anti-social towards one another the working of democracy is bound to give rise to cases of discrimination, neglect, partiality, suppression of the interests of one group at the hands of another group which happens to capture political power. The reason why in a heterogeneous society, democracy cannot succeed is because power instead of being used *impartially* and *on merits* and for the benefit of all is used for the aggrandisement of one group and to the detriment of another. On the other hand, a state which is homogeneous in its population can work for the true ends of democracy, for there are no artificial barriers or social antipathies which lead to the misuse of political power.

It follows that if democracy is to function properly the subjects of the State must be so distributed as to form a single homogeneous group. The constitution for the Provinces of India which is on the anvil is designed for a democratic form of Government. It follows that each Province must be homogeneous in its population if democracy in the Province is to be successful. This is simply another way of saying that each Province must be a linguistic unit if it is to be fitted to work a democratic constitution. Herein lies the justification for Linguistic Provinces.

## Can the creation of Linguistic Provinces be postponed?

Can the solution of this problem be postponed? In this connection, I would like to place before the Commission the following considerations:

(i) There is nothing new in the demand for Linguistic Provinces. Six Provinces (1) East Punjab, (2) United Provinces, (3) Bihar, (4) West Bengal, (5) Assam and (6) Orissa already exist as Linguistic Provinces. The Provinces which are clamouring for being reconstituted on linguistic basis are: (1) Bombay, (2) Madras and (3) Central Provinces. When the principle of Linguistic Provinces is accepted in the case of six Provinces, the other Provinces which are asking the same principle to be applied to them cannot be asked to wait indefinitely.

(ii) The situation in the Non-Linguistic Provinces has become exasperating if not dangerous and is in no way different from the situation as it existed in the old Turkish Empire or in the old Austro-Hungarian Empire.

(iii) The demand for Linguistic Provinces is an explosive force of the same character which was responsible for blowing up the old Turkish Empire or Austro-Hungarian Empire. It is better not to allow it to get too hot when it may become difficult to prevent an explosion.

(iv) So long as the Provinces were not democratic in their constitutions, and so long as they did not possess the widest sovereign powers which the new constitution gives them, the urgency of Linguistic Provinces was not very great. But with the new constitution, the problem has become very urgent.

## The solution of the difficulties

If the problem must be dealt with immediately what is to be the solution? As has already been pointed out, the solution must satisfy two conditions. While accepting the principle of Linguistic Provinces it must provide against the break-up of India's unity. My solution of the problem therefore is that, while accepting the demand for the re-constitution of Provinces on linguistic basis, the constitution should provide that the official language of every Province shall be the same as the official language of the Central Government. It is only on that footing that I am prepared to accept the demand for Linguistic Provinces.

I am aware of the fact that my suggestion runs counter to the conception of Linguistic Provinces which is in vogue. It is that the language of the Province shall be its official language. I have no objection to Linguistic Provinces. But I have the strongest objection to the language of the Province being made its official language where it happens to be different from the official language of the Centre. My objection is based on the following considerations:

(1) The idea of having a Linguistic Province has nothing to do with the question of what should be its official language. By a Linguistic Province, I mean a Province which by the social composition of its population is homogeneous and therefore more suited for the realisation of those social ends which a democratic Government must fulfil. In my view, a Linguistic Province has nothing to do with the language of the Province. In the scheme of Linguistic Provinces, language has necessarily to play its part. But its part can be limited to the creation of the Province, i.e., for demarcation of the boundaries of the Province. There is no categorical imperative in the scheme of Linguistic Provinces which compels us to make the language of the Province its official language. Nor is it necessary, for sustaining the cultural unity of the Province, to make the language of the Province its official language. For, the cultural unity of the Province, which already exists, is capable of being sustained by factors other than language such as common historic tradition, community of social customs, etc. To sustain Provincial cultural unity which already exists, it does not require the use of the Provincial language for official purposes. Fortunately for the Provincialists there is no fear of a Maharashtrian not remaining a Maharashtrian because he spoke any other language. So also there is no fear of a Tamilian or an Andhra or a Bengali ceasing to be a Tamilian, Andhra or Bengali if he spoke any other language than his own mother-tongue.

(2) The out-and-out advocates of Linguistic Provinces would, no doubt, protest that they have no intention of converting the Provinces into separate nations. Their *bona fides* need not be doubted. At the same time, it often happens that things do take a shape which their authors never intended. It is therefore absolutely necessary to take from the very beginning every step to prevent things taking an evil shape in course of time. There is therefore nothing wrong if the loosening of the ties in one direction is accompanied by their being tightened up in another direction.

(3) We must not allow the Provincial language to become its official language even if it was natural that the Provincial language should be the official language of the Province. There is no danger in creating Linguistic Provinces. Danger lies in creating Linguistic Provinces with the language of each Province as its official language. The latter would lead to the creation

of Provincial nationalities. For the use of the Provincial languages as official languages would lead Provincial cultures to be isolated crystallised, hardened and solidified. It would be fatal to allow this to happen. To allow this is to allow the Provinces to become independent nations, separate in everything and thus open the road to the ruination of United India. In Linguistic Provinces without the language of the Province being made its official language the Provincial culture would remain fluid with a channel open for give and take. Under no circumstances, we must allow the Linguistic Provinces to make their Provincial languages their official languages.

The imposition of an All-India official language on a Linguistic Province which may happen to be different from the language of the Province cannot come in the way of maintaining Provincial culture. Official language will be used only in the field occupied by Government. The nonofficial field or what may be the purely cultural field will still remain open to the Provincial language to play its part. There may be a healthy competition between the official and non-official language. One may try to oust the other. If the official language succeeds in ousting the non-official language from the cultural field, nothing like it. If it fails, there cannot be much harm. Such a position cannot be said to be intolerable. It is no more intolerable than the present position in which we have English as the official language and the Provincial language as its non-official language. The only difference is that the official language will not be English but some other.

### The requirements of a satisfactory solution

I am aware of the fact that my solution is not an ideal solution. It makes working of the constitution in the Provinces on democratic lines possible. But it does not make possible the democratic working of the constitution at the Centre. That is because mere linguistic unity, i.e., the facility to speak a common language does not ensure homogeneity which is the result of many other factors. As stated before, the representatives selected by the Provinces to the Central Legislature will remain what they are, namely, Bengalis, Tamilians, Andhras, Maharashtrians, etc., even though they may be speaking the official language of the Centre and not their mother-tongue. But an ideal solution which can be put into effect immediately, I cannot see. We must be content with the next best. The only thing we must be sure about is that the solution we adopt immediately must satisfy two conditions: (i) It must be the very next best to the ideal; and (ii) It must be capable of developing itself into the ideal. Judged in the light of these considerations, I venture to say that the solution which I have suggested satisfies these two conditions.

## WILL MAHARASHTRA BE A VIABLE PROVINCE?

### Tests of Viability

Coming to the specific question of Maharashtra Province it is necessary to be satisfied that it will be a viable Province. For being declared a viable Province, a Province must satisfy certain tests. It must be of a certain size, it must have a certain volume of population and a commensurate amount of revenue. A Province must not only be self-supporting—which any Province can be by choosing to live on a lower plane—but it must have sufficient revenue to provide for a minimum standard of administration required by efficiency and the needs of social welfare.

## Is Maharashtra Viable?

Does the Province of Maharashtra satisfy these tests? The following are the figures which show the size and population of the Maharashtra Province as constituted on a linguistic basis:

| *Territory* | *Area in square miles* | *Total Population of the territory* | *Total Marathi speaking population of the territory* | *Percentage of Marathi speaking population to total population* |
|---|---|---|---|---|
| Twelve districts of the Bombay Presidency | 47284 | 12913544 | 10045100 | 77.8 |
| Eight Districts of C.P. and Berar | 36865 | 7020694 | 5388300 | 76.7 |
| Total | 84151 | 19934238 | 15433400 | 77.4 |
| States within Bombay Presidency | 11314 | 2720207 | 2120700 | 77.9 |
| Marathi speaking Districts of Hyderabad State | 22766 | 4249272 | 3299300 | 77.6 |
| Goa | 1534 | 580000 | 520000 | 89.6 |
| State of Bastar | 13701 | 633888 | 212300 | 33.5 |
| Total | 49315 | 8183367 | 6142300 | – |
| GRAND TOTAL | 133466 | 28117605 | 21585700 | 76.8 |

## Area and population of Maharashtra

The above table gives figures for the Maharashtra Province in its two forms (1) abridged and (2) unabridged. In its unabridged form which means if all the area occupied by the Marathi-speaking people was constituted in one single Province the area and the population of Maharashtra will be 1,33,466 square miles with a population of 2,15,85,700. In its abridged form which means that if the area and population of the Marathi-speaking people comprised within the States was for the moment omitted, even then the proposed Maharashtra Province would comprise an area of 84,151 square miles with a population of 1,54,33,400.

## Revenue of Maharashtra

Turning to the revenue side of the Province, it has been estimated that the total annual revenue at the existing rate of taxation which will accrue to the abridged Maharashtra Province will be approximately Rs. 25,61,51,000.

## Comparison of Maharashtra with other Provinces

Some comparisons are necessary to get an idea if a Province of this size, with this population and with so much revenue will be viable. For this, I give below figures of the first or the biggest and the forty-seventh or the smallest states within the U.S.A. in order of their size and population:

| *States* | *Area in Square Miles* |
|---|---|
| 1st Texas | 2,67,339 |
| 47th Delaware | 2,057 |
| *States* | *Population* |
| 1st New York | 1,26,32,890 |
| 47th Wyoming | 2,57,108 |

It is obvious that Maharashtra whether one takes its abridged edition or the unabridged edition of it will be several times bigger than Delaware which is the smallest State in U.S.A. in point of area and also several times bigger than New York which is the biggest state in U.S.A. in point of population. Comparison of Maharashtra with the existing and prospective Linguistic Provinces of India may also be useful. Their position in point of area, population and revenue is as follows:

| *Province* | *Area in square miles* | *Population* | *Annual Revenue* |
|---|---|---|---|
| Existing Linguistic Province | | | |
| United Provinces | 106247 | 55020617 | 326508000 |
| Bihar | 69745 | 36340151 | 162678000 |
| Orissa | 32198 | 8228544 | 46062000 |
| New Linguistic Province | | | |
| Andhra | 70000 | 19000000 | – |
| Karnatak | 25000 | 4500000 | – |
| Kerala | 6000 | 3500000 | – |

These figures when compared with the figures for Maharashtra leave no doubt that Maharashtra will not merely be a viable Province but a strong province in point of area, population and revenue.

### SHOULD THE MAHARASHTRA PROVINCE BE FEDERAL OR UNITARY?

I will now turn to what are known to be points on which there is controversy. There is no controversy regarding the unification of Maharashtra into one Province. The controversy relates to the way it should he brought about. One view is that the new Maharashtra Province should be a unitary Province, with a single legislature and a single executive. The other view is that Maharashtra should be a Federation of two sub-provinces, one sub-province to consist of the Marathi-speaking districts of the Bombay Presidency and the other of the Marathi-speaking districts of the present Province of the Central Provinces and Berar. The idea of creating sub-Provinces has originated from the spokesmen of the Marathi-speaking districts of Central Provinces and Berar. I am satisfied that it is only the wish of a few high-caste politicians who feel that in a unified Maharashtra their political careers will come to an end. It has no backing from the people of ... that it gives me an opportunity to enunciate what I regard as a very vital principal. When it is decided to create a Linguistic Province, I am definitely of opinion that all areas which are contiguous and which speak the same language should be forced to come into it. There shouldn't be room for choice or for self-determination. Every attempt must be made to create larger provincial units. Smaller provincial units will be a perpetual burden in normal times and a source of weakness in an emergency. Such a situation must be avoided. That is why I insist that all parts of Maharashtra should be merged together in a single province.

### MAHARASHTRA AND THE CITY OF BOMBAY

#### Controversy over Bombay

Should the City of Bombay be included in Maharashtra or not is another point over which there has been a controversy. A meeting was held in Bombay in the building of the Indian Merchants Chamber. The meeting was attended by no more than sixty. With the exception of one Indian-Christian it was attended by only Gujarati-speaking merchants and industrialists. Although it was small and sectional meeting, its proceedings were flashed on the front page of every important newspaper in India and the *Times of India* was so impressed by its importance that it wrote an editorial which while mildly castigating the vituperative tone which the speakers at the meeting adopted against the Maharashtrians, supported the resolutions passed at the meeting regarding the future of Bombay. This proves what truth there is in the reply given by Lord Birkenhead to the Irish Leader, Mr. Redmond, in the course of the Irish controversy when he said that there are cases where a minority is a majority.

My memorandum would be woefully incomplete if I omitted to deal with the *pros* and *cons* of this controversy. This is because of two reasons: In the first place, the meeting has been recognized to be very important and secondly because the resolutions of the meeting have been supported by eminent University Professors.

### Proposals regarding Bombay

The meeting passed the following resolutions:

(1) That the question of the creation of Linguistic Provinces should be postponed, or
(2) That if it is not postponed, Bombay City should be constituted into a separate Province.

There is a third suggestion, namely, that Konkan should be constituted into a separate Province with Bombay as its capital. There is hardly any support to this plan. There is therefore no necessity to discuss it.

### Decision regarding Bombay must be made now

I have no complaint against that part of the Resolution which says the question of Linguistic Provinces be postponed provided the main question namely whether Bombay should or should not be included in Maharashtra is settled. If this question was settled it did not matter if it took five or ten years to give effect to the Settlement. But the resolution is only an escapism. It does not settle the issue. It only adjourns the controversy. The main question must therefore be tackled right now.

### Ground for the Exclusion of Bombay from Maharashtra

The arguments urged in favour of separating Bombay from Maharashtra are set out below:

(1) Bombay was never a part of Maharashtra.[1]
(2) Bombay was never a part of the Maratha Empire.[2]
(3) The Marathi-speaking people do not form a majority of the population of the City of Bombay.[3]
(4) Gujarathis have been old residents of Bombay.[4]
(5) Bombay is a trade centre for vast areas outside Maharashtra. Therefore, Bombay cannot be claimed by Maharashtra. It belongs to the whole of India.[5]
(6) It is the Gujarathi speaking people of Bombay who have built up the trade and industry of Bombay. The Maharashtrians have been only clerks and coolies. It would be wrong to place the owners of trade and industry under the political dominance of the working classes who form the bulk of Maharashtrians.[6]

[1] Prof. Gheewala—*Free Press Journal*, September 6, 1948, and Prof. Moraes—*Free Press Journal*, September 18, 1948.

[2] Ibid.

[3] Prof. C. N. Vakil, *Free Press Journal*, September 21, 1948.

[4] Prof. Gheewala, *Free Press Journal*, September 6, 1948.

[5] Prof. C. N. Vakil, *Free Press Journal*, September 11, 1948.

[6] Prof. C. N. Vakil, *Bombay Chronicle*.

(7) Maharashtra wants Bombay to be included in Maharashtra because it wants to live on the surplus of Bombay.[7]
(8) A multi-lingual State is better. It is not so fatal to the liberty of smaller people.[8]
(9) Regrouping of Provinces should be on rational lines and not on national lines.[9]

## Burden of Proof

On an examination of these points it is obvious that points (1) and (2) are preliminary in the sense that they help us to decide on whom rests the burden of proof. If it is proved that Bombay is part of Maharashtra, then the burden of proof for separating it from Maharashtra must fall upon those who urge that it should be separated and not upon those who claim that it should remain part of Maharashtra. I will therefore deal with these two points first.

## POINTS (1) AND (2)

### *Verdict of History*

These points can be considered both in the light of history as well as of geography. I am, however, convinced that history cannot help us to decide the issue. In the first place, how far back must we go to find the data on which to base our conclusion? It is obvious that the history of the ancient past would be of no use to us in this connection. What could be of use to us is the past of the present. One may go further and question any reliance being placed upon such a past of the present for drawing any conclusion that can have a bearing on the issue before us. Most of the contacts between people during historical times have been between conquerors and conquered. This is true of India as well as of Europe. But the results of such contacts have been quite different in Europe and in India. In Europe such contacts have produced assimilation of the conflicting social elements. Frequent inter-marriages have confounded the original stocks. One language, either the most useful or the most commonly spoken, has tended to supplant the other. If one civilisation is superior to the others in the same country it has automatically supplanted them. This natural tendency towards assimilation which we see in Europe is so strong that steps have to be taken to counteract it. What is the tendency in India? It is definitely against assimilation. The Musalmans conquered Hindus. But the Musalmans remained Musalmans and the Hindus remained Hindus. The Gujarathis were conquered by Maharashtrians and were ruled by them for some years. What effect has it produced upon the Gujarathis? Nothing. Gujarathis have remained Gujarathis and Maharashtrians have remained Maharashtrians. The Chalukyas conquered Maharashtrians and so did the Shilahars. But there

[7] Prof. C. N. Vakil, at the meeting of India Merchants Chamber.

[8] Prof. Dantwala, *Free Press Journal*, September 1, 1948

[9] Prof. Gheewala, *Free Press Journal*, September 11, 1948.

was no assimilation between them. The Shilahars and Chalukyas remained what they were and so did the Maharashtrians. This being the case, what help can Indian History give in the decision of the issue? The history of internal upheavals as well as of external aggressions has been nothing more than a passing show. Conquest means nothing and proves nothing.

### *Verdict of Geography*

Let us now turn to geography and ask for its verdict. It seems to be a better witness than history. For this purpose one must consider the location of Bombay in relation to the Province of Maharashtra. The Province of Maharashtra once it is created will be triangular in shape. One side of this triangle is formed by the Western Coast Line of India between Daman in the North and Karwar in the South. The City of Bombay lies in between Daman and Karwar. The Province of Gujarat starts from Daman and spreads northwards. The Kanada Province starts from Karwar and spreads southwards. It is about 85 miles South of Daman which is the starting point of Gujarat, and 250 miles North of Karwar, which is the starting point of Karnatak Province. If the unbroken territory between Daman and Karwar is geographically part of Maharashtra, how could Bombay be held not to be a part of Maharashtra? This is an incontrovertible fact of nature. Geography has made Bombay part of Maharashtra. Let those who want to challenge the fact of nature do so. To an unbiased mind it is conclusive proof that Bombay belongs to Maharashtra.

### *Bombay and the Maratha Empire*

That the Marathas did not care to make it a part of their Empire does in no way affect the validity of the conclusion drawn from geography. That the Marathas did not care to conquer it does not prove that Bombay is not a part of Maharashtra. It only means that the Maratha power was a land power and did not therefore care to spend its energy in the conquest of a seaport.

With the decision on Points (1) and (2), the burden must now shift on those who contended that Bombay should not be included in Maharashtra. Have they discharged the burden? This leads to the consideration of other points.

## POINT (3)

## Marathi-speaking Population—Majority or Minority

There is no unanimity on this question. Prof. Gadgil speaking for the inclusion of Bombay in Maharashtra asserts that the Marathi-speaking population of Bombay according to the census of 1941 is 51 per cent. Speaking against the inclusion of Bombay, Prof. Gheewala says that the Marathi-speaking population of Bombay is 41 per cent. Prof. Vakil has brought it down to 39 per cent which he regards as a very liberal estimate. I have not had time to check up these figures and I understand that the Census of Bombay does not render much help in arriving at a precise figure. However, if one reads the reasons assigned by Prof. Vakil, one would find his conclusion to be speculative it not wishful thinking. But assuming that the figures given by Prof. Vakil are correct, what of it? What conclusion can be drawn from it? Does it defeat the claim of Maharashtra to include Bombay? Ever since the British became the masters of India, India has been one country with a right to free movement from place to place. If people from all parts of India were allowed to come to Bombay and settle there, why should the Maharashtrians suffer? It is not their fault. The present state of the population cannot therefore be a ground for excluding Bombay from Maharashtra.

### POINT (4)

### Are Gujarathis Natives of Bombay?

Let us however fully consider the question. Are the Gujarathis natives of Bombay? If they are not, how did they come to Bombay? What is the source of their wealth? No Gujarathi would claim that the Gujarathis are the natives of Bombay. If they are not the natives of Bombay, how did they come to Bombay? Like the Portuguese, the French, the Dutch and the English on adventures to fight their way through and willing to take any risks? The answers which history gives to these questions are quite clear. The Gujarathis did not come to Bombay voluntarily. They were brought to Bombay by the officers of the East India Company to serve as commercial *Adatias* or go-betweens. They were brought because the East India Company's officers who had their first factory in Surat had got used to Surti Banias as their go-betweens in carrying on their trade. This explains the entry of Gujarathis in Bombay. Secondly, the Gujarathis did not come to Bombay to trade on the basis of free and equal competition with other traders. They came as privileged persons with certain trading rights given to them exclusively by the East India Company. Their importation into Bombay was considered for the first time in the year 1671 by Governor Aungier. This fact is referred to in the *Gazetteer of Bombay Town and Island*, Vol. I in the following terms:*

> "Another scheme for the advantage of Bombay in which Governor Aungier interested himself was the settlement of Surat Banias in Bombay. It appears that the Mahajan or committee of the Surat Bania community desired the assurance of certain privileges before risking the move to Bombay and that the company had given a general approval to the Mahajan's proposal. On the 10th January the Surat Council wrote to the Company. The Mahajan or Chief Council of the Banias have been much satisfied with the answer which you were pleased to give to their petition sent you by the ship *Samson* touching their privileges in Bombay. It seems they have determined once more to trouble Your Honours with a letter which they have ordered your broker Bhimji Parakh to write, representing their desires that the said privileges may be confirmed to them under your great seal, for which their

* *Bombay Gazetteer*, I, pp. 46–47.

request they give you their reason and ground in their own letter which they have sent us to be transmitted to you and now goes in your packet by ship *Falcon*. The argument they use to strengthen their request seems to have some weight. They say the Honourable Company are perpetual and their ordinances always of force, but their Presidents and Councils are mutable, and the succeeding Presidents and Councils, do alter often what their predecessors have granted on which score they hope your Honours will be pleased to grant their petition. As to our judgments hereon, we humbly offer that we cannot see any detriment can accrue to you thereby, rather a considerable advantage may follow; and as to the latitude and extent of what privileges you shall afford them, it must be totally referred to your own wisdoms howsoever you shall please to determine in this matter. We judge if your Honours would please to favour them with a line in answer to their letter, it would be a great comfort to them and no disadvantage to your interest."

What were the privileges which the Gujrarathi Banias had asked for from the East India Company? The following petition by one Nima Parakh, an eminent Bania belonging to the City of Diu, gives some idea of what they were:*

"(1) That the Honourable Company shall allot him so much ground in or near the present town free of rent as shall be judged necessary to build a house or warehouse thereon.

(2) That he with the Brahmans of Vers (Gors or priests) of his caste shall enjoy the free exercise of their religion within their own houses without the molestation of any person whatsoever; that no Englishman, Portuguese, or other Christian nor Muhammadan shall be permitted to live within their compound or offer to kill any living creature there, or do the least injury or indignity to them, and if any shall presume to offend them within the limits of their said compound, upon their complaint to the Governor (at Surat) or Deputy Governor (at Bombay), the offenders shall be exemplarily punished; that they shall have liberty to burn their dead according to their custom, also to use their ceremonies at their weddings ; and that none of their profession of what age, sex or condition whatever they be, shall be forced to turn Christians, nor to carry burthens against their wills.

(3) That he and his family shall be free from all duties of watch and ward, or any charge and duty depending thereon; that neither the Company nor the Governor, Deputy Governor or Council, or any other person, shall on any pretence whatsoever force them to lend money for public or private account or use any indirect.

(4) That in case there falls out any difference or suit in law between him or his vakil or attorneys or the Banias of his caste, and any other persons

* *Bombay Gazetteer*, I, pp. 74–76.

remaining on the island, the Governor or Deputy Governor shall not suffer him or them to be publicly arrested dishonoured or carried to prison, without first giving him due notice of the cause depending, that he or they may cause justice to be done in an honest and amicable way and in case any difference happen between him or his attorney and any Bania of their own caste, they may have liberty to decide it among themselves without being forced to go to law.

(5) That he shall have liberty of trade in his own ships and vessels to what port he pleases, and come in and go out when he thinks good; without paying anchorage, having first given the Governor or Deputy Governor or customer notice and taken their consent thereunto.

(6) That in case he brings any goods on shore more than he can sell on the island within the space of 12 months, he shall have liberty to transport them to what port he pleases, without paying custom for exportation.

(7) That in case any person be indebted to him, and also to other Banias, and be not able to pay all his debts, his right may be preferred before other Banias.

(8) That in case of war or any other danger which may succeed, he shall have a warehouse in the castle to secure his goods, treasure, and family therein.

(9) That he or any of his family shall have liberty of egress and regress to and from the fort or residence of the Governor or Deputy Governor; that they shall be received with civil respect and be permitted to sit down according to their qualities; that they shall freely use coaches, horses or palanquins and quitasols (that is barsums or umbrellas) for their convenience without any disturbances; that their servants may wear swords and daggers, shall not be abused, beaten or imprisoned except they offend, and that in case of any of his kindred or friends shall come to visit him or them from any other ports, they shall be used with civility and respect.

(10) That he and his assigns shall have liberty to sell and buy coconuts, betelnuts, pan or betel-leaves, and any other commodity not rented out without any molestation on the island."

How this petition of Nima Parakh was disposed of can be seen from the reply of the Deputy Governor of Bombay dated 3rd April, 1677, which was in the following terms:

> "According to order we have consider the articles of Nima Parakh Bania, which if we rightly understand we do not apprehend any prejudice connection the most of them being what the meanest enjoy.
>
> The first is very easy, the Company having vast ground enough, and we daily *do* the same to Banias and others who come to inhabit here. As to the second, the free exercise of religion is permitted to all with the use of their ceremonies at: weddings and feast, the Banias always burning

their dead without molestation. Neither do we permit any person to kill anything near the Banias who ail live by themselves, much less can any person presume to enter into anybody's house or compound without the owner's license; and, for forcing people to turn Christian against their wills, the whole world will vindicate us; neither are any persons forced to carry burdens against their wills. No Bania, Brahman, Moor, or such man is obliged to watch or ward or other duty, but if any person buys an oart or warge (vada) he is bound on every alarm to send a musquiter. But if he possesses no land no duty is exacted, so the articles may be granted to Nima, and when he goes about to buy any land he may be acquainted with that small encumbrance thereon.

The 4th article is indeed a privilege but no more than Girdhar, the Moody and some others have, which does not in the least exempt them from the hands of the law or justice, but does only ask that justice be done respectfully, which he need not doubt of ... and for matter of differences among themselves there is already his Honour's patent authorising them to decide such things.

As to the 5th, the great anchorage of a rupee per ton is wholly taken off. There remains only a small one of a rupee for every 100 tons, which is so inconsiderable a matter that we do not believe we will stick at it. If he does, it will amount but to a small matter being only for his own vessels that the Company may easily allow it.

The 6th if we rightly apprehend it, is no more than what all people enjoy, who are so far from paying custom at exportation of their own goods that they pay none for what goods they buy. But if he intends his goods must pay no custom at landing nor none at exportation of what he cannot sell, it will be so great a loss to the Company, they having farmed out the customs for two years, that the benefit of his settling here, will, we believe, not countervail it, till it comes into the Company's hands again.

As to the 7th, our law is such that if a person be indebted to several men, whosoever gets a judgment first in Court will be paid his full debt, but no man can be aggrieved at that, nor can any creditor have any pretence to what is once paid, and when judgment is given it is already paid in law, so that he *is* no longer proprietor of it. But when a person is indebted to two men and the first sues him and upon that the second comes in and sues him too, with what justice can we pay all the debtor's estate to the second creditor. Only of this he may be assured that all justice shall be done him with speed according to our law and the party forced to pay the full debts if able, and be in prison for the rest till he pleases to release him, which we suppose may well content him.

As to the 8th in case of war all person of quality have liberty to repair to the castle and secure their money and other things of value. Nor that I suppose *be* intends to fill up the castle with gari (coarse) goods; but for money, jewels household stuff, cloth goods of value that take up small

> room he may bring what he pleases and may have a warehouse apart allotted for himself and family.
>
> The 9th and 10th we may join together, they being only to fill up the number. They are plain optics to show the nature of those they live under which when they have experimented our Government, themselves will laugh at us, enjoying more freedom than the very articles demand for the meanest person is never denied egress and regress upon respectful notice given and for horses and coaches and the like he may keep as many as he pleases and his servants be permitted to wear what arms they please, a thing common to all. Nothing is more promoted by us than the free liberty for buying and selling which is the load-stone of trade.
>
> That last thing he asked of having 10 *mans* of tobacco free of all duties is the most difficult thing of all, for the farmers will ask a vast deal to grant such a licence, it being a very great profit they make in the sale of 10 *mans*, so that we know not which way this article can be condescended to, but in this your Honours can judge better than us.*

In reply on the 26th April, the Surat Council wrote:#

> "We observe your answer touching the articles proposed by Nima Parakh Bania in order to his settlement on Bombay. When we come again to treat with him thereon, we hope so to moderate the affair that the island shall not receive any the least prejudice thereby and we do not question but wholly to put him by his request to 10 *mans* of tobacco which he would annually receive or bring on the island free of all duties."

### POINT (5)

### Bombay—An Emporium of India

That Bombay is an emporium for the whole of India may be admitted. But it is difficult to understand how it can be said that because of this, Maharashtra cannot claim Bombay. Every port serves a much larger area than the country to which it belongs. No one, on that account, can say the country in which the port is situated cannot claim it as a part of its territory. Switzerland has no port. It uses either German or Italian or French Ports. Can the Swiss therefore deny the right of Germany, Italy or France, the territorial rights of their ports? Why then should Maharashtrians be denied the right to claim Bombay merely because it serves as a port for Provinces other than Maharashtra? It would be different if the Province of Maharashtra were to get a right to close the Port to Non-Maharashtrians. Under the constitution, it will not have that right. Consequently, the inclusion of Bombay in Maharashtra will not affect the right of non-Maharashtrians to use the port as before.

* This is probably new demand made by Nima Parakh.

# *Bombay Gazetteer*, I, p. 77.

POINT (6)

## Gujarathis—Owners of Trade and Industry of Bombay

It may be granted that the Gujarathis have a monopoly of trade. But, as has already been pointed out, this monopoly, they have been able to establish because of the profits they were able to make which was the result of the privileges given to them by the East India Company on their settlement in Bombay. Who built up the trade and industry of Bombay is a matter for which no very great research is necessary. There is no foundation in fact for the statement that the trade and industry of Bombay was built up by Gujarathis. It was built up by Europeans and not by Gujarathis. Those who assert that it is the Gujarathis who did it should consult the *Times of India Directory* before making such a claim. The Gujarathis have been just merchants which is quite a different thing from being industrialists.

Once it is established that Bombay belonged to Maharashtra the claim of Maharashtra to include Bombay cannot be defeated by the argument that the trade and industry of Bombay is owned by the Gujarathis. The claim of mortgagor to his land cannot be defeated by the mortgagee on the ground that the mortgagee has built up permanent structures on the land. The Gujarathis assuming they have built up the trade and industry of Bombay are in no better position than a mortgagee is.

But who have built up the trade and industry of Bombay seems to me quite irrelevant to the decision of the issue whether Bombay should or should not be included in Maharashtra. This argument based on monopoly of trade and industry is really a political argument. It means that the owners may rule the workers but the workers must not be allowed to rule the owners. Those who use this argument do not seem to know what they are up against. The one thing they are up against is whether this argument is to be confined only to the City of Bombay or whether it is to have a general application.

There is no reason why it should not have a general application. For just as in Bombay City society is divided into owners and workers or into capitalists and wage-earners, such also is the case of society in Gujarat or for the matter of that in every province of India. If the owners and capitalists of Bombay are to be protected by the exclusion of Bombay from Maharashtra because Maharashtrians belong to the working classes, what is the method they suggest for protecting the capitalists of Gujarat from the working classes of Gujarat? Those Gujarathi Professors like Vakils and Dantwalas who are searching their brains to supply arguments to the Gujarathi capitalists of Bombay have not thought of finding ways and means for protecting the Gujarathi capitalists of Gujarat against the working classes of Gujarat. The only remedy they can suggest is the abandonment of adult suffrage. That is the only way by which they can protect the capitalists if they are out to protect capitalists in general and not the Gujarathi capitalists of Bombay in particular.

There is however one argument which the Professors could urge. It is that the Maharashtrians being in a majority would discriminate against the Gujarathi capitalists of Bombay if Bombay was included in Maharashtra.

One could appreciate such an argument. But those who like to use this argument must remember two things:

(i) That Maharashtra is not the only place in which such a situation can arise. It may arise in any province. I like to refer to Bihar. In Bihar the land in which coal is found belongs to the people of Bihar. But the coal-owners are Gujarathis, Kathiawaris or Europeans. Is there no possibility of Biharis making a discrimination against Gujarathi and Kathiawari coal-owners? Are the coalfields of Bihar to be excluded from the Province of Bihar and constituted into a separate Province in the interest of Kathiawari and Gujarathi coal-owners?

(ii) The constitution of India has noted the possibility of discrimination being made against a minority and has made more than ample provision for preventing it. There the fundamental rights. There are the provisions against discrimination; there are the provisions of payment of compensation, and there are the High Courts with the inherent rights to issue high prerogative writs both against individuals and Governments to stop any harm, injustice or harassment being done to any citizen. What more protection do the Gujarathi traders and industrialists of Bombay want against the possibility of discrimination?

### POINT (7)

## Maharashtra's Eye on Bombay's Surplus

Before accusing Maharashtrians of having an eye on the surplus of Bombay it must be proved that Bombay has a surplus. What appears as surplus is due really to bad accounting. It is bad accounting where expenditure on overhead charges such as (1) the Governor and his establishment, (2) the Ministers and their establishments, (3) the Legislature and the expenditure thereon, (4) Judiciary, (5) Police and (6) Provincial establishments such as those of the Commissioners of Police and Directors of Public Instruction is not being taken into account. I doubt very much if on the existing basis of taxation, Bombay will have any surplus if expenditure on these items is charged to Bombay. It is a fallacy to charge all such expenditure to Maharashtra and exempt Bombay from it and then argue that Bombay has a surplus.

The statement that the Maharashtrians want Bombay because they want to live on the surplus revenue of Bombay, besides being wrong in fact raises a question of motive. I do not know if the Maharashtrians are actuated by any such motive. They are not a commercial community. Unlike other communities, the Maharashtrians have no nose for money, and I am one of these who believe that it is one of their greatest virtues. Money has never been their god. It is no part of their culture. That is why they have allowed all other communities coming from outside Maharashtra to monopolize the trade and industry of Maharashtra. But as I have shown there is no surplus and no question of Maharashtrians casting their eyes on it.

But supposing such a motive in the minds of the Maharashtrians, what is wrong in it? It is quite open to Maharashtrians to contend that they have a greater claim on Bombay's surplus because they have played and they will continue to play a greater part in supplying labour for the building up of the trade and industry of Bombay more than the people from other Provinces have done or likely to do. It would be difficult for any economist with any reputation to save who could deny that labour has as much claim on the wealth produced as capital if not more.

Secondly, the surplus from Bombay is not consumed by Maharashtra alone but is consumed by the whole of India. The proceeds of the Income-tax, Super-tax, etc. which Bombay pays to the Central Government are all spent by the Central Government for all-India purposes and is shared by all other Provinces. To Prof. Vakil it does not matter if the surplus of Bombay is eaten up by United Provinces, Bihar, Assam, Orissa, West Bengal, East Punjab and Madras. What he objects to is Maharashtra getting any part of it. This is not an argument. It is only an exhibition of his hatred for Maharashtrians.

Granting that, Bombay was made into a separate Province, what I don't understand is how Prof. Vakil is going to prevent Maharashtra from getting share of Bombay surplus revenue. Even if Bombay is made separate Province, Bombay will have to pay income-tax, super-tax, etc. and surely Maharashtra will get a part of the revenue paid by Bombay to the Centre either directly or indirectly. As I have said the argument has in it more malice than substance.

## POINT (8) AND (9)

## General Arguments against the Inclusion of Bombay in Maharashtra

I will now turn to the Points (8) and (9) which have been urged by Professors Dantwala and Gheewala. Their arguments strike at the very root of the principle of Linguistic Provinces. As such I should have dealt with them in Part I of this Memorandum. But as the aim of their argument is to exclude Bombay from being included in Maharashtra, I have thought it proper to deal with them in this Part of the Memorandum as they are really arguments against the inclusion of Bombay in Maharashtra.

The sum total of the arguments of the two Professors is that Linguistic Provinces are bad. This cry against Linguistic Provinces is too late. Since when two Professors having been holding these views is not known, are they opposed to Gujarat being reconstituted on Linguistic Provinces also has not been made clear by them. Or, is it that they believed in the principle of Linguistic Provinces but hurried to disavow it when they realized that the admission of the principle involves the surrender of Bombay to Maharashtra. It is perhaps one of these cases where a person not finding argument limited to his purpose is forced to resort to an argument which proves more than he is anxious to allow. I am, however, prepared to examine the substance of their argument.

Prof. Dantwala relies upon Lord Acton and quotes the following passage from his Essay on Nationality printed in his well-known book *The History of Freedom and Other Essays* in support of his own view against Linguistic Provinces. The quotation reads as follows:

> The combination of various nations in one State is a necessary condition of civilized life as the combination of men in society.

I am sorry to say that this quotation completely misrepresents Lord Acton. The quotation is only a few opening lines of a big passage. The full passage reads as follows:

> "The combination of different nations in one State is as necessary a condition of civilized life as the combination of men in society. Inferior races are raised by living in political union with races intellectually superior. Exhausting and decaying nations are revived by the contact of younger vitality. Nations in which the elements of organization and the capacity for Government have been lost, either through the demoralizing influence of despotism or the disintegrating action of democracy, are restored and educated anew under the discipline of a stronger and less corrupted race. This fertilizing and regenerating process can only be obtained by living under one Government. It is in the cauldron of the State that the fusion takes place by which the vigour, the knowledge and the capacity of one portion of mankind may be communicated to another."

Why Prof. Dantwala left out the rest of the passage, it is difficult to understand. I am not suggesting that it is a deliberate case of *suppresio veri* and *suggestio falsi*. The fact is that it does misrepresent Lord Acton. Why has the Professor relied upon this passage, I do not understand. It is quite obvious that if the inferior races are placed in common with the superior races, the inferior races may improve. But the question is who is inferior or who is superior. Are the Gujarathis inferior to Maharashtrians? Or are the Maharashtrians inferior to Gujarathis? Secondly, what is the channel of communion between Gujarathis and Maharashtrians which can assure the fusion of the two? Prof. Dantwala has not considered the question. He found a sentence in Lord Acton's Essay and jumped at it for he could find nothing else to support his case. The point is that there is nothing in the message which has any relevance to the principle involved in the question of Linguistic Province.

Prof. Gheewala also relies on Lord Acton. He quotes a portion of a passage from Lord Acton's Essay on Nationality. I reproduce below the passage in full:

> "The greatest adversary of the rights of nationality is the modern theory of nationality. By making the State and the nation commensurate with

> each other in theory, it reduces practically to a subject condition all other nationalities that may be within the boundary. It cannot admit them to equality with the ruling nation which constitutes the State, because the State would then cease to be national, which would be a contradiction of the principle of its existence. According, therefore, to the degree of humanity and civilization in that dominant body which claims all the rights of the community, the inferior races are exterminated, or reduced to servitude, or outlawed, or put in a condition of dependence."

I do not understand why the learned Professor has dragged in the name of Lord Acton. The passage does not really help him. There is one thing which seems to be uppermost in his mind. He thinks that if Bombay is included in Maharashtra the Province of Maharashtra will consist of two nationalities—one consisting of the Marathi-speaking people and the other of the Gujarathi-speaking people and the Marathi-speaking people who would be the dominant class will reduce the Gujarathi-speaking people to a subject condition. It is in support of this he thought of citing Lord Acton. Such a possibility is always there. There is no objection to the way in which he has presented the problem. But there are great objections to the conclusions he draws.

In the first place, in a country like India in which society is throughout communally organized it is obvious that in whatever way it is divided into areas for administrative purposes, in every area there will always be one community which by its numbers happens to be a dominant community. As a dominant community it becomes a sole heir to all political power, which the area gets. If Marathi-speaking people in a unified Maharashtra with Bombay thrown into it will become dominant over the Gujarathi-speaking people, will this prospect be confined to Maharashtra only? Will such a phenomenon not occur within the Marathi-speaking people? Will it not be found in Gujarat if Gujarat became a separate Province? I am quite certain that within the Marathi-speaking people who are sharply divided between the Marathas and the non-Marathas, the Marathas being a dominant class will reduce both Gujarathi-speaking and the non-Marathas to a subject condition. In the same way in Gujarat in some parts the Anavil Brahmins from a dominant class. In other parts it is the Patidars who form a dominant class. It is quite likely that the Anavils and the Patidars will reduce the condition of the other communities to subjection. The problem therefore is not a problem peculiar to Maharashtra. It is a general problem.

What is the remedy for this problem? Prof. Gheewala believes that the remedy lies in having a mixed State. So far as this remedy is concerned it is not his own. He has adopted it from Lord Acton. But I have no doubt that so far as Lord Acton advocates this remedy he is quite wrong. Lord Acton cites the case of Austria in support of his view. Unfortunately, Lord Acton did not live to see the fate of Austria. It was a mixed State. But far from providing for the safety of nationalities the clash of nationalities blew up Austria to bits. The real remedy is not a mixed State but an absolute State with no power to the people which is generally captured by a communal majority and exercised in the name of the people. Is Prof. Gheewala prepared for this remedy? One need have no doubt to what his answer would be.

In the second place, Prof. Gheewala has confounded nationality in the social sense of the term with Nationality in its legal and political sense. People often speak of nationality in speaking about Linguistic Provinces. Such use of the term can be only in the non-legal and non-political sense of the term. In my scheme there is no room even for the growth of separate provincial nationality. My proposal nips it in the bud. But even if the commonly suggested pattern of Linguistic Provinces with the language of the Province as the official language were adopted, Provinces cannot have that attribute of sovereignty which independent nations have.

It is very difficult to understand what exactly what Prof. Gheewala wants. Broadly he wants two things: He wants a mixed State and he also wants that a dominant section should not be in a position to reduce the smaller sections to subjection. I cannot see how Linguistic Provinces can come in the way of achieving it. For even after Provinces have been re-constituted on linguistic basis—

(1) Provinces will continue to be a conglomeration of communities which will give Prof. Gheewala the mixed State that he wants; (2) If Prof. Gheewala wants a more pronounced form of a mixed State to protect smaller communities or nationalities, he will certainly have it at the Centre.

As I have said, I do not think a mixed State is either a good State or stable State. But if Prof. Gheewala prefers it, he will have it in one form or another, both in the Provinces as well as at the Centre, in the former in the form of different communities and in the latter in the form of the representatives of different Provinces.

With regard to his second objective, there will be double protection. In the first place, the citizen will have such protection as a mixed State he thinks can give. Secondly, citizenship will be common throughout India.

There is no provincial citizenship. A Gujarathi in Maharashtra will have the same rights of citizenship in Maharashtra as Maharashtrian will have. Given these facts, I fail to understand what objection Prof. Gheewala can have to Linguistic Provinces? Prof. Gheewala has made two other recommendations. He says (1) if Provinces have to be reconstituted, constitute them on rational basis rather than on linguistic basis and (2) make nationality a personal thing.

To reconstitute Provinces on economic basis—which is what is meant by rational basis—appears more scientific than reconstituting them on linguistic basis. However, unscientific linguistic reorganization of Provinces I cannot see how they can come in the way of rational utilization of economic resources of India. Provincial boundaries are only administrative boundaries. They do not raise economic barriers for the proper utilization of economic resources. If the position was that the resources contained within a Linguistic Province must only be explained by the people of the Province and no other than it could no doubt be said that the scheme of Linguistic Provinces was mischievous. But such is not the case. So long as Linguistic Provinces are not allowed to put a ban on the exploitation of the resources of the people by any body capably of wishing to exploit them a Linguistic Province will yield all the advantages of a rationally planned Province.

The proposal of making nationality as a personal thing and put it on the same footing as religion may be dismissed as being to Utopian. It would raise many administrative problems. It will come when the world is one and all nationals are its citizens. Nationality will automatically vanish as being quite useless.

So far I have dealt with the arguments advanced by those who are opposed to the inclusion of Bombay in Maharashtra. I have taken pains to do so not because I felt that they were very weighty. I did so because I felt it desirable to prevent the common man from being misled. The possibility of this happening was there and for two reasons. In the first place, those who have come forward with these arguments are not ordinary men. They are University Professors. Secondly, these Professors came out with their arguments after Prof. Gadgil had put forth the case for the inclusion of Bombay in Maharashtra. Unfortunately, no attempt has so far been made to refute the arguments of the adversaries of Prof. Gadgil. The result has been the creation of an impression that Prof. Gadgil's adversaries have carried the day. It was absolutely essential to remove this impression.

## The Other Side

There are however arguments which the adversaries of Prof. Gadgil have not thought of but which may be advanced with justice as well as force in favour of the claim of Maharashtrians for the inclusion of Bombay in Maharashtra. It is quite possible that these arguments may suggest themselves to the Commission. But I don't like to leave it to chance. I therefore propose to set them out below even though the Commission might think that it was unnecessary.

## Calcutta and Bombay

In deciding upon the issue of exclusion of Bombay from Maharashtra the Commission will have to take into account the position of Calcutta. Like Bombay it is the chief emporium of the whole of eastern part of India. Like the Maharashtrians in Bombay the Bengalis in Calcutta are in a minority. Like the Maharashtrians in Bombay, the Bengalis do not own the trade and industry of Calcutta. The position of the Bengalis *vis-à-vis* Calcutta is worse than the position of the Maharashtrians *vis-à-vis* Bombay. For, the Maharashtrians can at least claim that they have supplied labour if not capital for the trade and industry of Bombay. The Bengalis cannot even say this. If the Commission can accept the arguments urged for the separation of Bombay from Maharashtra, it must be equally prepared to recommend the separation of Calcutta from West Bengal. For it is a very pertinent question to ask that if for the reasons given Bombay can be separated from Maharashtra why when the same reasons exist Calcutta be not separated from West Bengal.

### Is Bombay Viable?

Before Bombay can be separated it must be proved that financially Bombay is a viable Province. As I have already said if proper accounting of revenue and expenditure was made Bombay on the basis of present level of taxation may not be a self-sufficient Province. If that be so, the proposal for creating Bombay a separate Province must fall to the ground. It is no use comparing Bombay with Provinces like Orissa and Assam. The standard of administration, the standard of living and consequently the level of wages in Bombay are all so high that I doubt that even with a crushing rate of taxation Bombay will be able to raise the necessary amount of revenue to meet the expenditure.

### The Aim behind Greater Bombay

This doubt regarding viability of Bombay Province is heightened by the indecent haste shown by the Government of Bombay in creating Greater Bombay by including within the limits of Bombay the adjoining parts of Maharashtra. It seems that the object of including such area cannot but be to make Bombay viable. What else can it be? So long as Bombay remained part of Maharashtra it did not matter to Maharashtrians in which administrative area a portion of Maharashtra was included. But when Bombay is to be a separate Province it will take a long time to make Maharashtrians part with their territory to make Bombay greater and viable. What is more important is the scheme of greater Bombay casts responsibility upon the Linguistic Provinces Commission to decide whether they could, with justice force Maharashtrians not only to submit to the demand of the Gujarathis to give up Bombay but also to submit to their further demand to hand over a part of territory of Maharashtra to make Bombay a viable Province. The Commission cannot escape this responsibility.

Maharashtra and Bombay are not merely inter-dependent, they are really one and integral. Severance between the two would be fatal to both. The sources of water and electricity for Bombay lie in Maharashtra. The intelligentsia of Maharashtra lives in Bombay. To sever Bombay from Maharashtra would be to make the economic life of Bombay precarious and to dissociate the masses of Maharashtra from its intelligentsia without whose lead the masses of Maharashtra will be nowhere.

### Arbitration as a Solution

I have seen a suggestion made in some quarters that problem of Bombay should be settled by arbitration. I have never heard of a more absurd suggestion than this. It is as absurd as the suggestion to refer matrimonial case to arbitration. The matrimonial tie is too personal, to be severed by a third party. Bombay and Maharashtra are tied together by God to use a Biblical phrase. No arbitrator can put them asunder. The only agency which is authorized to do so is the Commission. Let it decide.”

# III

# Need for Checks and Balances

This article appeared in *Times of India* on 23 April 1953 after the death of Potti Sriramulu (16 March 1901–16 December 1952). Sriramulu had been on fast-unto-death demanding the creation of separate Andhra State since 19 October 1952 in Madras. This initiated a series of protests and processions by the people disrupting normal life in the state. When on 19 December 1952 Prime Minister Nehru announced the formation of a separate Andhra State; Ambedkar termed it as a *pindaadan* to the departed soul of Sriramulu. The state of Andhra was established with Kurnool as capital carving out from Madras State on 1 October 1953. Later, on 1 November 1956, Telangana, the Telugu-speaking part of Hyderabad State was also merged with Andhra.

Ambedkar in this article presents a history of the subject and argues that the genesis of the idea of creating linguistic provinces can be traced in a Constitution framed by the Congress in 1920 under the aegis of Gandhi. It was then that the Congress first proposed the creation of new provinces on the basis of language. But due to the circumstances prevalent in the country, this responsibility was thrust upon the Congress only when it assumed office in 1945. Strange as it may appear, the Congress, on the very first occasion when a member of Parliament moved a resolution for the creation of linguistic provinces in India, totally opposed the idea.

When Ambedkar—as Chairman of the Drafting Committee—presented the concern of linguistic provinces to the prime minister, the government set up the Dar Committee. However, before the Dar Committee report was submitted and a separate Andhra State could be formed, Potti Sriramulu sacrificed his life continuing his fast unto death. Ambedkar argued that, it was a sad commentary on the ruling party that Sriramulu had to die for a cause, the validity of which was accepted by all Congressmen. Ambedkar once again used this opportunity to remind the people about the need for linguistic states and the three conditions which, in his opinion, must be satisfied before bringing a linguistic state into being.

***

Reproduced below is the *Times of India* article by Ambedkar, published on 23 April 1953. It has been excerpted here from *Dr. Babasaheb Ambedkar Writings and Speeches*, ed. Vasant Moon, vol. 1, 129–36 (Bombay: Government of Maharashtra, 1979).

## "NEED FOR CHECKS AND BALANCES

The British who ruled India for more than 150 years never thought of creating linguistic States although the problem was always there. They were more interested in creating a stable administration and maintaining law and order throughout the country than in catering to the cultural craving of people in multi-lingual areas. It is quite true that towards the end of their career they did realise that the administrative set-up which they had built required some adjustment from the point of view of linguistic considerations, at any rate in cases where the conglomeration was very glaring. For instance, they did create Bengal, Bihar and Orissa as linguistic States before they left. It is difficult to say whether if they had continued to rule, they would have followed the path of forming linguistic States to its logical conclusion.

But long before the British thought of creating linguistic provinces the Congress under the aegis of Mr. Gandhi had already in the year 1920 framed a constitution for itself on the basis of linguistic provinces. Whether the ideology underlying the constitution of the Congress as framed in 1920 was a well thought out ideology or whether it was a sop to draw people inside the Congress fold, one need not now stop to speculate. There is, however, no doubt about it that the British did realise that linguistic considerations were important and they did give effect to them to a limited extent.

### OPPOSITION

Upto the year 1945, the Congress was, of course, not called upon to face the responsibility which it had created for itself by its constitution of 1920. It was only in the year 1945 when it assumed office that this responsibility dawned upon the Congress. Looking into the recent history of the subject the necessary momentum to the issue was given by a Member of Parliament by moving a resolution for the creation of linguistic provinces in India.

The duty of answering on behalf of the Government to the debate fell on me. Naturally I took the matter to the higher authorities in order to ascertain what exactly their point of view was. Strange as it may appear, it became clear to me that the High Command was totally opposed to the creation of linguistic provinces. In these circumstances, the solution that was found was that the responsibility to answer the debate had better be taken over by the Prime Minister. The Prime Minister in reply to the debate made statement promising the creation of an Andhra State immediately. On the basis of the statement made by the Prime Minister, the resolution was withdrawn. The matter rested there.

### SECOND TIME

As Chairman of the Drafting Committee, I had to deal with the matter a second time. When the draft Constitution was completed, I wrote a letter to the Prime Minister asking him whether I could include Andhra as a separate

State in Part A States of the Constitution in view of what he had said in the course of the debate on the Resolution. I have nothing with me here to refresh my memory as to what exactly happened. But the President of the Constituent Assembly, Dr. Rajendra Prasad, appointed a Committee to investigate into the formation of linguistic States, under the Chairmanship of Mr. Dhar, a lawyer from U.P.

People will remember the Dhar Committee for one thing if not for any other. The Committee said that under no circumstances should Bombay City be included in Maharashtra if Maharashtra was made a linguistic State. That report was then considered by the Jaipur session of the Congress. The Jaipur Congress appointed a Three-Man Committee consisting of the Prime Minister, Mr. Vallabhbhai Patel and Dr. Pattabhi Sitaramayya. They produced a report, the gift of which was that an Andhra province should be created immediately but the city of Madras should remain with the Tamils. A committee was appointed to go into the details. It produced a more or less unanimous report. But the report was opposed by substantial elements among the Andhras including Mr. Prakasam who were not prepared to relinquish their claim to Madras, and the thing lay dormant there.

After that comes the incident of Shri Potti Sriramulu who had to sacrifice his life for the sake of an Andhra province. It is a sad commentary on the ruling party that Mr. Sriramulu should have had to die for a cause the validity of which was accepted by all Congressmen. The creation of a new Andhra province now being thought of is only a pindadan to the departed soul of Mr. Sriramulu by the Prime Minister. Whether such action on the part of the Government would have been tolerated in any other country is a matter on which there is no use speculating.

There are, in my opinion, three conditions which must be satisfied before a linguistic State is brought into being. The first condition is that it must be a viable State. This rule was accepted as absolute when the question of the merger of the Indian States was under consideration during the making of the Constitution. Only those Indian States which were viable were allowed to remain as independent States. All others were merged into the neighbouring States.

### A SAHARA?

Is the proposed Andhra State a viable State? Mr. Justice Wanchoo had very candidly admitted that the annual revenue deficit of the proposed Andhra State will be of the magnitude of Rs. 5 crores. It is possible for the proposed Andhra State to reduce this gap either by increase of taxation or decrease in expenditure? The Andhras must face this question. Is the Centre going to take the responsibility of meeting this deficit? If so, will this responsibility be confined to the proposed Andhra State or will it be extended to all similar cases? These are questions which are to be considered.

The new Andhra State has no fixed capital. I might incidentally say that I have never heard of the creation of a State without a capital. Mr.

Rajagopalachari (the staunchest Tamilian tribesman) will not show the Government of the proposed Andhra State the courtesy of allowing it to stay in Madras city even for one night—courtesy which is prescribed by the Hindu Dharma on all Hindus for an *atithi*. The new Government is left to choose its own habitat and construct thereon its own hutments to transact its business. What place can it choose? With what can it construct its hutments? Andhra is Sahara and there are no oases in it. If it chooses some place in this Sahara it is bound to shift its quarters to a more salubrious place, and the money spent on this temporary headquarters would be all a waste. Has the Government considered this aspect of the case? Why not right now give them a place which has the possibility of becoming their permanent capital.

It seems to me that Warangal is best suited from this point of view. It is the ancient capital of the Andhras. It is a railway junction. It has got quite a large number of buildings. It is true that it lies within that part of Andhra which is part of Hyderabad State. As a matter of principle Hyderabad State which is a monstrosity should have been broken up and a complete Andhra State might have been created. But if the Prime Minister has some conscientious objection to the proposal, can he not create an enclave in the Andhra part of Hyderabad and join it to the new Andhra State and make a way to Warangal? An enclave is not a new thing in India. But the Prime Minister wants to work against the will of God in Hyderabad as well as in Kashmir. I am sure he will very soon learn the consequences of it.

### FIRST CONDITION

This is just incidental. My main point is that a linguistic State must be viable. This is the first consideration in the creation of a linguistic State. The second consideration is to note what is likely to happen within a linguistic State. Unfortunately no student has devoted himself to a demographic survey of the population of India. We only know from our census reports how many are Hindus, how many are Muslims, how many Jews, how many Christians and how many untouchables. Except for the knowledge we get as to how many religions there are this information is of no value. What we want to know is the distribution of castes in different linguistic areas. On this we have very little information. One has to depend on one's own knowledge and information. I don't think it would be contradicted if it is said that the caste set-up within the linguistic area is generally such that it contains one or two major castes large in number and a few minor castes living in subordinate dependence on the major castes.

### COMMUNAL SET-UP

Let me give a few illustrations. Take the Punjab of PEPSU. The Jats dominate the whole area. The untouchables live in subordinate dependence on them. Take Andhra—there are two or three major communities spread over the linguistic area. They are either the Reddis or the Kammas and the Kappus. They hold all the land, all the offices, all the business. The untouchables live in subordinate dependence on them. Take Maharashtra. The Marathas are a huge majority in every village in Maharashtra. The Brahmins, the Gujars, the Kolis and the untouchables live in subordinate co-operation. There was a time when the Brahmins and the banias lived without fear. But times have changed. After the murder of Mr. Gandhi, the Brahmins and the banias got such a hiding from the Marathas that they have run away to the towns as safety centres. Only the wretched untouchables, the Kolis and the Malis have remained in the villages to bear the tyranny of the Maratha communal majority. Anyone who forgets this communal set-up will do so at his peril.

In a linguistic State what would remain for the smaller communities to look to? Can they hope to be elected to the Legislature? Can they hope to maintain a place in the State service? Can they expect any attention to their economic betterment? In these circumstances, the creation of a linguistic State means the handing over of Swaraj to a communal majority. What an end to Mr. Gandhi's Swaraj! Those who cannot understand this aspect of the problem would understand it better if instead of speaking in terms of linguistic State we spoke of a Jat State, a Reddy State or a Maratha State.

**THIRD ISSUE**

The third problem which calls for consideration is whether the creation of linguistic States should take the form of consolidation of the people speaking one language into one State. Should all Maharashtrians be collected together into one Maharashtra State? Should all Andhra area be put into one Andhra State? This question of consolidation does not merely relate to new units. It relates also to the existing linguistic provinces such as U.P, Bihar and West Bengal. Why should all Hindi-speaking people be consolidated into one State as has happened in U.P.? Those who ask for consolidation must be asked whether they want to go to war against other States. If consolidation creates a separate consciousness we will have in course of time an India very much like what it was after the break-up of Maurya Empire. Is destiny moving us towards it?

This does not mean that there is no case for linguistic provinces. What it means is that there must be definite checks and balances to see that a communal majority does not abuse its power under the garb of a linguistic State.”

# IV

# On the Andhra State Bill

The Bill for the creation of a separate Andhra State after being passed by the House of People (Lok Sabha) on 27 August 1953 was introduced in the Council of States (Rajya Sabha) by the Minister for Home Affairs and States (K. N. Katju) on 1 September 1953. The minister while moving the Bill termed the day as historic in the life of people of Andhra Pradesh. He also informed the Upper House that the discussions in the Lok Sabha had categorically rejected the idea that looking at reorganisation of states would lead to disintegration of the country even in the remotest sense. Rather, it had accepted the view that reorganisation would add strength to the Indian democracy. Smaller Houses of Legislature may function efficiently. Although the minister accepted that with one or even two languages people's views would be heard better and they would be able to manage their affairs in a more intelligent manner, the Bill he introduced had no mention of the word 'linguistic'.

Ambedkar spoke on this occasion on 2 September 1953. Unlike those who were celebrating the creation of Andhra as the victory of the struggle for linguistic and cultural identity, he chose to draw attention to the contradictions and vacillations in the position of the central government with regard to the reorganisation of the states in India. He discussed the Bill clause-by-clause and spoke on issues from the capital of the new state, the financial position of the new state, the demographic and social composition, to the condition of the Scheduled Castes, the question of land, and even the administration. In other words, he once again verified the Bill on the variables of his theory of viability. Ambedkar took the opportunity to point out that the conditions under which the Andhra State was formed not only encouraged regionalism among other linguistic groups but also gave the impression that New Delhi was more responsive to violence than peaceful agitation.

Ambedkar also used this occasion to raise the concern of the small linguistic areas and groups within the state who, in the future, he felt, may find themselves discriminated and oppressed at the hands of the majority. He, therefore, suggested that there should be some kind of a safeguard to ensure that the interests of certain small linguistic areas or linguistic groups remain protected. Ambedkar wanted to protect the interests of the Rayalaseema area from the domination of the coastal people, who were generally able to get larger funds for their area. At the end, he requested the house to examine carefully some of the important points.

***

Reproduced below are excerpts from *Dr. Babasaheb Ambedkar Writings and Speeches*, ed. Vasant Moon, vol. 15, 851–64 (Bombay: Government of Maharashtra, 1997).

### "SPEECH DELIVERED IN THE RAJYA SABHA ON 2 SEPTEMBER 1953

This is a Bill, the object of which is to create a new State for the Andhras. As such it is the subject matter of the Andhras themselves. Others who are not Andhras can only take part in it in a general way, and solely because this new Province is a portent of probably some other linguistic provinces to come into existence. It is only because of the feeling of the latter that I have stood up today to say a few words.

... when one goes into the Bill, one is very much puzzled as to whether one should congratulate the Government on the Bill such as has been brought forward before this House, or whether one should congratluate the Andhras who are clamouring for a separate Province. As anyone in this House knows, as soon as the Congress Party was organised and had a constitution in the year 1921, the first thing it did was to incorporate the principle of linguistic provinces. I have no idea that any time from the year 1921 up to the year 1949 or thereabout, the Congress either ever withdrew that principle from its constitution or regretted having entered that principle in its constitution. In 1949 I believe—if I am wrong my friends will correct me—but I think that is about the year, when the Drafting Committee was sitting, and one Member of then Assembly tabled a resolution for the formation of the linguistic provinces. I was in charge of the Law Department and as such the Resolution fell within my portfolio. I had to consult my cabinet colleagues in order to know what sort of reply I should give to this Resolution. They said the better thing would be for me to transfer the Resolution either to the Prime Minister or to the late Sardar Vallabhbhai Patel which I very gladly did, because I did not want the responsibility to fall upon my shoulder for the answer that might be given to that Resolution. It was then arranged between the mover of the Resolution and the members of the high command of the Congress, that although they were not prepared to accept the Resolution in all its generality so as to apply to all the multi-lingual provinces then existing, they were prepared to consider the question of creating an Andhra Province. The members of the Drafting Committee were waiting to know what exactly they should enter Andhra as a separate province in the Schedule of the States. Hon. Members who are particular to know about this will find in a foot-note to the first draft of the Drafting Committee's report that I referred to the Prime Minister in order to let me know whether Andhra should be entered in the Schedule to the Constitution. I got no reply, with the result that Andhra then did not become a separate province. It was a great surprise to me that when practically for twenty years, a party had stood by the principle of linguistic provinces, it should have developed cold feet after twenty years. Surely, 20 years was a long period for even the greatest dullard to think over the matter and come to a clear conclusion as to whether the principle that was adopted in 1921 was a mistaken principle and ought completely to be withdrawn, or whether it was a principle which should be pursued with certain modifications. The result has been that from 1949 up to this period, there has been a vacillating attitude on the part of the Government, once saying that there shall be no linguistic provinces, at another time saying, "Yes, we shall create an Andhra Province". And unless and until one honourable gentleman had sacrificed his life for the sake of creating an Andhra Province, the Government did not think it fit to move in the matter. I have no idea and I do not wish to be harsh on the Government; but I am dead certain in my mind that if in any other country a person had to die in order to invoke a principle which had already been accepted, what would have happened to the Government. It is quite possible that the Government might have been lynched. But here nothing has happened. The Government is playing with the proposition.

The argument that has been brought forth by the Government is that if you create linguistic provinces, you will break up the unity of India. That has been the argument which one heard time and again from every member of the Government. ... I am surprised that such an argument should have been used. If anyone were to look up the Schedule of States attached to the Constitution, he would find that there are altogether 27 States filling up different parts—Part A, Part B and Part C. I am not taking into account Part D. Now, if you take up these 27 States, you will find that 23 States are linguistic States. Only 4 are multi-lingual. I should like to ask my honourable friend, the Home Minister, whether he thinks that the 23 linguistic States which have existed from the very beginning of the Constitution have in any way done anything in order to disrupt the unity of this country. I would like him to answer that question. These 23 linguistic States have not been able to disrupt the unity of India. I am as keen as he is on maintaining the unity of India and I shall not support any step which will bring about the break-up of this country.

We have, by God's grace achieved not only independence but also unity, and it is our bounden duty, no matter to what party we belong, to see that this independence and this unity is retained. But, to say, in the face of this fact, with 23 linguistic states, that linguistic States would break up the unity of India is to say something which is puerile. They must produce some very weighty arguments in support of their contention that they cannot pursue a policy of creating linguistic States.

... Coming to the Andhras on whom this blessing is showered by the Government after such a long delay, what do they get by it? First of all, as I look at the Bill, I do not find anywhere mention about the capital of this new State of Andhra. The capital is the very life source of a State. I cannot understand how one can imagine a State without its capital. In fact, it is the capital that gives life to the States. There is no mention of it at all. Who is to create this capital? Is it the Legislature of the new Andhra State which is to meet and decide what is to be its capital? Is it the Executive Government of the new State which is to sit at some place and decide that the capital of the new Andhra State will be this? There is no indication at all in the Bill, as to which is the authority which is to create this capital. Reading from the newspapers it does appear that there is no unanimity among the Andhras on the question of the capital. There is a section which wants Vijaywada, there is a section which wants Kurnool and those in favour of Kurnool I think, won by one vote or so. In a situation of this kind, I think the Government would not have fallen—I am sure about it, they have an enormous majority to beat down any opposition—if they had taken courage in both hands and said that, "in our judgement this should be the capital", leaving liberty to the Andhras at a later stage to change it if they so liked.

... In connection with this question of the capital, there is one point which I would like to mention. I do not know, what is the town that is going to be selected as the capital of the Andhra State? But, any how, everybody seems to be taking that whatever town is selected for the purpose of a capital, it shall be a temporary capital. That is what I hear. ... it strikes me—whether they select a town which is Vijaywada or Kurnool or some other place—that they may be spending a certain amount of money for the construction of the necessary buildings for the housing of the capital. Surely, there must be the Secretariat: surely, there must be the houses for the Ministers and various other things in order that the capital may come into existence. I have no idea of the amount of money the new Andhra Government proposes to spend on the creation of this temporary capital. After what is being said that this will only be a temporary capital and that the permanent capital will be selected at a later stage, what would happen? In my judgement, what would happen is this: the five crores of rupees or so that might be spent initially on the construction of a temporary capital would all be a waste and another five or ten crores of rupees will have to be spent on what the Andhras might regard as the permanent capital for their new State. I do not know whether the Hon. the Home Minister or the Hon. the Finance Minister who, I believe, in his most charitable way gives grants to anybody who wants to come and ask for a grant, is prepared to give five crores of rupees for a temporary capital and another five or ten crores for a permanent capital. That would certainly be a wonderful way of managing the finances of this country.

... Looking at the financial position of the new State, it has been shown that the new State will begin with a deficit of Rs. 5 crores. Many optimistic Andhras who are more keen on having an Andhra State than on stability told the investigator—Mr. Justice Wanchoo—that, in their judgement there were a variety of means whereby they could bridge the gap and make the State self-sufficient. Mr. Justice Wanchoo examined every one of the suggestions that were made to him by the various parties of the Andhra people; and he has, in unmistakable terms, said that all these are fertile imagination and that it is neither possible to increase the revenues of the new State, nor is it possible to reduce the expenditure; at the most, anything may happen either by the way of increasing the revenue or by the way of reducing the expenditure. Nonetheless, the new Andhra State will begin with a deficit of Rs. 2 crores. That is the least that the Andhras will have to face to begin with. Well, it is the concern of the Andhras whether they could make good deficit which may be Rs. 5 crores or which may be Rs. 2 crores; we have not much to say about it; it is for them.

Then there is a third point which I would like to put to my Hon. Friend the Home Minister. It seems to me that my Hon. Friend has not considered what I might call the demographic picture of the Andhra State. What is the social composition of this State? When I am dealing with the social composition of Andhra, I beg of my Andhra friends not to mistake me. It is not that I am making the statement, which I am about to make, by way of accusation against the Andhras, but it is a general proposition which I am enunciating and which I shall develop at the conclusion of my speech. ... I am not an Andhra. But I belong to what might be called a political group—I shall not give it the honorific name of a 'Party'—which is called the Scheduled Caste Federation. As the Leader of that group, I had the occasion to move round in the Andhra country in order to see what the condition of the Scheduled Castes there is. My picture is this that, in this Andhra country, there are, as everywhere else, as I am going to show, some big communities and some very small communities. Of the big communities, the biggest, I believe, is the Reddy community; below the Reddys come the Kamma; below the Kammas come the Kappu; and below them come the unfortunate Scheduled Castes people working as landless labourers. That is primarily the picture of this area. As I said, this is not a lonely case. There are many other areas of the same pattern.

The second thing I noticed is this that all the lands practically are in possession of the Reddys. The Reddys are the biggest landlords there. Next, probably, come, the Kammas, to which my friend Professor Ranga belongs. I was told very recently how great this evil is. I was told in a very vivid way by one of the Congressmen himself. I do not know whether he would feel offended if I mention his name. It would lend great authority to the statement that I am making, but I shall not mention his name as I have not asked him .... When we were discussing this question, my friend told me that that was by no means peculiar. There was a certain village in the Andhra area. The entire land of the village measured 1,400 acres. Out of that, only 14 acres were owned by private individuals; the rest of it was owned by a single Reddy. One has just to imagine the picture .... The third fact he told me was that all trade in the village was in the hands of the Reddys. The lowest village officer is also a Reddy; the 'mulki' is also a Reddy. ... I want to know for myself, especially in view of the fact whether the reservation, which was so blissfully granted to us by the Congress Party for ten years, is going to disappear ....

... In view of the situation that is obtaining there, you can imagine what is likely to be the position of the Scheduled Castes. What provision has my hon. Friend made for the purpose of granting protection against tyranny, against oppression, against communalism, that is sure to be rampant not only in the Andhradesh but everywhere in the States similarly situated? One of the greatest regrets that I have is that the Home Member, whose duty it is to see that every citizen is well protected against the tyranny of the majority, has come here with a Bill with no idea, with no conception as to what the State is likely to be and what is likely to happen to millions of people. I know, ... he is a high born person.[1] ... these are the three considerations which I thought I, should urge before my hon. Friend, the Home Minister, for his consideration. There is still time even in this House, if he likes. ...[2]

We are not going to finish our troubles with the creation of the Andhra State. There are plenty of other States which are making a similar demand and I think it is therefore necessary for the Government to find out whether there are any other ways and means whereby we could keep the multi-lingual provinces as they are, and remove the feelings and the lots of blemishes that arise therefrom and only in excusable cases resort to the creation of a linguistic State, I have been devoting a certain amount of attention to this question because I know that this is going to be one of our most crucial questions. ... my suggestions are two-fold. Wherever I find a multi-lingual State I would vest the Governor there with certain special powers to protect the minorities in that State. That is one proposition that I would place before the Government for its consideration. I shall presently cite some authority in order that they may not think that this is my imagination. I am going to cite some constitutional precedents. And the second thing that I would like to be done would be that in all such States where there are multi-lingual people you should establish by law committees of members belonging to different linguistic sections which would have the right to hear and the right to ask the Ministry whether they are doing justice to their problems. Also they should have the right to appeal to the Governor to set aside any act of injustice that might have been done to anyone section. I think, if these three things are done, we should be able to keep the States as they are, at any rate in the first stage. If ultimately we find that we do not succeed even with these measures, then fate may take us to the logical extreme end, namely, to have a linguistic State.

... In the case of creation of linguistic States, in my judgement there appears to me to be two considerations. One is that the linguistic State must be a viable State. It may be that this is a small State which has got a culture and which has got a language and which has got a separate feeling and an entity. Yet it is so small that it cannot find the means of carrying on its Administration. People do not live on culture. People do not live on language. People live on the resources they possess. But if God has given them culture and God has given them language but God has not given them resources, I am afraid they cannot have the luxury of having a separate linguistic State. The second thing is this. It is only in our country that we find that linguistic provinces create difficulty. I would like to ask the question as to why there are no difficulties in Switzerland although Switzerland itself is a multilingual unit. The Cantons have French, German and Italian. Yet they are a very happy nation and they are the most prosperous nation today. Why is it, that Switzerland has no provinces although it is a multi-lingual unit? The answer which I can give is this that linguism in Switzerland is no loaded with communalism. But in our country linguism is only another name for communalism. What happens when you create a linguistic province is that you hand over the strings of Administration to one single community which happens to be the majority community and I can cite many provinces where this is likely to happen. That community charged with a feeling of its own sacred existence begins to practice the worst kind of communalism which otherwise is called discrimination. Discrimination creates injustice and injustice creates ill-feeling. If our linguism was not charged with communalism our linguism would not be a danger to us at all; but the fact is that it is. But it seems to me that in order to do away with the community practicing communalism being in office these two remedies are worthwhile, namely, to give the power to the Governor to override and, secondly, to appoint small committees who can make representations either to the Ministry or to the Governor.

... we have inherited a tradition. People always keep on saying to me: "Oh, you are the maker of the Constitution". My answer is I was a hack. What I was asked to do, I did much against my will ....[3]

... we have inherited, on account of our hatred of the British, certain ideas about democracy which, it seems to me are not universally accepted. We inherited the idea that the Governor must have no power at all, that he must only be a rubber stamp. If a Minister, however scoundrel he may be, however corrupt he may be, if he puts up a proposal before the Governor, he has to do it. That is the kind of conception about democracy which we have developed in this country ....[4]

We happened to develop a theory of democracy, simply because of our opposition to the British. The British must go and the British must have no power. A Governor must have no power. Let me cite two cases. One case which I propose to cite is about the Constitution of Canada and I refer to section 93 of that Constitution. As everyone in this House knows, Canada, like us is a bilingual place. A part of it speaks English; a part of it speaks French. And what is worse still is that the English-speaking people are Protestants; the French are Roman Catholics. In 1864, when the Constitution of Canada was made, the Catholics were very much afraid as to what might happen to them under the English Protestant majority and they were not prepared to come into the Constitution of a united Canada. Therefore the Parliament enacted section 93 in the Canadian Constitution. That section does two things. It says that if any province—naturally, the reference was to provinces in Protestant areas—where Roman Catholics lived, passed any law with regard to certain matters which the Roman Catholics regarded as their special privilege based upon religion, they had the right to appeal to the Governor General that a wrong was done to them, and the Governor General by section 93 had the right to look into their complaint. It was a statutory right of complaint. Not only did section 93 give the Catholics a statutory right of appeal against the decision of the majority to have a certain measure annulled, but it goes much further and says that the Governor General shall have the right to enact a positive measure in protection of the Catholic minority. I would like to ask my friend, the Home Member, whether, with the inclusion of section 93 in the Canadian Constitution, he regards the Canadian Constitution to be democratic or undemocratic. What is his answer?[5]

... therefore, my submission is this that no harm can be done to democracy and to democratic Constitution if our Constitution was amended and powers similar to those given to the Governor General under section 93 were given to the Governor. At any rate, that would be some kind of a safeguard to certain small linguistic areas or linguistic groups who find that the majority in the State are, not doing justice to them. The second suggestion that I would like to make is from the English Constitution. My hon. Friend must be aware of the position of Scotland in the British Constitution and therefore I would not go into greater details. But he will remember two things. One is this that although Scotland and England are one—nobody can say that they are two separate countries—still there is a special Secretary of State for Scotland under the British Constitution to look after the interests of the Scottish people. He must have gone to London, I think, various times ....[6] Surely, he must have passed by the Parliament Street and just by the side of 10, Downing Street, there is a big brass board 'Scottish Office' which is the place where the Secretary of State for Scotland sits. That is the one provision which the British have made. They have not argued, as my friends have argued, that this is a recognition of communalism. Have they? Scotland came and joined England some hundreds of years ago and yet the British people, in order to recognise the sentiments of the Scots, in order to respect their feelings, have created statutorily an office called the Secretary of State for Scotland.

The second thing to which I would like to refer is this that in the British Parliament there are two Committees. One is a Committee for Wales and Monmouthshire and there is another Committee for Scotland consisting of Scottish members. All Bills referring to Scotland have to be sent to the Scottish Committee so that the Scottish members may have their full say in the matter. In the same way, the members of Wales and Monmouthshire are also brought on committees connected with their affairs. It is by placating the sentiments of smaller communities and smaller people who are afraid that the majority may do wrong, that the British Parliament works. ... my friends tell me that I have made the Constitution. But I am quite prepared to say that I shall be the first person to burn it out. I do not want it. It does not suit anybody. But whatever that may be, if our people want to carry on, they must not forget that there are majorities and there are minorities, and they simply cannot ignore the minorities by saying, "Oh, no. To recognise you is to harm democracy." I should say that the greatest harm will come by injuring the minorities. I fear sometimes that if the minorities are treated in the way in which they are being treated in our Bombay State—I do not want to be parochial, but my friends have been telling me, as I am not there and I do not take any interest in my State, as you know, and I do not even like to call myself a Maharashtrian—I do not know what will ultimately happen. I am fond of Hindi, but the only trouble is that the Hindi-speaking people are the greatest enemies of Hindi ....

... I am told that the Ministers are drawn from the two provinces. The clever members of the Ministry draw all the funds for developing the resources in that particular area, and the other area gets nothing. The same is being said about the Rayalaseema area, that the coastal people are generally able to get larger funds for their area and the Rayalaseema people get nothing. If my friend could make a provision in the Constitution that there shall be constituted lawfully under this very Bill a committee consisting of the members belonging to Rayalaseema, who will have the right to represent to the Governor and to the members of the Ministry that their part is to be included, I think a large part of the grievance would disappear. Similarly, ... I find that our Bengali Members are considerably agitated over the fact that part of Bihar—they say is Bengal. I do not know; it may be, because originally Bengal spread over everywhere. The Governor General had a very large area, and wherever the Governor General went, the Bengalis also went with him ....[7]

My illustration is this that supposing such was the case that the Biharis were not treating the Bengalis well. Well, the only way open for solving this problem would be that there should be a committee of the Legislature consisting of the members who are Bengalis and who would have the right to represent their grievances to the Ministry as well as the Governor or to the President. When all these things fall, then I suppose we shall have to go to the naked proposition that we shall be linguists first and linguists last, and that we shall not recognize India. If that is to be our ultimate aim, well, God save us. But, ... my submission to my hon. Friend is this that he should examine carefully some of the points I have made, particularly in the last part of my speech, and see whether he can find any solution to the problem of linguistic provinces, based on the suggestions that I have made, in the new measure that he may have to bring—he may not be very willing to bring a new measure, but he may have to bring it.”

## Notes

1. Ambedkar was referring to Dr K. N. Katju. Katju interrupted him by saying that he started life in a normal manner. But, Ambedkar replied, 'the fact is that he is a Kashmiri Pandit. Even if he takes to the profession of a Bhangi he will still remain a Kashmiri Pandit. He may never suffer. All people may respect him for his ancestry, for his noble birth, for his learning. What about us who have been tyrannised for the last 2,000 years?' At this point when H. P. Saksena of Uttar Pradesh said that all respected Dr Ambedkar also, he replied, 'I may die in ten years time.'
2.. There was an interruption at this point by K. S. Hegde who wanted to clarify whether Ambedkar was suggesting a different tradition altogether for Andhra or was that a general proposition. Ambedkar replied that it would be applicable to all the States.
3 Interruptions by P. Sundarayya.
4. Interruptions by M. S. Ranawat.
5. K. N. Katju interrupted to reply that the Constitution was drafted by Ambedkar himself. To this Ambedkar responded that naming him for all the mistakes would merely be an act of accusation for their own blemishes. The Chairman at this moment intervened saying 'he has said that he defended the present constitution because it was the majority decision. Get along.'
6. The Hon. Minister indicated by sign—three.
7. At this point the Chairman reminded him to restrict his speech only to the Andhra Bill.

# V

# Thoughts on Linguistic States

During the period when the creation of linguistic states became a burning question in the country, Ambedkar could not participate in the discussion in great detail, either in Parliament or in the campaign carried outside, owing to his illness. However, his engagement with this issue since the days of participation on the debate for a separate Karnatak Province in the BLA in 1938 had been quite long and therefore, he could not ignore the question to sleep over in silence. He decided to set out his views in writing once again in 1955.

In his writing, Ambedkar accepts that there has been a significant change in his views, as his former opinions were made on the basis of fragmentary data. It was only after the submission of the report of the SRC that he could visualise a complete picture. Therefore, while writing this work, he chose responsibility over consistency. He opined that formation of linguistic states, although essential, should not be decided by any sort of hooliganism. It must be solved only by reasoning alone.

Ambedkar divided his monograph into six parts. He starts by examining the report of the SRC and points to some of the faulty recommendations which in his opinion were hidden but which very important to be understood. In the second part, he goes on to describe the pros and cons of linguism. Discussing about the solutions in the third part, Ambedkar suggests the division of the large northern states, namely Bihar (into two states), Uttar Pradesh (into three states) and Madhya Pradesh (into three states) (with maps attached in the sixth part). He then goes to discuss the solution for Maharashtra. Examining all the proposals suggested by different groups, Ambedkar came at a conclusion that Maharashtra should be divided into four states: (1) Maharashtra City State, (2) Western Maharashtra, (3) Central Maharashtra, and (4) Eastern Maharashtra.

In the fourth part, Ambedkar once again examines the problems of linguistic states. He discusses the issues of viability and majority-minority. Ambedkar believed that two safeguards were necessary for the protection of minorities: (1) creation of smaller states, and (2) provision for representation in the Legislature. Since the old types of representation provided in the Constitution, namely (1) number of reserved seats, and (2) separate electorates have been given up in the new Constitution; it would be necessary to have plural member constituencies (of two or three) with cumulative voting in place of the system of single-member constituency embodied in the present Constitution. This will allay the fears which the minorities have about linguistic states.

At the end, he discussed the necessity for a second capital for India. He felt that the location of Delhi, due to its distance form the south was not satisfactory. According to Ambedkar, there was a need to make a second capital of the country which not only would help the smooth functioning of the administration but would also help in the hour of crisis such as war. He found Hyderabad as the perfect place for India's second capital, as it would not only satisfy the above mentioned necessity but would also remedy for easing the tension between the North and the South.

***

Reproduced below are excerpts from *Dr. Babasaheb Ambedkar Writings and Speeches*, ed. Vasant Moon, vol. 1, 137–204 (Bombay: Government of Maharashtra, 1979).

## "THOUGHTS ON LINGUISTIC STATES

### PART-1
### THE WORK OF THE COMMISSION

### Chapter 1
### Linguism and Nothing Else

The present Constitution of India recognises the following States which are enumerated in the Schedule:

| *Part "A" States* | *Part "B" States* | *Part "C" States* |
|---|---|---|
| 1. Andhra | 1. Hyderabad | 1. Ajmer |
| 2. Assam | 2. Jammu & Kashmir | 2. Bhopal |
| 3. Bihar | 3. Madhya Bharat | 3. Coorg |
| 4. Bombay | 4. Mysore | 4. Delhi |
| 5. Madhya Pradesh | 5. Patiala | 5. Himachal Pradesh |
| 6. Madras | 6. Rajasthan | 6. Kutch |
| 7. Orissa | 7. Saurashtra | 7. Manipur |
| 8. Punjab | 8. Travancore - Cochin | 8. Tripura |
| 9. Uttar Pradesh | | 9. Vindhya Pradesh |

Article 3 of the Constitution gives power to Parliament to create new States. This was done because there was no time to reorganize the States on linguistic basis for which there was a great demand. In pursuance of this incessant demand the

Prime Minister appointed the States Reorganisation Commission to examine the question. In its report the States Reorganisation Commission has recommended the creation of the following States:

**Proposed New States**

| *Name of the State* | *Area (Sq. Miles)* | *Population (Crores)* | *Language* |
|---|---|---|---|
| Madras | 50,170 | 3.00 | Tamil |
| Kerala | 14,980 | 1.36 | Malyalam |
| Karnatak | 72,730 | 1.90 | Kanarese |
| Hyderabad | 45,300 | 1.13 | Telugu |
| Andhra | 64,950 | 2.09 | Telugu |
| Bombay | 151,360 | 4.02 | Mixed |
| Vidarbha | 36,880 | 0.76 | Marathi |
| Madhya Pradesh | 171,200 | 2.61 | Hindi |
| Rajasthan | 132,300 | 1.60 | Rajasthani |
| Punjab | 58,140 | 1.72 | Punjabi |
| Uttar Pradesh | 113,410 | 6.32 | Hindi |
| Bihar | 66,520 | 3.82 | Hindi |
| West Bengal | 34,590 | 2.65 | Bengali |
| Assam | 89,040 | 0.97 | Assamese |
| Orissa | 60,140 | 1.46 | Oria |
| Jammu and Kashmir | 92,780 | 0.14 | Kashmiri |

The important thing is to compare the size of the states. Taking population as the measuring red the result may be presented as follows:

There are 8 states with a population between 1 and 2 crores each. There are 4 states with a population between 2 and 4 crores each. There is one state above 4 crores. There is one state above 6 crores. The result, to say the least, is fantastic. The Commission evidently thinks that the size of a state is a matter of no consequence and that the equality in the size of the status constituting a federation is a matter of no moment. This is the first and the most terrible error cost which the commission has committed. If not rectified in time, it will indeed be a great deal.

## Chapter 2
## Linguism in Excelsis

In the first chapter it has been pointed out that one result of the recommendations of the States Reorganisation Commission is the disparity in the size of the different States the Commission has suggested for creation. But there is another fault in the recommendation of the commission which perhaps is hidden but which is nonetheless real. It lies in not considering the North in relation to the South. This will be clear from following table:

| *Southern States* | | *Central States* | | *Northern States** | |
|---|---|---|---|---|---|
| *Name* | *Population (in crores)* | *Name* | *Population (in crores)* | *Name* | *Population (in crores)* |
| Madras | 3.00 | Maharashtra | 3.31 | Uttar Pradesh | 6.32 |
| Kerala | 1.36 | Gujarat | 1.13 | Bihar | 3.85. |
| Karnataka | 1.90 | Saurashtra | 0.4 | Madhya Pradesh | 2.61 |
| Andhra | 1.09 | Kutch | 0.5 | Rajasthan | 1.60 |
| Hyderabad | 1.13 | | | Punjab | 1.72 |

* I have included certain centrally situated states because by language they are all affiliated to one another.

This scheme of dividing India in the name of Linguistic States cannot be overlooked. It is not so innocuous, as the Commission thinks. It is full of poison. The poison must be emptied right now. The nature of Union of India expresses only an idea. It does not indicate an achievement. Bryce in his "*American Commonwealth*" relates the following incident which is very instructive. This is what he says:

> "A few years ago the American Protestant Episcopal Church was occupied at its annual conference in revising liturgy. It was thought desirable to introduce among the short sentence prayers a prayer for the whole people; and an eminent New England Divine proposed the words 'O Lord, bless our Nation'. Accepted one afternoon on the spur of the moment, the sentence was brought up next day for reconsideration, when so many objections were raised by the laity to the word, 'Nation', as importing too definite recognition of national unity, that it was dropped, and instead there were adopted the words, 'O Lord, bless these United States'."

India is not even mentally and morally fit to call itself the United States of India. We have to go a long way to become the United States of India. The Union of India is far, far away, from the United States of India. But this consolidation of the North and balkanisation of the South is not the way to reach it.

## PART-2
## THE LIMITATIONS OF LINGUISM

# Chapter 3
# The Pros and Cons of a Linguistic State

"One State, one language" is a universal feature of almost every State. Examine the constitution of Germany, examine the constitution of France, examine the constitution of Italy, examine the constitution of England, and examine the constitution of the U.S.A. "One State, one language" is the rule.

Wherever there has been a departure from this rule there has been a danger to the State. The illustrations of the mixed States are to be found in the old Austrian Empire and the old Turkish Empire. They were blown up because they were multi-lingual States with all that a multi-lingual State means. India cannot escape this fate if it continues to be a congery of mixed States.

The reasons why a unilingual State is stable and a multi-lingual State unstable are quite obvious. A State is built on fellow feeling. What is this fellow-feeling? To state briefly it is a feeling of a corporate sentiment of oneness which makes those who are charged with it feel that they are kith and kin. This feeling is a double-edged feeling. It is at once a feeling of fellowship for ones own kith and kin and anti-fellowship for those who are not one's own kith and kin. It is a feeling of "consciousness of kind" which on the one hand, binds together those who have it so strongly that it over-rides all differences arising out of economic conflicts or social gradations and, on the other, severs them from those who are not of their kind. It is a longing not to belong to any other group.

The existence of this fellow-feeling is the foundation of a stable and democratic State. This is one reason why a linguistic State is so essential. But there are other reasons why a State should be unilingual. There are two other reasons why the rule "one State, one language" is necessary. One reason is that democracy cannot work without friction unless there is fellow-feeling among those who constitute the State. Faction fights for leadership and discrimination in administration are factors ever present in a mixed State and are incompatible with democracy.

The present State of Bombay is the best illustration of the failure of democracy in a mixed State. I am amazed at the suggestion made by the States Reorganisation Commission that the present Bombay State should be continued as it is to enable us to gain experience of how a mixed State flourishes. With Bombay as a mixed State for the last 20 years, with the intense enmity between the Maharashtrians and Gujaratis, only a thought less or an absent-minded person could put forth such a senseless proposal. The former State of Madras is another illustration of the failure of democracy in a mixed State. The formation of a mixed State of United India and the compulsory division of India into India and Pakistan are other illustrations of the impossibility of having democracy in a mixed State.

Another reason why it is necessary to adopt the rule of "one State, one language" is that it is the only solvent to racial and cultural conflicts. Why do Tamils hate Andhras and Andhras hate Tamils? Why do Andhras in Hyderabad hate Maharashtrians and Maharashtrians hate Andhras? Why do Gujaratis hate Maharashtrians and Maharashtrians hate Gujaratis? The answer is very simple. It is not because there is any natural antipathy between the two. The hatred is due to the fact that they are put in juxtaposition and forced to take part in a common cycle of participation, such as Government. There is no other answer.

So long as this enforced juxtaposition remains, there will be no peace between the two. There will be people who would cite the cases of Canada, Switzerland and South Africa. It is true that these cases of bilingual States exist. But it must not be forgotten that the genius of India is quite different from the genius of Canada, Switzerland and South Africa. The genius of India is to divide—the genius of Switzerland, South Africa and Canada is to unite.

The fact that they have been held together up till now is not in the natural course of things. It is due to the fact that both of them are bound by the Congress discipline. But how long is the Congress going to last? The Congress is Pandit Nehru and Pandit Nehru is Congress. But is Pandit Nehru immortal? Anyone who applies his mind to these questions will realise that the Congress will not last till the sun and the moon. It must one day come to an end. It might come to an end even before the next election. When this happens the State of Bombay will find itself engaged in civil war and not in carrying on administration.

We therefore want linguistic States for two reasons. To make easy the way to democracy and to remove racial and cultural tension. In seeking to create linguistic States India is treading the right road. It is the road which all States have followed. In the case of other linguistic States they have been so, from the very beginning. In the case of India she has to put herself in the reverse gear to reach the goal. But the road she proposes to travel is well-tried road. It is a road which is followed by other States.

Having stated the advantages of a linguistic State I must also set out the dangers of a linguistic State. A linguistic State with its regional language as its official language may easily develop into an independent nationality. The road between an independent nationality and an independent State is very narrow. If this happens, India will cease to be Modern India we have and will become the medieval India consisting of a variety of States indulging in rivalry and warfare.

This danger is of course inherent in the creation of linguistic States. There is equal danger in not having linguistic States. The former danger a wise and firm statesman can avert. But the dangers of a mixed State are greater and beyond the control of a statesman, however eminent.

How can this danger be met? The only way I can think of meeting the danger is to provide in the Constitution that the regional language shall not be the official language of the State. The official language of the State shall be

Hindi and until India becomes fit for this purpose English. Will Indians accept this? If they do not, linguistic States may easily become a peril.

One language can unite people. Two languages are sure to divide people. This is an inexorable law. Culture is conserved by language. Since Indians wish to unite and develop a common culture it is the bounden duty of all Indians to own up Hindi as their language. Any Indian who does not accept this proposal as part and parcel of a linguistic State has no right to be an Indian. He may be a hundred per cent Maharashtrian, a hundred per cent Tamil or a hundred per cent Gujarathi, but he cannot be an Indian in the real sense of the word except in a geographical sense. If my suggestion is not accepted India will then cease to be India. It will be a collection of different nationalities engaged in rivalries and wars against one another.

God seems to have laid a heavy curse on India and Indians, saying 'Ye Indians ye shall always remain divided and ye shall always be slaves!' I was glad that India was separated from Pakistan. I was the philosopher, so to say, of Pakistan. I advocated partition because I felt that it was only by partition that Hindus would not only be independent but free. If India and Pakistan had remained united in one State Hindus though independent would have been at the mercy of the Muslims. A merely independent India would not have been a free India from the point of view of the Hindus. It would have been a Government of one country by two nations and of these two the Muslims without question would have been the ruling race notwithstanding Hindu Mahasabha and Jana Sangh. When the partition took place I felt that God was willing to lift his curse and let India be one, great and prosperous. But I fear that the curse may fall again. For I find that those who are advocating linguistic States have at heart the ideal of making the regional language their official language.

This will be a death knell to the idea of a United India. With regional languages as official languages the ideal to make India one United country and to make Indians, Indians first and Indians last, will vanish. I can do no more than to suggest a way out. It is for Indians to consider it.

## Chapter 4
## Must There be One State for One Language?

### What does a linguistic State mean?

It can mean one of two things. It can mean that all people speaking one language must be brought under the jurisdiction of one State. It can also mean that people speaking one language may be grouped under many States provided each State has under its jurisdiction people who are speaking one language. Which is the correct interpretation?

The Commission took the view that the creation of one single State for all people speaking one and the same language was the only rule to be observed. Let the reader have a look at map No. 1. He will at once note the disparity between the Northern and Southern States. This disparity is tremendous. It will be impossible for the small States to bear the weight of the big States.

How dangerous this disparity is, the Commission has not realised. Such disparity no doubt exists in the United States. But the mischief it might cause has been prevented by the provisions in the Constitution of the United States. One such safeguard in the Constitution of the United States has been referred to by Mr. Pannikar in his dissenting minute to the Report.... I give below the following extract from his minute:

> "I consider it essential for the successful working of a federation that the units should be fairly evenly balanced. Too great a disparity is likely to create not only suspicion and resentment but generate forces likely to undermine the federal structure itself and thereby be a danger to the unity of the country. This is clearly recognised everywhere. In most federal constitutions, though wide variation exists in respect of the population and resources of the unit, care is taken to limit the influence and authority of the larger States. Thus in the United States of America, for example, though the States are of varying population and resources and the Slate of New York has many times the population, say of Nevada, the constitution provides for equal representation of every State in the Senate."

On this point Mr. Pannikar also refers to the Soviet Union and old Germany. This is what he says:

> "In the Soviet Union also, in which great Russia has a larger population than most other units of the Federation taken together, representation in the House of Nationalities is weighed against her so that the other units of the Federation may not be dominated by the larger unit. In the Bismarckian Reich again, though Prussia had a dominant position from the point of view of population, she was given less representation in the *Reichsrat* or the house representing the states than she was entitled to (less than one-third) and the permanent presidency of that body was vested in Bavaria, clearly demonstrating that even here—where there was concentration of political, military and economic power in one State—it was considered necessary, in the interest of the union, to give weightage to the smaller units and also to reduce Prussia to the position of minority in the *Reichsrat,* States Council, which enjoyed greater powers than the *Reichstag* or the House of the People."

Mr. Pannikar has however not mentioned one other safeguard in the Constitution of the United States against the evils of disparity. In our Constitution the two Houses are not co-equal in authority. But the position in the Constitution of the United States is quite different. In the U.S.A. the two Houses are co-equal in authority. Even for money Bills the consent of the Senate is necessary. This is not so in India. This makes a great difference to the disparity in the population. This disparity in the population and power between the States is sure to plague the country. To provide a remedy against it is most essential.

## Chapter 5
## The North versus the South

What the Commission has created is not a mere disparity between the States by leaving U.P. and Bihar as they are, by adding to them a new and a bigger Madhya Pradesh with Rajasthan it creates a new problem of North *versus* South.

The North is Hindi speaking. The South is non-Hindi speaking. Most people do not know what the size of the Hindi-speaking population is. It is as much as 48 per cent of the total population of India. Fixing one's eye on this fact one cannot fail to say that the Commission's effort will result in the consolidation of the North and the balkanisation of the South.

Can the South tolerate the dominance of the North?

It may now not be a breach of a secret if I revealed to the public what happened in the Congress Party meeting when the Draft Constitution of India was being considered, on the issue of adopting Hindi as the national language. There was no article which proved more controversial than Article 115 which deals with the question. No article produced more opposition. No article, more heat. After a prolonged discussion when the question was put, the vote was 78 against 78. The tie could not be resolved. After a long time when the question was put to the Party meeting the result was 77 against 78 for Hindi. Hindi won its place as a national language by one vote. I am stating these facts from my personal knowledge. As Chairman of the Drafting Committee I had naturally entry to the Congress Party enclosure.

These facts reveal how much the South dislikes the North. This dislike may grow into hatred if the North remains consolidated and the South becomes disintegrated and if the North continues to exercise a disproportionate influence on the politics of India (See Map 1).[1]

To allow one State to have such preponderating influence in the Centre is a dangerous thing. Mr. Pannikar has referred to this aspect of the case. In his dissenting minute he says:

> "The consequence of the present imbalance, caused by the denial of the federal principal of equality of units, has been to create feelings of distrust and resentment in all the States outside Uttar Pradesh. Not only in the Southern States but also in the Punjab, Bengal and elsewhere the view was generally expressed before the Commission that the present structure of government led to the dominance of Uttar Pradesh in all-India matters. The existence of this feeling will hardly be denied by anyone. That it will be a danger to our unity, if such feelings are allowed to exist and remedies are not sought and found now, will also not be denied."

There is a vast difference between the North and the South. The North is conservative. The South is progressive. The North is superstitious, the South is rational. The South is educationally forward, the North is educationally backward. The culture of the South is modern. The culture of the North is ancient.

Did not Prime Minister Nehru on the 15th of August 1947 sit at the Yajna performed by the Brahmins of Benares to celebrate the event of a Brahmin becoming the first Prime Minister of free and independent India and wear the Raja Danda given to him by these Brahmins and drink the water of the Ganges brought by them? How many women have been forced to go Sati in recent days and immolate themselves on the funeral pyre of their dead husbands? Did not the President recently go to Benares and worship the Brahmins, washed [*sic*] their toes and drank the water? The North still has its Satis, its Nanga Sadhus. What havoc the Nanga Sadhus made at the last Hardwar Fair! Did anyone in U.P. protest against it? How can the rule of the North be tolerated by the South? Already there are signs of the South wanting to break away from the North.

Mr. Rajagopalachari has made a statement on the recommendations of the States Reorganisation Commission which has appeared in the *Times of India* of the 27th November 1955. This is what he says:

> "If it is impossible to put the States Reorganisation Schemes in cold storage for the next 15 years, the only alternative is for the Centre to govern India as a unitary state and deal with district officers and district boards directly, with regional commissioners' supervision. It would be utterly wrong to fritter away national energy in dispute over boundaries and divisions conceived in the drawing room and not on the background of conditions that have resulted historically. Apart from the general convictions of mine, I feel that a large southern State is absolutely essential for preserving the political significance of that part of the country. To cut the South up into Tamil, Malayalam and other small States will result only in complete insignificance of everybody and, in the net result, India as a whole will be the poorer."

Mr. Rajagopalachari has not expressed himself fully. He did do so fully and openly to me when he was the Head of the State and I was the Law Minister in charge of drafting the constitution. I went to Mr. Rajagopalachari for my usual interview which was the practice of the day. At one such interview Mr. Rajagopalachari, referring to the sort of constitution which the Constituent Assembly was making, said to me,

> "You are committing a great mistake. One federation for the whole of India with equal representation for all areas will not work. In such a federation the Prime Minister and President of India will always be from the Hindi speaking area. You should have two Federations, one Federation of the North and one Federation of the South and a Confederation of the North and the South with three subjects for the Confederation to legislate upon and equal representation for both the federations."

These are the real thoughts of Mr. Rajagopalachari. They came to me as a revelation coming as they did from the innermost heart of a Congressman. I now regard Mr. Rajagopalachari as a prophet predicting the break-up of

India into the North and the South. We must do everything to falsify Mr. Rajagopalachari's prophecy.

It must not be forgotten that there was a civil war in the U.S.A. between the North and the South. There may also be a civil war between the North and the South in India. Time will supply many grounds for such a conflict. It must not be forgotten that there is a vast cultural difference between the North and the South and cultural differences are very combustible. In creating this consolidation of the North and balkanisation of the South the Commission did not realise that they were dealing with a political and not a merely linguistic problem. It would be most unstatesmanlike not to take steps right now to prevent such a thing happening. What is the remedy?

# PART-3
# SOLUTION

## Chapter 6
## The Division of the North

The problem having been realised we must now search for a solution. The solution lies obviously in adopting some standard for determining the size of a State. It is not easy to fix such a standard. If two crores of population be adopted as a standard measure most of the Southern States will become mixed States. The enlargement of the Southern States to meet the menace of the Northern States is therefore impossible. The only remedy is to break up the Northern States of U.P., Bihar and Madhya Pradesh. How did this solution not strike the Congress Working Committee I am unable to understand? It is so obvious.

### Division of the Northern States

As I have said the Commission in designing linguistic States has created a consolidation of the North and balkanisation of the South. The Commission has not I am sure done this intentionally. But intentionally or unintentionally the fact is there. Its evil consequences are also clear.

It is therefore necessary that this situation must be rectified. The only way to do this is to divide the three States of (1) Uttar Pradesh, (2) Bihar and (3) Madhya Pradesh into smaller units. In this behalf I make bold to offer certain tentative proposals. This division does not conflict with the underlying principles of a linguistic State. For, if these States are divided in the way suggested, each resulting State will be a linguistic State. I am happy to find Mr. Pant saying in the recent debate in Parliament on the subject that he has no objection to the cutting up of the U.P. What he said for U.P. may well be taken as applicable to Bihar and Madhya Pradesh.

***Division of Uttar Pradesh***—My proposal with regard to the Uttar Pradesh is to divide it into three States. Each of these three States should have a population of approximately two crores which should be regarded as the standard size of population for a State to administer effectively. Where the boundary lines of these three States should be drawn I have shown in the accompanying Map No. 2.[2] The three States of the Uttar Pradesh could have as their capitals (1) Meerut (2) Cawnpore and (3) Allahabad. They are situated quite in the centre of each of these three States.

***Division of Bihar***—My proposal with regard to Bihar is to divide it into two States. Each of these two States will have a population of little over one and half crores. It is not a small population for one Government to administer. Where the boundary lines should be drawn I have shown in the accompanying Map No. 3.[3] The two States of Bihar could have as their capitals (1) Patna and (2) Ranchi. They are situated quite in the centre of the two States.

***Division of Madhya Pradesh***—Madhya Pradesh stands before us in two forms. The old Madhya Pradesh and the new Madhya Pradesh. The old Madhya Pradesh consisted of: (1) the Province at one time known as C. P. and Berar, and (2) some Indian States out of the States known as the Eastern States. This old State of Madhya Pradesh had a population of 2 1/2 crores. It consisted of 22 districts. Its legislature had 223 members. The new Madhya Pradesh as planned by the Commission will consist of (1) the 14 districts of the old Madhya Pradesh, (2) the whole of Bhopal, (3) the whole of Vindhya Pradesh, (4) Madhya Bharat except Sunel enclave of Mandasaur district, and (5) the Sironj sub-division of Kola district of Rajasthan.

The total population of this new Madhya Pradesh will be 26.1 million and its area will be about 171,200 square miles. I suggest that it should be divided into two States: (1) Northern Madhya Pradesh, (2) Southern Madhya Pradesh (See Map 4).[4] The State of New Madhya Pradesh should consist of the following areas: (1) The whole of Vindhya Pradesh, and (2) The whole State of Bhopal. The State of Southern Madhya Pradesh should consist of (1) the whole State of Indore, and (2) the 14 districts of Mahakosal. The population of this Indore State will be about 2 crores and the population of this Vindhya Pradesh will be about 1.30 crores.

Why the Commission created this Monster State, it is no way to know. Even Prime Minister Nehru was surprised at its creation. All that one can think of is that the Commission has been under the impression that one language, one State is a categorical imperative from which there is no escape. As I have shown one language, one State can never be categorical imperative. In fact one State, one language should be the rule. And therefore people forming one language can divide themselves into many States.

## Chapter 7
## The Problems of Maharashtra

### I
### The Proposals to Deal with Maharashtra

Maharashtra is another area which is a subject of controversy. There are four proposals in the field: (1) to retain the Bombay State as it is i.e. to retain it as a mixed State consisting of Maharashtra, Gujarat and Bombay; (2) to disrupt the existing State and to separate Maharashtra and Gujarat and make them into two separate States; (3) to make united Maharashtra with Bombay as one State; (4) to separate Bombay from Maharashtra and make it a separate City State.

I would like to state what my proposals are. They are as follows: Bombay as a mixed State should be done away with. I would divide Maharashtra into four States (See Map 5):[5]

(1) Maharashtra City State (Bombay)
(2) Western Maharashtra,
(3) Central Maharashtra and
(4) Eastern Maharashtra.

Maharashtra City State—The City of Bombay plus such area of Maharashtra as would enable it to be a good and strong City State.
Western Maharashtra— (1) Thana, (2) Kolaba, (3) Ratnagiri, (4) Poona, (5) North Satara, (6) South Satara, (7) Kolhapur and (8) the Marathi-speaking territories given over to Karnataka.

Central Maharashtra (1) Dang, (2) East Khandesh, (3)West Khandesh, (4) Nasik, (5)Ahmednagar, (6) Aurangabad, (7) Nanded, (8) Parbhani, (9) Beed, (10) Usmanabad, (11) Sholapur City and the Marathi-speaking area of Sholapur District and (12) the Marathi-speaking territories given over to Telangana.

Eastern Maharashtra—(1) Buldhana, (2) Yeotmal, (3)Akola, (4) Arnraoti, (5) Wardha, (6) Chanda, (7) Nagpur, (8) Bhandara and (9) the Marathi-speaking territories given to Hindi States.

I will next proceed to examine the merits of these proposals.

## II
## Maharashtrians Under the Mixed State

Should Bombay remain a mixed State? It is a most unusual procedure. The City of Calcutta is not a separate City State. Madras is not a separate City State. Why Bombay alone be made the exception? Secondly, it is already a mixed State. What is the experience of the Maharashtrians under this mixed State? The Maharashtrians have suffered terribly under this mixed State. What is the position of the Maharashtrians in the Bombay Cabinet? Let us consider the distribution of Ministership:

| | |
|---|---|
| Gujarathi Ministers | 4 |
| Marathi Ministers | 4 |
| Kannada Ministers | 1 |
| **Total** | **9** |

Gujarathi members in the Assembly are only 106, Marathi members are 149 and yet the number of Gujarathi Ministers is equal to that of Maharashtrian Ministers. Let us come to Deputy Ministers:

| | |
|---|---|
| Marathi speaking | 5 |
| Gujarathi speaking | 2 |
| Kannada speaking | 2 |
| **Total** | **9** |

Only among Deputy Ministers do the Maharashtrians have a majority of one. But how the power and subjects are distributed among the Ministers and Deputy Ministers is the most important matter. It shows what power and authority the Maharashtrian Ministers possess in this mixed Cabinet of the Bombay State.

## Allocation of Subjects among Ministers

| | *Gujarathi Ministers* | | | *Maharashtrian Ministers* | | |
|---|---|---|---|---|---|---|
| 1 | Morarji Desai | 105 | subs | Hirey | 49 | subs |
| 2 | Dinkerrao Desai | 26 | subs | Nimbalkar | 20 | subs |
| 3 | Jivaraj Mehta | 43 | subs | Tapase | 15 | subs |
| 4 | Shantilal Shah | 28 | subs | Chavan | 4 | subs |

The allocation of subjects among Deputy Ministers is also done on the same pattern.

## Allocation of Subjects among Deputy Ministers

| | *Gujarathi Deputy Ministers* | | | *Maharashtrian Deputy Ministers* | | |
|---|---|---|---|---|---|---|
| 1 | Indumati Sheth | 12 | subs | Wandrekar | 12 | subs |
| 2 | Babubhai J Patel | 3 | subs | Deshmukh | 4 | subs |
| | | | | Naravane | 5 | subs |
| | | | | Sathe | 5 | subs |
| | | | | Faki | 3 | subs |

Let us now consider how much money is spent on development in Maharashtra and in Gujarath. The following figures will give an idea of the Per Capita Expenditure for the three years on Maharashtra and Gujarath:

**Per Capita Expenditure on Development in Rupees**

| | | Years | | |
|---|---|---|---|---|
| | *Population* | *1950–51* | *1951–52* | *1952–53* |
| Maharashtra | 21720091 | 1.7 | 2.3 | 1.8 |
| Gujarath | 11896789 | 2.9 | 3.1 | 3.2 |

What a differential treatment? What discrimination? What an injustice? Can anybody blame the Maharashtrians if they felt disputed with the mixed State of Bombay? Such a position of subordination no Maharashtrian can tolerate. The idea of a mixed State must be blown off once for all.

## III
## The Position of the City of Bombay

The Bombay City is an area which is a subject matter of controversy. The controversy has become very acute. Maharashtrians want the City to be part of Maharashtra. Gujarathis want the City to be a separate State. Heads have been broken over the controversy. But there has been no agreement. It is therefore necessary to go to the root of the matter.

The Gujarathis do not claim Bombay City as their own. But will not let go their hold on it. They claim a sort of easement over it by reason of the fact that they control the trade and industry of the City. The issue is: should it become part of Maharashtra or should it be constituted into a separate State? The Gujarathis and Maharashtrians are sharply divided on the issue. The Maharashtrians want that Bombay should become exclusively a part of the new Maharashtra State. The Gujarathis are stoutly opposed to it. They have presented two alternatives. One alternative is not to break up the existing bi-lingual State of Bombay into two linguistic units of Gujarath and Maharashtra. The Congress Working Committee's decision is to make the city of Bombay into a separate State.

The Gujarathis are happy. The Maharashtrians are naturally angry. The resentment of the Maharashtrians is well justified. The arguments urged against the claim of the Maharashtrians have no force at all. The first argument that is urged is that the Marathi-speaking population of Bombay City does not form a majority of the total population of the City. The total population of Bombay City is very large.[6] Marathi-speaking population is 48 per cent. Those who use this kind of argument do not seem to realise the weakness of it. The total Marathi population of Bombay City is no doubt less than 50 per cent but it has to be valued against two factors. One is that geographically no one can deny that Bombay is part of Maharashtra even if the Maharashtrians are in a minority in the City. Even Mr. Morarji Desai admitted in the course of his speech in the meeting of the Gujarath Pradesh Congress Committee that Bombay is part of Maharashtra.

The second point to be taken into consideration in valuing the population factor is the continued influx of population from the rest of India who come to Bombay either for making profits or for earning their bread. None of them regard Bombay as their home; they should not therefore be counted as permanent residents of Bombay City. Many come for a few months and go back. Bombay is a home only to the Maharashtrians and none else. It is not therefore logical or fair to count the non-Maharashtrians for the purpose of coming to the conclusion as to who form the majority of population in the Bombay City.

Again it is not realised that the increase in the non-Marathi-speaking people in the Bombay City is due to the absence of a local law restricting citizenship. If Bombay State had such a law all this influx into Bombay from all parts of India could have been shut out and the Maharashtrian majority retained. It is also not realised that the influx of the non-Maharashtrians in Bombay is due to the fact that Bombay is a port, and it is a port on the Western Coast. The route from Europe to Bombay is much shorter than the route from Europe to Calcutta or Europe to Madras. That is why, large number of poor people from other parts of India leave their homes and come to Bombay as temporary residents. It is easier to find a job in Bombay than elsewhere.

Really speaking the matter has to be looked at from a different point of view. People have been coming to Bombay for the last two hundred years or so. Yet this influx has not reduced the Maharashtrian population in the city below 48 per cent. After two hundred years, the bedrock of its population remains Maharashtrian in its composition. This is due to the migratory character of City.[7] The Gujarathis are migratory population.

There are also other arguments which could be urged in favour of allowing Bombay to remain as part of Maharashtra. Bombay is not the only composite city in India. Calcutta and Madras are also composite cities. If Calcutta can be part of Western Bengal and Madras can be part of Madras State what objection can there be to Bombay being made part of Maharashtra? This is the question that every Maharashtrian will ask. I see no answer to this question. The only answer that comes to one's mind is that the Congress High Command thinks that Maharashtrians are unfit to rule others. This is a slur on the Maharashtrian character and they will not tolerate it.

It is said that Bombay has been built up by the capital belonging to non-Maharashtrians. That may be so. But has Madras been built by the capital of Madrasees? Has Calcutta been built by the capital of Bengalees? Without the capital of Europeans Madras and Calcutta would have been villages. Then why urge this point against the Maharashtrians when they claim Bombay to themselves? Maharashtrians have at least contributed labour without which Bombay could not have been what it is. It must always be remembered that the life lines of Bombay lie in Maharashtra. The sources of its electricity lie in Maharashtra. Sources of its water supply lie in Maharashtra. The sources of its labour lie in Maharashtra. Maharashtra can at any time make the city of Bombay *'Mohenjodaro'* a City of the Dead.

The Gujarathi population is filled with fear that Maharashtrians will practise discrimination against them. But under our Constitution discrimination is not possible for the reason that the Constitution contains a list of fundamental rights and remedies by way of writs from the High Court and the Supreme Court which can immediately provide redress for a wrong. For every wrong of a discriminative character there is a remedy provided by the Constitution. Why should the Gujarathis have any fear?

Let us now consider what benefit the Gujarathis are going to get from Bombay being made a separate City State. Their population in the Bombay State is only ten per cent. How many seats can they get in the Bombay City State Legislature? Not even ten per cent. How can ten per cent protect their clients against 90 per cent?

It must be remembered that the feelings between the Maharashtrians and the Gujarathis would hereafter be running high as never before. A Maharashtrian will not vote for a Gujarathi candidate and a Gujarathi voter will not vote for a Maharashtrian candidate. Hitherto the Gujarathis have been able to plough the sands of Maharashtra with their money. But money may not succeed once self-respect is aroused. The Gujarathis must consider whether goodwill is not a better protection than a paltry share in the Government of the City.

While the case of Maharashtra is as strong as steel there are some points on the other side which they must not fail to consider in their anger. They want Bombay to be within Maharashtra. But the question which they must consider is: What do they want? Do they want prosperous Bombay or do they want decadent Bombay? Can Bombay be prosperous under Maharashtra? This in other words means: can Maharashtra provide the capital necessary for the growing trade and industry of the City? No Maharashtrian can answer this question in the affirmative. The Maharashtrians may be able to supply the need for capital after a course of years. But certainly not now.

The second point is: what would be the effect on the standard of living of Maharashtrians living in Bombay if the City's prosperity declines either by flight of capital or removal of business houses. The Maharashtrians must not forget, however it may hurt their pride, that they are a nation of clerks and coolies. What employment can they get in a declining city?

The Maharashtrian should consider the question of Bombay from this point of view. There is a saying which goes as follows, *sarvanashe samutpanne ardha tyajati panditah.*[8]

There is also another reason why Bombay City should be made a separate state. The minorities and the Scheduled Castes who are living in the village are constantly subjected to tyranny, oppression, and even murders by the members of the majority communities. The minorities need an asylum, a place of refuge where they can be free from the tyranny of the majority. If there was a United Maharashtra with Bombay included in it where they can go to for safety? The same tyranny was practised over the Brahmins, Marwaris and Gujarathis living in the villages when Godse killed Mr. Gandhi. All the Brahmins, Marwaris and Gujarathis who were once living in villages ran away and are now living in towns and forgetting their experiences are shouting for United Maharashtra, after having reached a safe harbour.

It seems to me that Maharashtrians will do well to accept the decision of the Congress High Command for the time being. The Maharashtrians need have no fear of losing Bombay. Nobody can dispossess Maharashtrians of Bombay. Much less can there be any ouster of them by anybody. The real objection to the creation of Bombay as a separate State arises from the fact that the name Bombay does not carry within it the sense that it is part of Maharashtra. It is to remove this objection that I propose that the new State of Bombay should be renamed by another name which will carry on its face the word Maharashtra.

Supposing in terms of this suggestion instead of saying that Bombay be made a separate State it is said that Maharashtra be divided into four States, (1) Maharashtra City State (which is Bombay City), (2) Western Maharashtra, (3) Central Maharashtra, (4) Eastern Maharashtra; what objection can there be to the creation of a separate State of Bombay?

This also involves the separation of Bombay. With this change in the name of the City I like to know which Maharashtrian can raise objection to the creation of Bombay as a separate City State on the ground that this scheme separates Bombay from Maharashtra? To say that Bombay be made a separate State is merely stating that Maharashtra be divided into four States. If there is no objection to Maharashtra being divided into *two* or *three* States what objection can there be to Maharashtra being divided into four? I can see none. For the sake of similarity in language I propose that Calcutta be called Bengal City State and Madras be called Tamil City State.

This is one proposal which I make to ease the tension between Maharashtrians and Gujarathis.

The Maharashtra City State will be a surplus State. Those who want United Maharashtra with Bombay are hoping to get the benefit of this surplus for Maharashtra. The surplus revenue of the City State arises because of (1) The Property Tax and (2) The Electricity Tax. Can the revenue from these two sources be appropriated by Maharashtra if Bombay becomes a separate City State?

Nothing can be done to take away the yield of the Property Tax from the Bombay City State Property Tax. It is a local tax, on local situated property. The State within which the property is situated is entitled to the yield of the Tax. With regard to the Electricity Tax the situation is different.

When Gujarath and Maharashtra are separated—and they must be—Gujarath will claim the revenue derived from electricity produced and consumed within Gujarath. Maharashtra will claim the revenue derived from electricity produced and consumed within Maharashtra. Bombay City as a State will do the same. Can Bombay be allowed to do so and appropriate the revenue to itself? Is it just? Bombay City does not produce electricity. It is produced outside Bombay City in Maharashtra. Therefore the new Bombay City State has no right to appropriate to itself the whole revenue derived from electricity. The proper thing to do is to apply the principle of the segregation of the sources and division of the yield well known to all students of State Finance.

To put it in concrete shape let the Centre take over the taxation of Electricity and divide the yield among the four States of Maharashtra—(1) Bombay, (2) Western Maharashtra, (3) Central Maharashtra, (4) Eastern Maharashtra according to their needs. It will also ease the financial strain that the three Maharashtras are likely to suffer on account of the separation of Bombay.

## IV
## United or Divided?

I have said that Bombay be given a new area and made into a separate City State. There now remains the question of how to deal with the rest of the Maharashtra. I have suggested that the rest of the Maharashtra should be divided into three States. From very ancient times Maharashtra has been divided into three States.

Maharashtra first comes to be known in history during the time of Ashok. It is mentioned in *Mahavansa* in connection with reference to the missionaries sent by Ashok to different parts of India for the purpose of propagating Buddhism. But thereafter the Pali literature speaks of *Trai Maharashtrika* or three Maharashtras. It means that from very ancient times there have been three Maharashtras. My proposal is not therefore new. The distribution of population, area and revenue would be as shown in Table below.

The accompanying map No. 5[9] will show the area and boundaries of each of the three divisions. For the present, from the point of view of area and population there is nothing to complain against the three divisions. From the earliest times they have always been spoken of as *Trai Maharashtras*.

The division does no wrong to the language principle. In fact if all the three Maharashtras have the same language it can help to develop the Marathi language if it is worth their while to do so. The question of viability I will consider later on. I propose to deal with it separately in a special chapter. Bombay was then unknown. Otherwise it would have been the fourth part of Maharashtra.

Of the remaining three parts what I call Eastern Maharashtra is already a separate State. All that required is that it should be allowed to remain separate. It has got a well-established administration system, a well-established revenue system and a well-established judicial system. It has been separated from the trammels of the Hindi-speaking people. The only problem that remains is how to divide the area covered by the Maharashtra which is part of the present Bombay State and the Marathwada of the Hyderabad State. Instead of forming a merger of the two into one and joining it to the third which I call Eastern Maharashtra, why not divide the Maharashtra part of Bombay and Marathwada into two equal States? This is my scheme. I transfer six districts of Maharashtra part of the Bombay State and make them part of Marathwada. The distribution of the area and population of the three Maharashtras are shown below:

The population area and revenue of the three Maharashtra states

| *Name of State* | *Total Population of the territory* | *Area in square miles* | *Total Revenue* | *Total expenditure* |
|---|---|---|---|---|
| Western Maharashtra | 12677316 | 30028 | 262420441 | not known |
| Central Maharashtra | 12409044 | 55482 | 216380095 | not known |
| Eastern Maharashtra | 8027130 | 39004 | 94111012 | not known |
| Total | 33113490 | 124514 | 572911548 | not known |

I will now proceed to state my reasons in support of my plan.

I have said that Maharashtra has always been divided into three. This is a historical argument. It at least shows that the tradition, the way of life and the social and economic condition of what is called United Maharashtra is not one. Those who are in a hurry to have United Maharashtra may not take it seriously. But there are other arguments which arise out of the present condition and which cannot be ignored. I mention a few.

My first argument is that a single Government cannot administer such a huge State as United Maharashtra. The total population of the Marathi-speaking area is 3,30,83,490. The total area occupied by the Marathi-speaking people is 1,74,514 sq. miles. It is a vast area and it is impossible to have efficient administration by a single State. Maharashtrians who talk about Samyukta Maharashtra have no conception of the vastness as to the area and population of their Maharashtra. But why there should be one single Maharashtrian State. I am quite unable to understand. To have a separate Maharashtra State is one thing. To have a single Maharashtra State is quite a different thing. I am in favour of a separate Maharashtra, separate from Gujarathis and separate from Hindi-speaking people. But I am unable to understand why a free Maharashtra should be made into one single State. The Maharashtrians are not planning to declare war on U.P. and therefore they need not have a common front.

Even from the point of view of Marathas why should there be this consolidation? What affiliation has a Maratha of Satara got with the Maratha of Aurangabad? What affiliation has a Maratha of Nasik got with the Maratha of Ratnagiri? What care and interest a Maratha of Satara is going to bestow upon the problems of the Maratha of Aurangabad? What care and interest a Maratha of Nasik is going to bestow upon the problems of the Maratha of Ratnagiri? The consolidation has no meaning and can serve no purpose. All Maratha Ministers in the present Bombay Cabinet come from Satara District or Nasik District. There is none from Konkan.

The second consideration is the economic inequality between the three parts of Maharashtra. Marathwada has been solely neglected by the Nizam. What guarantee is there that the other two Maharashtras will look after the interests of what I call the Central Maharashtra?

The third consideration is industrial inequality between the three parts of Maharashtra. Western Maharashtra and Eastern Maharashtra are industrially well developed. What about the Central Maharashtra? What guarantee is there of its industrial development? Will Western Maharashtra and Eastern Maharashtra take interest in the industrial development of Central Maharashtra?

The fourth consideration is the inequality of education between Eastern and Western Maharashtra on the one hand and Central Maharashtra on the other. The inequality between them is marked. If the Central Maharashtra goes under the Poona University its destiny is doomed.

I am greatly worried about Marathwada. It was hitherto part of the Nizam's Territory for the last 200 years. The Nizam had criminally neglected this area. He took no interest in it. There is not a mile of canal irrigation in Marathwada. There is hardly a high school in taluka places in Marathwada. There is hardly a youth in Nizam's public service from Marathwada. I speak from knowledge and experience. People are not only down and out they are ignorant. They are being grabbed by highly advanced people on both sides. When their avenues of employment are closed there will be further degradation in their position.

I shudder to think what would happen when Marathwada goes under the Poona University. The standard of education in the schools and colleges under the Poona University is so high that hardly any boy from Marathwada can hope to pass the examination. It is quite possible that with the madness for united Maharashtra there will develop a madness for a single and common University. The creation of United Maharashtra will be followed by the onrush of Poona and Nagpur Brahmins in Marathwada to pick up the jobs.

There is a further reason why Maharashtra should be divided into three.

The total strength of the Bombay Legislative Assembly is 315, Out of them 149 members are Marathi-speaking. The total strength of the Bombay Legislative Council *is* 72; out of them 34 are Marathi-speaking. Obviously some Marathi-speaking person should have been the Chief Minister of the Bombay State. Mr. Hirey stood up as a candidate foı the Chief Ministership, but he was made to sit down by the Congress High Command. Not only was Mr. Hirey made to sit down but he was forced to move that Mr. Morarji Desai be made the Chief Minister. What a humiliation for a Maharashtrian leader! And what value does the Congress High command attach to the political intelligence of Maharashtrians?

The same incapacity of the Maratha Ministers is clear from the division of subjects referred earlier. It is obvious from the facts given above that the Marathas are lacking in political talent. There is no man of eminence among them such as Tilak, or Gokhale or Ranade.

The Maharashtrian today counts for nothing. The Congress Maharashtrian coin is for much less in the Congress. The non-Congress Maharashtrian also counts for nothing. It is therefore absolutely essential to train up Maharashtrians in political life. This political training has become fundamental because of the transfer of power to the masses. The word Marathas is used in two senses. In one sense it means all those who speak the Marathi language. In another sense it means all those who are Marathas by caste. They are all spoken of as Marathas. But they all fail to make the distinction between Marathas i.e. those who speak the Marathi language and Marathas i.e. those who are Marathas by caste.

Those who are going to rule Maharashtra are not Marathas by speech but Marathas by caste, notwithstanding the hopes of the Brahmins. Now it cannot be denied that Marathas are politically the most backward community. It is fundamental that they should receive political training. If there is only one Maharashtra only *one* Maratha can be trained as Chief Minister and five or six as Ministers. On the other hand if there are three Maharashtra States, three Marathas can find training as Chief Ministers and thirty Marathas can get training as Ministers. We can do real service to ourselves by helping to educate our Masters.

The only way of educating the Marathas is to give them more fields for developing their abilities and exercising their abilities. Only the creation of three Maharashtras can do this. There is a story which is very appropriate to the occasion. The father of a young girl had taken her for an outing in a jungle. She found that under big trees there stood small shrubs. Finding this to be uniformly so, she asked her father why these small shrubs under the big trees do not grow. The father not being a botanist could not give an answer. So he said: Oh! I do not know. He, however, felt that the question was very significant. He was a Professor in a college. Next day he went to the college and put the question to his Botanist colleague. The Botanist replied: Why! The answer is simple. The big trees use up all the sun's rays to themselves. The shrubs do not get any rays. That is why they do not grow. The Marathwada people must not forget the moral of this story.

The only argument in favour of United Maharashtra is that it is like a meeting of the two brothers Rama and Bharat in Ramayana after a long separation. It is a silly argument, not worth consideration. There are some Maharashtrians who are satisfied with some kind of Political Treaty with Western Maharashtra guaranteeing some concessions. Treaties are like scraps of paper. They cannot be enforced. Instead of political treaties which nobody can enforce is it not better to have power in one's own hands? What a poor and wretched show by Maharashtrians in the Government of Bombay! If this is the show that the most advanced and educated part of Maharashtrians can make, what can be expected from the people of Marathwada? I advise the people of Marathwada or Central Maharashtra to have a State of their own so that they have power in their own hands to improve their own lot.

## V
## Reclamation of Lost Territory

Should all the Marathi-speaking people be huddled up under one State? Or should they be divided into two or more States. How to dispose of the remainder when Bombay is separated is the next question. The remainder consists of two parts: (1) Gujarath, (2) Maharashtra.

I am concerned with Maharashtra. While creating Linguistic Provinces the Commission has given over Marathi-speaking areas to non-Marathi-speaking areas. The number of such excluded areas is as follows:

1. Belgaum Taluka with the City of Belgau; 2. Khanapur Taluka; 3. Chikori Taluka including Nipani; 4. Supa Taluka; 5. Karwar Taluka; 6. Nilanga Taluka in Bidar; 7. Ahamadpur Taluka in Bidar; 8. Udgir Taluka in Bidar; 9. Rajgir Taluka in Adilabad; 10. Some portion from Vidarbha given to the neighbouring Hindi-speaking State.

The Maharashtrians excluded from Maharashtra come to 13,89,648 in terms of population. The Commission in retaining the mixed State of Bombay had to secure two most important objects. One is not to allow Bombay to go into the hands of Maharashtrians. This the Commission did by creating a mixed State. The second thing they had to do was to secure equality between Maharashtrians and the Gujarathis. The necessity of equality between the two in the future Legislature of the Bombay State as planned by the Commission had become urgent as the members of Karnatak in the old Assembly on whom the Gujarathis depended for their majority *were* to disappear in the new Karnatak State. This the Commission did by clipping the wings of Maharashtra by handing over Marathi-speaking people to non-Marathi-speaking States. There seems to be no other reason for this political vandalism.

This wrong done by the Commission to Maharashtra must now be remedied and fortunately it can be undone. The proposal of a mixed State is gone and there is no necessity for equality between Maharashtrians and Gujarathis.

## Chapter 8
## Summary of Principles Governing the Issue

For the sake of the reader I summarise below the principles which should underly the creation of Linguistic States which are already enunciated in the foregoing pages but which lie about scattered. These principles may be stated as below:

(1) The idea of having a mixed State must be completely abandoned.
(2) Every State must be a unilingual State. One State, one language.
(3) The formula one State, one language must not be confused with the formula of one language, one State.
(4) The formula one language, one State means that all people speaking one language should be brought under one Government irrespective of area, population and dissimilarity of conditions among the people speaking the language. This is the idea that underlies the agitation for a united Maharashtra with Bombay. This is an absurd formula and has no precedent for it. It must be abandoned. A people speaking one language may be cut up into many States as is done in other parts of the world.

(5) Into how many States a people speaking one language should be cut up, should depend upon (a) the requirements of efficient administration, (b) the needs of the different areas, (c) the sentiments of the different areas, and (d) the proportion between the majority and minority.

(6) As the area of the State increases the proportion of the minority to the majority decreases and the position of the minority become precarious and the opportunities for the majority to practise tyranny over the minority become greater. The States must therefore be small.

(7) The minorities must be given protection to prevent the tyranny of the majority. To do this the Constitution must be amended and provisions must be made for a system on plural member constituencies (two or three) with cumulative voting.

## PART-4
## THE PROBLEMS OF LINGUISTIC STATES

### Chapter 9
### Viability

Will the three Maharashtrian States be viable? Will their Revenue be sufficient to meet their expenditure? Such a question is bound to be asked. It is not that such a question can be asked about Maharashtra alone. It can be asked about many other States in India. I give four statements relating to Part A States, Part B States and the Central Government from Part III of the Report of the Taxation Inquiry Committee presided over by Dr. John Mathai. From these statements the following propositions stand out: (1) that up to a certain year in the life of the States there was no deficit. They were all viable. It is only after Congress came into office that States ceased to be viable; (2) that since the Congress came into office the Excise Revenue has begun to dwindle. It has gone down to a vanishing point; (3) that Income Tax and Sales Tax have increased enormously.

These are the causes which explain why States have ceased to be viable. The Excise Revenue is being sacrificed for a false ideology which has no meaning, no sense and no reality. To regard to the Policy of Prohibition followed by the Congress, the following conclusions can be drawn without fear of challenge: (1) An enormous amount of revenue is sacrificed for nothing; (2) people have not ceased to drink. There is enormous amount of illicit manufacture of liquor which is being sold to the public clandestinely; (3) the money lost by Government is picked up by the illicit manufacturer; (4) prohibition has demoralised Society. Formerly only male members of the family drank because they alone could go to the liquor shop; now illicit liquor manufacture has become a Home Industry. Liquor being now made at home both men and women drink. (5) In addition to the loss of revenue on account of Prohibition Government has to undertake increased expenditure on Police to enforce Prohibition which, however, they never do.

What good is this Prohibition which does not prohibit? The Congress threatens to extend this Prohibition to the whole of India. God bless the

Congress! It *is* said that God first makes them mad whom He wishes to destroy. God is doing the same with Congressmen. It is enough for me to say that Congress cannot have both viability and Prohibition.

Coming to the Land Revenue it could certainly be increased. But the Congress is afraid to touch the agriculturist for fear of losing votes. It is therefore raising money from the Sales Tax and the Income Tax both of which fall so heavily on the urban classes as is apparent from Table above. It is therefore clear that viability is no problem. Only the Congress has to revise its Taxation Policy. Viability is a question of capacity to bear taxation and will to tax. There is enough capacity. What is wanted, is will. The whole of the Indian Taxation system requires to be changed. It is a question of altering the Constitution. I cannot deal with it now. I must reserve it for another occasion.

## Chapter 10
## Majorities and Minorities

Politics is nothing if not realistic. There is very little in it that is academic. It is therefore follows that before passing any judgement on any scheme of politics it is essential that one must consider the ground plan. Someone may ask what I mean by "Ground Plan". To me the ground plan means the social structure of a community to which the political plan is sought to be applied. It needs no argument to show that the political structure rests on the social structure. Indeed the social structure has a profound effect on the political structure. It may modify it in its working. It may nullify it or it may even make a mockery of it.

In the case of India the social structure is built up on the caste system, the special product of Hindu civilisation and culture. The caste system is so well known that one need not wait to explain its nature. One can straight proceed to show what effect it is likely to have on Linguistic States. There are some peculiar features of the caste system which must however be noted—

(1) Castes are so distributed that in any given area there is one caste which is major and there are others which are small and are subservient to the major caste owing to their comparative smallness and their economic dependence upon the major caste which owns most of the land in the village.

(2) The caste system is marked not merely by inequality but is affected by the system of graded inequality. All castes are not on a par. They are one above the other. There is a kind of ascending scale of hatred and a descending scale of contempt.

(3) A caste has all the exclusiveness and pride which a nation has. It is therefore not improper to speak of collection of castes as a collection of major and minor nations.

I am sorry; I cannot illustrate these points by reference to facts and figures. The census which is the only source of information on these points fails to help me. The last census omits altogether the caste tables which had been the feature of the Indian census ever since its birth. The Home Minister of the Government of India who is responsible for this omission was of the opinion that if a word does not exist in a dictionary it can be proved that the fact for which the word stands does not exist. One can only pity the petty intelligence of the author.

The consequences of the caste system on politics are quite obvious. The interesting part is to see what effect it has upon elections, which is the foundation of Representative Government which is reared up on a system of single member constituencies.

The effects may be summarised as follows:

(1) Voting is always communal. The voter votes for the candidate of his community and not for the best candidate.
(2) The majority community carries the seat by sheer communal majority.
(3) The minority community is forced to vote for the candidate of the majority community.
(4) The votes of the minority community are not enough to enable the candidate to win the seat against the candidate put up by the majority community.
(5) As consequence of social system of graded inequality the voter of the higher (major) communities can never condescend to give his vote to a candidate of a minority community. On the other hand the voter of the minority community who is socially on a lower level takes pride in giving his vote to the candidate of the majority community. That is another reason why a candidate of a minority community loses in election.

The Congress always wins, so it is found. But no one asks why does the Congress win? The answer is that Congress is very popular. But why is the Congress popular? The true answer is that Congress always puts up candidates which belong to castes which are in the majority in the constituencies. Caste and Congress are closely linked. It is by exploiting the caste system that the Congress wins. These evil consequences of the caste system are sure to be sharpened by creation of Linguistic States. Minority communities may be crushed. If not crushed they may be tyrannised and oppressed. They are sure to be discriminated against and denied equality before law and equal opportunity in public life.

The history of nations and the changes in their ideologies have been well traced by Lord Action:

> "In the old European system, the rights of nationalities were neither recognised by governments nor asserted by the people. The interest of the reigning families, not those of the nations, regulated the frontiers, and the administration was conducted generally without any reference to popular desires. Where all liberties were suppressed, the claims of national

> independence were necessarily ignored, and a princess, in the words of Fenelon, carried a monarchy in her wedding portion."

Nationalities were at first listless. When they became conscious:

> "They first rose against their conquerors in defence of their legitimate rulers. They refused to be governed by usurpers. Next came a time when they revolted because of the wrongs inflicted upon them by their rulers. The insurrections were provoked by particular grievances justified by definite complaints. Then came the French Revolution which effected a complete change. It taught the people to regard their wishes and wants as the supreme criterion of their right to do what they like to do with themselves. It proclaimed the idea of the sovereignty of the people uncontrolled by the past and uncontrolled by the existing state."

The caste is a nation but the rule of one caste over another may not be admitted to be the same as the rule of one nation over another. But supposing the case is not carried so far but is limited to majority and minority even then the question remains: What right has the majority to rule the minority? The answer is that whatever the majority does it is right. What complain the minorities can have?

People who rely upon majority rule forget the fact that majorities are of two sorts: (1) Communal majority and (2) Political majority. A political majority is changeable in its class composition. A political majority grows. A communal majority is born. The admission to a political majority is open. The door to a communal majority is closed. The politics of a political majority are free to all to make and unmake. The politics of a communal majority are made by its own members born in it. How can a communal majority run away with the title deeds given to a political majority to rule? To give such title deeds to a communal majority is to establish a hereditary Government and make the way open to the tyranny of that majority. This tyranny of the communal majority is not an idle dream. It is an experience of many minorities. This experience to Maharashtrian Brahmins being every recent it is unnecessary to dilate upon it.

What is the remedy? No doubt some safeguards against this communal tyranny are essential. The question is: What can they be? The first safeguard is not to have too large a State. The consequences of too large a State on the minority living within it are not understood by many. The larger the State the smaller the proportion of the minority to the majority. To give one illustration—if Mahavidarbha remained separate, the proportion of Hindus to Muslims would be four to one. In the United Maharashtra the proportion will be fourteen to one. The same would be the case of the Untouchables. A small stone of a consolidated majority placed on the chest of the minority may be borne. But the weight of a huge mountain it cannot bear. It will crush the minorities. Therefore creation of smaller States is a safeguard to the minorities.

The second safeguard is some provision for representation in the Legislature. The old types of remedy provided in the Constitution were (1) certain number of reserved seats and (2) separate electorates. Both these safeguards have been given up in the new Constitution. The lambs are shorn of the wool. They are feeling the intensity of the cold. Some tempering of the wool is necessary. Separate electorates or reservation of scats must not be restored to. It would be enough to have plural member constituencies (of two or three) with cumulative voting in place of the system of single-member constituency embodied in the present Constitution. This will allay the fears which the minorities have about Linguistic States.

## PART-5
## THE NEED FOR A SECOND CAPITAL

### Chapter 11
### India and the Necessity of a Second Capital
### A way to remove tension between the north and the south

Can India afford to have one Capital? That India has now one capital does not close the question. If the Capital of India is not satisfactorily located, now is the time for considering the question. Since the departure of the British, India has only one capital and that is Delhi. Before the British, India has always had two capitals. During the Moghal period, India had Delhi as one Capital and Shrinagar in Kashmir as another Capital. When the British came they too had two capitals, one was Calcutta and another was Simla. Even when they left Calcutta for Delhi, they retained Simla as their summer Capital. The two capitals maintained by the Moghuls and by the British were the results of climatic conditions. Neither the British nor the Moghuls were able to live in Delhi or in Calcutta continuously for 12 months. The summer months in Delhi were unbearable to the Moghuls. They made Shrinagar their second capital for summer months. The summer months in Calcutta were equally unbearable to the British. They, therefore, established a second capital. To these climatic conditions must now be added three other conditions. There was no popular Government when the Moghuls ruled or when the British ruled. Now we have popular Government and the convenience of the people is an important factor. Delhi is most inconvenient to the people of the South. They suffer the most from cold as well as distance. Even the Northern people suffer in the summer months. They do not complain because they are nearer home and they are nearer the seat of power. Second is the feeling of the Southern people and the third is the consideration of Defence. The feeling of the Southern people is that the Capital of their Country is far away from them and that they are being ruled by the people of Northern India. The third consideration is of course more important. It is that Delhi is a vulnerable place. It is within bombing distance of the neighbouring countries. Although India is trying to live in peace with its neighbours it cannot be assumed that India will not have to face war sometime or other and if war comes, the Government of India will have to leave Delhi and find another place for its location. Which is the place to which the Government of India can migrate? A place that one can think of is Calcutta. But Calcutta is also within bombing distance from Tibet. Although India and China today are friends, how long the friendship would last no one can definitely say. The possibility of conflict between India and China remains. In that event Calcutta would be useless. The next town that could be considered as a refuge for the Central Government is Bombay. But Bombay is a port and our Indian Navy is too poor to protect the Central Government if it came down to Bombay. Is there a fourth place one could think of? I find Hyderabad to be such a place. Hyderabad, Secunderabad and Bolarum should be constituted into a Chief Commissioner's Province and made a second capital of India. Hyderabad fulfils all the requirements of a capital for India. Hyderabad is equidistant to all States. Anyone who looks at the table of distances given below will realise it:

| | *From Delhi – miles* | *From Hyderabad – miles* |
|---|---|---|
| To Bombay | 798 | 440 |
| To Calcutta | 868 | 715 |
| To Madras | 1198 | 330 |
| To Karnul | 957 | 275 |
| To Trivandrum | 1521 | 660 |
| To Patiala | 124 | 990 |
| To Chandigarh | 180 | 1045 |
| To Lucknow | 275 | 770 |

From the defence point of view it would give safety to the Central Government. It is equidistant from all parts of India. It would give satisfaction to the South Indian people that their Government is sometimes with them. The Government may remain in Delhi during winter months and during other months it can stay in Hyderabad. Hyderabad has all the amenities which Delhi has and it is a far better City than Delhi. It has all the grandeur which Delhi has. Buildings are going cheap and they are really beautiful buildings, far superior to those in Delhi. They are all on sale. The only thing that is wanting is a Parliament House which the Government of India can easily build. It is a place in which Parliament can sit all the year round and work, which it cannot do in Delhi. I do not see what objection there can be in making Hyderabad a second capital of India. It should be done right now while we are reorganising the States.

Hyderabad, Secunderabad and Bolarum should be constituted into a second capital of India. Fortunately, it can be very easily done with satisfaction to the whole of South India, to Maharashtra and to the Andhras. This is another remedy for easing the tension between the North and the South.

***

## Appendix I
## Population by Linguistic Families

| *Language Groups* | *No. of languages spoken* | *No. of speakers as mother-tongue and subsidiary 1931 (bilinguals shown twice)* | *No. of speakers 1931* | *No. of speakers mother-tongue 1931* | *Difference between columns 4 & 5 (increase in 1931 + decrease in 1931 -)* | *Difference between columns 4 & 3 (increase + decrease -)* |
|---|---|---|---|---|---|---|
| Language of India and Burma | 225 | 366,430,537 | 315,525,177 | 349,887,527 | +94,362,350 | +50,905,360 |
| (I) Austric Languages | | | | | | |
| 1. Indonesian Languages | 2 | 6542 | 5561 | 6542 | +981 | +981 |
| 2. Mon-Khmer Languages | 10 | 734,204 | 549,917 | 726,578 | +176,661 | +184,287 |
| 3. Munda Languages* | 7 | 4,710,685 | 3,973,873 | 4,609,588 | +635,715 | +736,812 |
| (II) Tibeto-Chinese Languages | | | | | | |
| 1. Tibeto-Burman Languages | 128 | 14,167,611 | 11,959,011 | 12,982,840 | +1,023,829 | +2,208,600 |
| 2. Tai-Chinese Languages | 11 | 1,150,220 | 926,335 | 1,027,656 | +101,321 | +223,885 |
| 3. Man and Karen Languages** | 17 | 1,351,291 | 1,114,617 | 1,342,278 | +227,661 | +236,674 |

* The correct classification of these two languages is doubtful. Pizyluski treats them as Tai (Meillet and Cohen, *tongues du Monde* 380), but it is probable they have Austric affinities.

** The correct classification of these two languages is doubtful. Pizyluski treats them as Tai (Meillet and Cohen, *tongues du Monde* 380), but it is probable they have Austric affinities.

(Appendix I contd.)

| *Language Groups* | *No. of languages spoken* | *No. of speakers as mother-tongue and subsidiary 1931 (bilinguals shown twice)* | *No. of speakers 1931* | *No. of speakers mother-tongue 1931* | *Difference between columns 4 & 5 (increase in 1931 + decrease in 1931 -)* | *Difference between columns 4 & 3 (increase + decrease -)* |
|---|---|---|---|---|---|---|
| (III) Dravidian Languages | | | | | | |
| 1. Dravida Languages | 7 | 47,032,874 | 37,285,594 | 41,454,593 | +4,168,999 | +9,747,280 |
| 2. Intermediate Languages | 5 | 3,661,277 | 3,056,598 | 3,609,418 | +552,820 | +604,679 |
| 3. Andhra Languages | 1 | 28,195,824 | 23,601,492 | 26,373,727 | +2,772,235 | +4,594,332 |
| 4. N.W. Languages | 1 | 231,581 | 184,368 | 207,049 | +22,681 | +47,213 |
| (IV) Indo-European Languages | | | | | | |
| 1. Eranian Languages | 3 | 2,457,134 | 1,981,675 | 2,270,466 | +288,791 | +475,459 |
| 2. Dardic Languages | 5 | 1,354,031 | 1,304,319 | 1,522,936 | +218,617 | +238,712 |
| 3. Indo-Aryan Languages | 19 | 261,105,909 | 229,560,555 | 253,699,403 | +24,138,848 | +31,545,354 |
| (V) Unclassed Languages | | | | | | |
| 1. Andamanese | 2 | 466 | 580 | 466 | +114 | -114 |
| 2. Burushashi | 1 | 26,076 | – | 26,076 | +26,076 | +26,076 |
| 3. Gipsy dialects* | 6 | 25,999 | 15,018 | 25,999 | +10,981 | +10,981 |

* These dialects are drawn from various Indian languages and contain such diverse elements that they cannot fairly be allotted to one family rather than another.

(Appendix I contd.)

(Appendix I contd.)

| *Language Groups* | *No. of languages spoken* | *No. of speakers as mother-tongue and subsidiary 1931 (bilinguals shown twice)* | *No. of speakers 1931* | *No. of speakers mother-tongue 1931* | *Difference between columns 4 & 5 (increase in 1931 + decrease in 1931 -)* | *Difference between columns 4 & 3 (increase + decrease -)* |
|---|---|---|---|---|---|---|
| 4. Languages not returned and unspecified | – | 29,813* | 5,664 | 2,912 | +3,752 | +24,149 |
| B. Languages of other Asiatic counties and Africa | 17 | 305,386 | 211,894 | 302,324 | +90,430 | +93,492 |
| C. Languages of Europe | 10 | 452,099 | 319,112 | 339,706 | +20,594 | +132,987 |

* Includes Hill and aboriginal subsidiary languages (27,841).

**APPENDIX II**

## Area and population of states of United States of America

| *Name of State* | *Area sq. miles* | *Population Est. 1944* |
|---|---|---|
| *1* | *2* | *3* |
| 1. Alabama | 51,609 | 2,818,083 |
| 2. Arirona [sic] | 113,909 | 638,412 |
| 3. Arkansas | 53,102 | 1,776,446 |
| 4. California | 158,693 | 8,746,989 |
| 5. Colorado | 104,247 | 1,147,269 |
| 6. Connecticut | 5,009 | 1,176,807 |
| 7. Delaware | 2,057 | 283,802 |
| 8. Florida | 58,560 | 3,367,217 |
| 9. Georgia | 58,876 | 3,223,727 |
| 10. Idaho | 83,557 | 531,573 |
| 11. Illinois | 56,400 | 7,729,720 |
| 12. Indiana | 36,291 | 3,419,707 |
| 13. Jowa [sic] | 56,280 | 2,269,759 |
| 14. Kansas | 82,276 | 1,774,447 |
| 15. Kentucky | 40,395 | 2,630,194 |
| 16. Louisiana | 48,523 | 2,535,385 |
| 17. Maine | 33,215 | 793,600 |
| 18. Maryland | 10,577 | 2,127,874 |
| 19. Massachusetts | 8,257 | 4,162,815 |
| 20. Michigan | 58,216 | 5,429,641 |
| 21. Minnesota | 84,008 | 2,508,663 |
| 22. Mississippi | 47,716 | 2,175,877 |
| 23. Missouri | 69,674 | 3,589,538 |
| 24. Montana | 147,138 | 464,999 |
| 25. Nebraska | 77,237 | 1,213,792 |
| 26. Nevada | 110,540 | 156,445 |
| 27. New Hampshire | 9,304 | 457,231 |
| 28. New Jersey | 7,836 | 4,167,840 |
| 29. New Mexico | 121,666 | 532,212 |
| 30. New York | 49,576 | 12,632,890 |
| 31. North Carolina | 52,712 | 3,534,545 |

(Appendix II contd.)

(Appendix II contd.)

| *Name of State* | *Area sq. miles* | *Population Est. 1944* |
|---|---|---|
| *1* | *2* | *3* |
| 32. North Dakota | 70,665 | 528,071 |
| 33. Ohio | 41,222 | 638,667 |
| 34. Oklahoma | 69,919 | 2,064,679 |
| 35. Oregon | 96,981 | 1,214,226 |
| 36. Pennsylvania | 45,332 | 9,247,088 |
| 37. Rhode-Island | 1,214 | 778,972 |
| 38. South Carolina | 31,055 | 1,923,354 |
| 39. South Dakota | 77,047 | 558,629 |
| 40. Tennessee | 42,246 | 2,870,158 |
| 41. Texas | 267,339 | 6,876,248 |
| 42. Utah | 84,916 | 606,994 |
| 43. Vermont | 9,609 | 310,941 |
| 44. Virginia | 40,815 | 3,119,115 |
| 45. Washington | 68,192 | 2,055,378 |
| 46. West Virginia | 24,181 | 1,715,984 |
| 47. Wisconsin | 56,154 | 2,975,910 |
| 48. Wyoming | 97,914 | 257,108 |

## APPENDIX III

### The population of the Bombay City according to the communities given in the census of 1941

| | |
|---|---|
| Hindu | 8,99,398 |
| Scheduled Castes | 1,21,352 |
| Muslims | 2,51,518 |
| Indian Christians | 1,22,683 |
| Anglo-Indians | 8,787 |
| Parsees | 58,813 |
| Sikhs | 2,418 |
| Jains | 33,281 |
| Buddhists | 912 |
| Tribes | 4,606 |
| Others | 29,84 |
| Total | 1,489,883 |

The area of the Bombay City according to the Census of 1941 was 30 sq. miles.

## APPENDIX IV

### Inter-provincial immigration and emigration in India
### Variation as compared with 1921 in the volume of migration within India

| *Province or State* | *Net gain + or loss* | *1931* | | *Net gain + or loss -* | *1921* | | *Variation 1921–31* | |
|---|---|---|---|---|---|---|---|---|
| | | *Immigrants* | *Emigrants* | | *Immigrants* | *Emigrants* | *Immigrants* | *Emigrants* |
| *1* | *2* | *3* | *4* | *5* | *6* | *7* | *8* | *9* |
| Provinces or States which gain | | | | | | | | |
| Assam | + 1,241,011 | 1,314,047 | 73,036 | +1,140,752 | 1,216,661 | 75,909 | +97,386 | - 2,873 |
| Bengal | + 771,936 | 1,726,370 | 954,434 | 1,132,192 | 1,817,775 | 685,581 | -91,405 | + 68,853 |
| Burma | + 593,3244 | 617,521 | 24,197 | + 553,471 | 572,530 | 19,059 | -44,991 | + 5,138 |
| Bombay | - 596,707 | 1,188,901 | 592,194 | - 472,023* | 1,039,622 | 567,599* | +256,074 | +318,2801# |
| Central Provinces and Berar. | + 27,003 | 649,064 | 422,061 | +197,323 | 603.924 | 406,601 | +45,140 | +15,460 |
| Mysore | +215,462 | 340,700 | 125,238 | +210,064 | 309,850 | 99,786 | +30,850 | + 25,452 |
| Delhi | +189,736 | 259,163 | 69,427 | +113,158 | 182,485 | 69,327 | -76,678 | +100 |
| Baroda | +127,907 | 333,077 | 105,176 | +10,674 | 231,880 | 221,206 | +101,197 | -16,030 |
| Central India Agency | + 115,566 | 598,102 | 482,536 | + 58,056 | 544,688 | 486,632 | +53,414 | - 4,096 |
| Travancore | + 83,919 | 133,852 | 49,933 | + 49,732 | 71,973 | 22,241 | +61,879 | + 27,692 |
| Ajmer-Merwara | + 44,029 | 104,938 | 60,909 | + 66,033 | 108,452 | 42,419 | -3,514 | +18,490 |
| Cochin | + 41,424 | 87,214 | 45,790 | +15,792 | 39,689 | 23,897 | -47,525 | + 21,893 |
| Coorg | + 35,388 | 38619 | 3,231 | + 30,988 | 33,838 | 2,850 | +4,781 | +381 |

* Includes Western India Agency.
\# Includes Punjab States Agency.

(Appendix IV contd.)

(Appendix IV contd.)

| *Province or State* | *Net gain + or loss* | *1931* | | *Net gain + or loss -* | *1921* | | *Variation 1921–31* | |
|---|---|---|---|---|---|---|---|---|
| | | *Immigrants* | *Emigrants* | | *Immigrants* | *Emigrants* | *Immigrants* | *Emigrants* |
| *1* | *2* | *3* | *4* | *5* | *6* | *7* | *8* | *9* |
| Baluchistan | + 23,779 | 66,542 | 42,763 | + 5,924 | 66,166 | 60,242 | +376 | -17,479 |
| North West Frontier Province. | +21,187 | 111,868 | 90,681 | + 50,835 | 118,395 | 67,560 | -6,527 | + 23,121 |
| Andamans and Nicobars. | +13,703 | 14,255 | 582 | +14,080 | 14,396 | 316 | -141 | +236 |
| Provinces or States which Lose | | | | | | | | |
| Sikkim | - 4,782 | 2,403 | 7,212 | - 2,297 | 1,836 | 4,133 | +594 | + 3,079 |
| Gwalior | -14,471 | 281,350 | 296,821 | +632 | 289,657 | 289,025 | -8,307 | + 7,796 |
| Jammu and Kashmir | - 33,266 | 61,189 | 94,445 | - 22,685 | 61,561 | 84,246 | -372 | +10,029 |
| Punjab | - 67,792 | 635,025 | 702,817 | + 60,940 | 591,885 | 530,942 | +43,140 | +171,875 |
| Hyderabad | -19,788 | 312,814 | 332,602 | -166,326 | 197,127 | 363,453 | +115,687 | - 30,851 |
| Western India States Agency | -186,890 | 106,795 | 293,685 | Included against Bombay | | | | |
| Rajputana | -516,898 | 329,913 | 864,811 | - 625,650 | 242,234 | 8,67,893 | +87,670 | - 21,082 |
| Madras | - 888,339 | 246,892 | 1,135,231 | - 718,183 | 196,609 | 914,792 | +50,283 | + 220,439 |
| United Provinces | - 1,063,143 | 494,308 | 1,557,451 | - 974,642 | 425,152 | 1,399,794 | +69,156 | +157,657 |
| Bihar and Orissa | - 1,291,567 | 466,563 | 1,758,130 | -1,567,968 | 387,068 | 1,955,036 | +79,495 | -196,906 |

*Note*—The figures for provinces include those for the States attached to them except in the case of Madras, where they exclude Cochin and Travancore. Migration figures to and from countries outside British India are excluded.

## APPENDIX V

### Provincial/State revenue

| | Yield (Crores of Rupees) | | | | | Share in total revenue (per cent) | | | | |
|---|---|---|---|---|---|---|---|---|---|---|
| | *1921–22* | *1936–37* | *1938–39* | *1944–45* | *1953–54 (R. E.)* | *1921–22* | *1936–37* | *1938–39* | *1944–45* | *1953–54 (R. E.)* |
| | *1* | *2* | *3* | *4* | *5* | *6* | *7* | *8* | *9* | *10* |
| Total Revenue | 58.48 | 74.86 | 76.78 | 193.87 | 462.04 | 100.0 | 100.0 | 100.0 | 100.0 | 100.0 |
| Land Revenue | 29.08 | 25.96 | 25.40 | 30.21 | 69.20 | 49.7 | 34.7 | 33.1 | 15.6 | 15.0 |
| State Excise | 15.67 | 13.63 | 13.08 | 43.42 | 44.81 | 26.8 | 18.2 | 17.0 | 22.4 | 9.7 |
| Stamps | 10.14 | 10.80 | 9.53 | 15.20 | 23.50 | 17.3 | 14.4 | 12.4 | 7.8 | 5.1 |
| Registration | 1.07 | 1.11 | 1.09 | 2.39 | 3.91 | 1.8 | 1.5 | 1.4 | 1.2 | 0.9 |
| General Sales Tax | | | . | 7.91 | 57.25 | | | | 4.1 | 12.4 |
| Forests (net) | 0.66 | 0.71 | 0.63 | 4.58 | 10.82 | 1.1 | 0.9 | 0.8 | 2.4 | 2.3 |
| Irrigation works for which capital accounts are kept (net). | 5.55 | 7.53 | 7.57 | 10.14 | 8.09 | 9.5 | 10.0 | 9.9 | 5.2 | 1.8 |
| Devolution of revenue and grants from the Centre. | 9.02 | 2.67 | 6.45 | 36.89 | 117.92 | | 3.6 | 8.4 | 19.1 | 25.6 |
| Share of income tax assigned to States | 3.09 | 0.04 | 1.47 | 25.75 | 56.90 | 5.3 | 0.1 | 1.9 | 13.3 | 12.3 |

(Appendix V contd.)

(Appendix V contd.)

| | Yield (Crores of Rupees) | | | | | Share in total revenue (per cent) | | | | |
|---|---|---|---|---|---|---|---|---|---|---|
| | *1921–22* | *1936–37* | *1938–39* | *1944–45* | *1953–54 (R. E.)* | *1921–22* | *1936–37* | *1938–39* | *1944–45* | *1953–54 (R. E.)* |
| | *1* | *2* | *3* | *4* | *5* | *6* | *7* | *8* | *9* | *10* |
| Share of jute duty assigned to States | | 2.13 | 2.51 | 1.48 | | | 2.8 | 3.3 | 0.8 | |
| Share of Central excise duty assigned to States | | | | | 15.94 | | | | | 3.5 |
| Grant of aid etc. from the Centre. | 12.11 | .5 | 2.47 | 9.66 | 45.08 | | .7 | 3.2 | 5.0 | 9.8 |

Figures for 1921–22 exclude those for Burma but include Sind as part of Bombay. Figures for 1936–37 exclude those for Burma, Sind and N.W.F.P.

Transfers from funds are excluded, receipts under forests are taken net after deducting entire expenditure from gross receipts, for other public utilities and State undertaking net receipts (after deducting working expenses) are included.

## APPENDIX VI

### Budgetary Position of the States on Revenue Account

Figures for 1938–39 and 1944–45 are for nine Provinces excluding Sind and N.W.F.P.
Figures for 1953–54 relate to all Part A, Part B and Six Part C States.

*Part "A" States*

| | *1950–51* | *1951–52* | *1952–53* | *1953–54 (R.E.)>** | *1954–55 (B.E.)* |
|---|---|---|---|---|---|
| Revenue | 93.33 | 106.70 | 108.12 | 112.21 | 121.76 |
| Expenditure | 81.93 | 100.33 | 105.88 | 115.85 | 127.65 |
| Surplus (+) or deficit (-) | (+) 1.45 | (+) 6.17 | (+) 3.24 | (-) 3.64 | (-) 5.89 |
| Surplus (+) or deficit (-) (excluding transfers from and to Revenue Reserve Funds) | (+) 1.45 | (+) 5.97 | (+) 3.24 | (-) 3.64 | (-) 5.89 |

>* Figures for 1953–54 include budget estimates for the composite state of Madras and revised estimates are available for later six months only.

*Part "B" States*

| | *1950–51* | *1951–52* | *1952–53* | *1953–54 (R.E.)* | *1954–55 (B.E.)* |
|---|---|---|---|---|---|
| Revenue | 214.37 | 315.60 | 229.32 | 357.49 | 367.17 |
| Expenditure | 293.08 | 309.10 | 329.37 | 371.64 | 400.89 |
| Surplus (+) or deficit (-) | (+) 1.29 | (+) 6.50 | (-) 0.15 | (-) 14.15 | (-) 33.72 |
| Surplus (+) or deficit (-) (excluding transfers from and to Revenue Reserve Funds) | (-) 3.15 | (-)2.25 | (-) 12.01 | (-) 20.82 | (-) 39.86 |

## Appendix VII

## Central Revenues (Selected Years)

| | *1921–22* | | *1936–37* | | *1938–39* | | *1944–45* | | *1953–54 (R.E.)* | |
|---|---|---|---|---|---|---|---|---|---|---|
| Total Revenue*> | 80.00 | 100 | 81.45 | 100 | 82.90 | 100 | 334.40 | 100 | 394.34 | 100 |
| Customs (net) | 31.61 | 39.5 | 38.11 | 46.8 | 40.51 | 48.9 | 39.77 | 11.9 | 160.00 | 40.6 |
| Taxes on income (net) | 18.74 | 23.4 | 14.33 | 18.8 | 13.74 | 16.6 | 80.52 | 24.1 | 69.31 | 17.6 |
| Corporation tax | | | | | 2.04 | 2.5 | 84.22 | 25.2 | 38.4 | 9.7 |
| Central excise duties (net) | 2.80 | 3.5 | 13.35 | 16.4 | 8.66 | 10.5 | 38.14 | 11.4 | 78.00 | 19.8 |
| Salt duty | 6.34 | 7.9 | 8.81 | 10.8 | 8.12 | 9.8 | 9.29 | 2.8 | | |
| Commercial Departments— | | | | | | | | | | |
| Railways (net contribution) | (-) 9.09 | | | | 1.37 | 1.7 | 32.00 | 9.6 | 7.50 | 1.9 |
| Posts & Telegraphs (net) | | | 0.14 | 0.2 | 0.19 | 0.2 | 10.25 | 3.1 | 2.02 | 0.5 |

*> Total revenue includes net receipts under opium, irrigation. Forests, electricity and road transport schemes. Figures for 1921–22 and 1936–37 are inclusive of those for Burma. Figures for 1921–38–39 and 1944–45 relate to undivided India.

## Appendix VIII

## Population of the Indian Union by Communities

| | HINDUS | | | | | | | | | | | |
|---|---|---|---|---|---|---|---|---|---|---|---|---|
| | Population | | | Scheduled Castes | | | Others | | | Muslims | | |
| | Persons | Males | Females | Persons | Males | Females | Persons | Males | Females | Persons | Males | Females |
| | 1 | 2 | 3 | 4 | 5 | 6 | 7 | 8 | 9 | 10 | 11 | 12 |
| Madras | 49841 | 24800 | 25040 | 8152 | 4064 | 4088 | 35095 | 17466 | 17630 | 3927 | 1939 | 1987 |
| Bombay | 29384 | 15184 | 14200 | 2526 | 1217 | 1256 | 20691 | 1068 | 10011 | 2463 | 1321 | 1142 |
| West Bengal | 21837 | 11834 | 10003 | 3520 | 1847 | 1673 | 11206 | 6160 | 5046 | 5544 | 3011 | 2533 |
| United Provinces | 56346 | 29542 | 26804 | 11931 | 6128 | 5803 | 34923 | 18411 | 16512 | 8692 | 4574 | 4117 |
| East Punjab | 12697 | 6853 | 5844 | 1028 | 540 | 487 | 4489 | 2435 | 2053 | 4427 | 2380 | 2047 |
| Bihar | 36546 | 18325 | 18220 | 4344 | 2135 | 2209 | 22263 | 11252 | 11010 | 4719 | 2340 | 2379 |
| C.P. & Berar | 19948 | 9845 | 9802 | 3310 | 1639 | 1671 | 10920 | 5491 | 5428 | 811 | 425 | 387 |
| Assam | 7685 | 4068 | 3617 | 377 | 203 | 174 | 2885 | 1564 | 1321 | 1754 | 939 | 815 |
| Orissa | 13768 | 6706 | 7062 | 1865 | 906 | 956 | 8187 | 3963 | 4224 | 166 | 81 | 85 |
| Ajmer | 589 | 310 | 279 | 1 | 0.5 | 0.5 | 30 | 198 | 182 | 90 | 49 | 41 |
| Andaman & Nicobar Islands | 34 | 21 | 12 | – | – | – | 8 | 6 | 3 | 8 | 6 | 2 |
| Bilaspur | 110 | 57 | 53 | 16 | 8 | 7 | 93 | 48 | 45 | 1 | 0.8 | 0.6 |
| Bhopal | 785 | 410 | 375 | 187 | 96 | 91 | 410 | 215 | 195 | 110 | 59 | 51 |

(Appendix VIII contd.)

(Appendix VIII contd.)

| | HINDUS | | | | | | | | | | | |
|---|---|---|---|---|---|---|---|---|---|---|---|---|
| | *Population* | | | *Scheduled Castes* | | | *Others* | | | *Muslims* | | |
| | *Persons* | *Males* | *Females* | *Persons* | *Males* | *Females* | *Persons* | *Males* | *Females* | *Persons* | *Males* | *Females* |
| | *1* | *2* | *3* | *4* | *5* | *6* | *7* | *8* | *9* | *10* | *11* | *12* |
| Coorg | 169 | 92 | 76 | 26 | 15 | 11 | 105 | 56 | 49 | 14 | 9 | 6 |
| Cutch | 501 | 239 | 262 | 39 | 19 | 20 | 279 | 135 | 144 | 117 | 57 | 60 |
| Delhi | 918 | 535 | 383 | 23 | 69 | 53 | 445 | 262 | 182 | 305 | 176 | 128 |
| Himachal Pradesh | 935 | 495 | 441 | 229 | 120 | 109 | 672 | 356 | 316 | 29 | 16 | 13 |
| Manipur | 512 | 249 | 263 | – | – | – | 304 | 148 | 156 | 30 | 15 | 15 |
| Tripura | 513 | 272 | 241 | 12 | 6 | 6 | 336 | 178 | 158 | 124 | 66 | 57 |
| Vindhya Pradesh | 3569 | 1819 | 1750 | 399 | 202 | 197 | 2851 | 1455 | 1397 | 95 | 49 | 46 |
| Madhya Pradesh | 7141 | 3734 | 3407 | 437 | 221 | 216 | 5025 | 2648 | 2377 | 475 | 251 | 224 |
| P.E.P.S.U. | 3424 | 1868 | 1557 | 214 | 112 | 102 | 978 | 530 | 448 | 899 | 483 | 416 |
| Rajasthan | 13085 | 6868 | 6217 | – | – | – | 9878 | 5196 | 4682 | 1256 | 663 | 593 |
| Saurashtra | 3556 | 1809 | 1747 | 242 | 122 | 120 | 2737 | 1402 | 1336 | 436 | 220 | 226 |
| Travancore Cochin | 7493 | 3742 | 3751 | 537 | 269 | 268 | 3902 | 1931 | 1971 | 543 | 276 | 268 |
| Hyderabad | 16339 | 8347 | 7992 | 2928 | 1487 | 1442 | 10382 | 5303 | 5073 | 2097 | 1080 | 1017 |
| Kashmir | 4022 | 2130 | 1892 | 113 | 61 | 53 | 694 | 369 | 325 | 3074 | 1627 | 1446 |
| Mysore | 7329 | 3763 | 3566 | 1405 | 723 | 682 | 5282 | 2702 | 2580 | 485 | 258 | 227 |

## APPENDIX IX

## Statistics of Chief Castes

| *Caste* | *Strength* | *Where chiefly found* |
|---|---|---|
| Agri | 265,285 | Bombay. |
| Ahar, Ahir,Gopi, Goshi, Goala, Golla, Gowari, Gaura, Kavundan Idaiyan. | 14,170,032 | Most Provinces. |
| Ahom | 249,434 | Assam. |
| Arain, Kunjra, Koeri, Kachli, Murao. | 5,048,849 | Most Provinces. |
| Arora, Bhansali, Lohana | 1,499,407 | Baluchistan, Bombay, N.W.F.P., Panjab, Jammu and Kashmir, W.I. States |
| Babhan, Bhuinihar | 1,113,541 | Bihar and Orissa, U.P.C.P. |
| Baidya | 110,739 | Bengal. |
| Baiga, Bhania, Binjwar, Bharia, Kadar, Bhumia, Bhunjia, Bhuiya, Ghatwar, Naiya, Pao. | 1,050,760 | Bengal, Bihar and Orissa, C.P., C.I, Rajputana, Sikkim. |
| Bairagi | 838,285 | Most Provinces. |
| Baloch | 1,333,215 | Baluchistan, Bombay, Punjab, N.W.F.P. |
| Baniya, Bhatia, Chetti, Khatri, Kamati (Vaishya). | 5,176.383 | Most Provinces, |
| Banjara, Lumbadi, Labana, Lamani. | 951,022 | Bombay, C.P., C.L.Gvvalior-Hyderabad, Mysore, Rajputana |
| Bania, Bhalia, Chodhra, Gedia, Khant, Koli, Kotwal, Naikda, Patclia, Patanwadia, Thakarda, Talabda, Valvi. | 3,418,643 | Most Provinces. |
| Bauri, Bagdi | 1,671,481 | Bengal, Bihar and Orissa, Rajputana. |
| Bawaria, Bavari, Baori, Bagari, Vagri,Badhik. | 309,720 | Most Provinces. |
| Bayar, Barmanu, Dhangar, Musahar. | 811,746 | Bengal, Bihar and Orissa, U.P„Central India. |
| BeDar, Boya | 991,536 | Bombay, Madras, Hyderabad, C.P. |

(Appendix IX contd.)

(Appendix IX contd.)

| Caste | Strength | Where chiefly found |
|---|---|---|
| Bhandari, Idiga, Iruvan, Siyal | 1,253,403 | Bihar and Orissa, Cochin, Mysore, Madras, Travancore, Rajputana. Baroda. |
| Bhangi | 797,599 | Ajmer-Merwara, Bombay, U.P., Baroda, Gwalior, Rajputana, W. I. States |
| Bharwad, Dhangar, Gadariya, Kumba. | 1,816,283 | Most Provinces. |
| Bhat, Barhmabhatt, Chamn, Jasondhi. | 397,274 | Most Provinces |
| Bhatra, Pardhana, Parja | 353,183 | Madras, C.P. and Berar. |
| Bhil, Barda Bhilala, Dhanka, Mankar,Mavchi, Pathia, Rathia, Tadvi. | 1,454,144 | Most Provinces. |
| Bhisti, Bhoi, Dhimar, Jhinwar, Kabar, Machhi, Tiyar. | 3,575,941 | Most Provinces. |
| Bohra | 212,752 | Bombay, Baroda, C.I., Gwalior, C.P., Rajputana, W.I. States, Travancore. |
| Brahman | 15,207,277 | Most Provinces. |
| Brahui | 224,415 | Baluchistan, Bombay. |
| Chamar, Khalpa, Samagara | 12,195,516 | Most Provinces. |
| Chasa, Raju | 835,236 | Bengal, Bihar and Orissa. |
| Chasi, Kajbartta (Mahisya) | 2,381,266 | Bengal. |
| Chuhra | 721,981 | N.W.F. Prov. Punjab, Delhi. |
| Dhanuk, Kandra | 758,671 | Bihar and Orissa, Bengal, C.P., C.I., Ajmer-Merwara, Rajputana, Delhi, Gwalior. |
| Dhobi, Parit, Vanran, Velutte-dan. | 3,161,428 | Most Provinces. |
| Dom, Dombar, Bansphor, Dharkar, Dholi. | 907,776 | Most Provinces. |
| Dhor, Chakkliyan | 671,926 | Bombay, C.P., Madras, Cochin, Travancore, W.I. States. |
| Dusadh | 1,400,878 | Bengal, Bihar and Orissa, U.P. |

(Appendix IX contd.)

(Appendix IX contd.)

| Caste | Strength | Where chiefly found |
|---|---|---|
| Fakir | 820,577 | Punjab, U.P., C.P., Rajputana, C.I.,Agency Gwalior. |
| Garo, Hajong, Kachari, Mech, Rabha. | 695,648 | Assam, Bengal. |
| Gond, Dhanwar, Kalota, Kamar, Karwar,Kolam, Kondh, Konda, Dora, Koya, Maria, Muria Nagarchi. | 4,719,222 | Andamans and Nicobars, Bengal, Bihar and Orissa, Bombay, C.P., and Berar, Madras, U.P., C.I. Hyderabad, Gwalior, Rajputana. |
| Gujar | 2,430,669 | Ajmer-Merwara, Bombay, C.P. and Berar, Delhi, N.W. Frontier, Punjab, U.P., C.I., Rajputana. |
| Guria, Halwai | 246,583 | Bihar and Orissa, U.P., C.I., Rajaputana, Gwalior. |
| Hajjam, Ambattan, Bhandari, Kelashi,Mhali, Nadig, Nai "Naibrahman", Napit, Nhavi, Pandithar, Vellakat-talavan. | 3,725,860 | Most Provinces. |
| Hari | 418,830 | Assam, Bengal, Bihar and Orissa Madras. |
| Jat | 8,377,819 | N.W. Frontier, Punjab, U.P. Kashmir, Rajputana. |
| Jogi | 111,586 | Gwalior, C.I., Agency, Rajputana, Jammu and Kashmir. |
| Kaikolan | 419,078 | Madras, Cochin, Travancore. |
| Kalar | 1,017,179 | Ajmer-Merwara, Bengal, C.P. and Berar, U.P., Baroda, C.I., Gwalior, Hyderabad, Rajputana, Sikkim. |
| Kallavan, Maravan | 948,630 | Madras, Cochin, Travancore. |
| Kamalan, Viswabrahman, Panchal. | 7,735,393 | Most Provinces. |
| Karen | 1,367,673 | Burma. |
| Kayastha, Karan, Prabhu | 2,946,228 | Most Provinces. |
| Kewat, Kaibartta | 1,813,278 | Assam, Bengal, Bihar and Orissa C.P., and Berar, U.P. |

(Appendix IX contd.)

(Appendix IX contd.)

| *Caste* | *Strength* | *Where chiefly found* |
|---|---|---|
| Kolita | 109,250 | Bihar and Orissa, C.P. and Berar. |
| Koshti, Devang | 921,201 | Bengal, Bombay, C. P. and Berar, Madras, C.I., Hyderabad, Mysore, Gwalior, Cochin. |
| Khandayat, Paik | 1,060,587 | Bihar and Orissa, Bengal, Madras. |
| Kisan | 431,044 | Bengal, Bihar and Orissa, U.P. |
| Khasi, Synteng. | 232,595 | Assam, Andamans and Nicobars. |
| Khatik, Chick | 412,520 | U.P., C.P., Bengal, Delhi, Ajmer-Merwara, Baluchistan Hyderabad, Rajputana Gwalior. |
| Kori, Katia, Balai, Chaupal, Jugi. | 2,165,953 | Most Provinces. |
| Korku, Korwa | 246,765 | Bihar and Orissa, C.P., C.I., U.P. |
| Kumhar, Kusavan | 3,580,143 | Most Provinces. |
| Kunbi, Karbi, Kurmi, Kshatriya, Kapu, Kapewar, Raddi, Vakkaliga, Vellala | 11,082,108 | Most Provinces. |
| Labbai | 374,829 | Coorg, Madras, Mysore, Travancore. |
| Lodhi | 1.742,470 | C.P. and Berar, U.P., C.I., Bengal, Delhi, Rajputana, Hyderabad, Gwalior. |
| Lushei, Sokte, Thado | 192,520 | Assam, Bengal, Burma. |
| Mahar, Mehra, Dhed, Vankar, Holiya,Pulayan, Cheruman. | 4,729,405 | Most Provinces. |
| Mala | 852,050 | C.P. and Berar, Madras. |
| Mali, Phulmali, Saini, Malakar | 2,332,143 | Most Provinces. |
| Mailah, Goriya, Gonrhi | 894,951 | Bengal, Bihar and Orissa, U.P., N.W. Frontier, C.I., Gwalior, Rajputana. |

(Appendix IX contd.)

(Appendix IX contd.)

| *Caste* | *Strength* | *Where chiefly found* |
|---|---|---|
| Mang, Megh, Meghwal, Madgi, Madiga. | 2,556,765 | Most Provinces. |
| Mapilla | 139,621 | Travancore, Cochin, Coorg, Burma. |
| Maratha | 6,113,061 | Bombay, C.P. and Berar, Gwalior, Hyderabad, Baroda, Mysore, C.L |
| Meithei | 330,545 | Assam, Burma. |
| Mina, Meo | 1,110,479 | Most Provinces. |
| Mirasi | 283,637 | Punjab, N.W. Frontier, Rajputana, Ajmer-Merwara, Jammu and Kashmir, C.I., Gwalior. |
| Mochi, Jiagar, Dabgar | 1,026,405 | Most Provinces. |
| Momin | 3,122,100 | Most Provinces. |
| Munda, Mawasi, Ho, Kol, Kharwar, Kharia,Bhogia, Bhumji, Kora. | 2,315,276 | Bihar and Orissa, Bengal, C.P. and Berar, C.Y., U.P., Raj-plitena. |
| Naga | 272,529 | Assam, Burma, Gwalior. |
| Namasudra | 2,265,476 | Assam, Bengal. |
| Nayar | 1,550,641 | Madras, Travancore, Cochin. |
| Nepali | 371,906 | Most Provinces. |
| Nunlya, Od, Beldar, Bind, Rehgar. | 561,926 | Most Provinces. |
| Oraon | 1,021,334 | Bengal, Bihar arid Orissa. C.P. and Berar. |
| Pallan | 825,224 | Madras. |
| Pan, Panka, Ganda, Paidi, Baraik. | 1,241,322 | Bengal. Bihar and Orissa, C.P. and Berar, Madras, C.I. |
| Paraiyan, Turi | 1,277,365 | Madras, Bombay, Baroda, Cochin, W.I.States, Coorg. |
| Pasi, Arakh | 1,743,166 | Bihar and Orissa, U.P., Bengal, C. I. |
| Oinjara, Sarahira, Dhunia | 565.254 | U. P., Bombay, Rajputana Gwalior, N. W. Frontier, Punjab, C.I., Mysore, W.I States, Jammu and Kashmir. |

(Appendix IX contd.)

(Appendix IX contd.)

| *Caste* | *Strength* | *Where chiefly found* |
|---|---|---|
| Rajbhar, Rajjhar, Rajwar Bhar. | 630,708 | U. P., Bihar and Orissa, Bengal, C.P. and Berar. |
| Rajput | 10,743,001 | Most Provinces. |
| Santal, Saunta, Karmali | 2,524,472 | Bengal, Bihar and Orissa, C.I. |
| Saun | 480,131 | U.P., C.I. |
| Sawara, Saonr, Savar, Saharia | 675,628 | Bihar and Orissa, C.P., Madras, U.P., C.I., Rajputana, Gwalior. |
| Shaha, Sunri | 533,825 | Bengal, Madras, Sikkirn. |
| Shan | 900.204 | Burma. |
| Silpkar | 333,036 | U.P. |
| Singpho, Kachin | 156,253 | Burma, Assam. |
| Talavla, Dubla | 229,190 | Bombay, Baroda, W.L States. |
| Tamboli, Barai | 452,423 | Bengal U.P., C.I., Rajputana, Gwalior, Baroda. |
| Tankkshatriya | 926.274 | Most Provinces. |
| Tanti, Tatwa, Bhulia, Chadar, Sali. | 1,132,563 | Bengal, Bihar, and Orissa, Bombay, C.P. and Berar. |
| Telaga | 1,669,559 | C. |
| Teli, Tili, Chakkan. Ganig, Chanchi,Varniyan. | 5,024,496 | Madras, Hyderabad, Coorg. |
| Thakkar, Rathi, Rawat, Kanet, Ghirath. | 71 4,503 | Bombay, Punjab, C.I., Gwalior, Jammu and Kashmir, Rajputana. |

## APPENDIX X
## Relative Population of Different Communities

### Distribution by Religion of 10,000 persons in India, in the Provinces and in the States, 1921 and 1931

| *Province etc.* | *Year* | *Hindu* | *Muslim* | *Buddhist* | *Tribal* | *Christian* | *Sikh* | *Jain* | *Others* |
|---|---|---|---|---|---|---|---|---|---|
| *1* | *2* | *3* | *4* | *5* | *6* | *7* | *8* | *9* | *10* |
| India | 1921 | 6,856 | 2,174 | 366 | 309 | 150 | 103 | 37 | 5 |
| | 1931 | 6,824 | 2,216 | 365 | 236 | 179 | 124 | 36 | 20 |
| Provinces | 1921 | 6,606 | 2,407 | 465 | 280 | 123 | 96 | 18 | 5 |
| | 1931 | 6,548 | 2,469 | 468 | 213 | 142 | 118 | 17 | 25 |
| Ajmer-Merwara | 1921 | 7,356 | 2,055 | | 96 | 112 | 4 | 372 | 5 |
| | 1931 | 7,755 | 1,734 | | 27 | 124 | 6 | 348 | 6 |
| Andamans and Nicobars | 1921 | 3,278 | 1,515 | 979 | 3,387 | 586 | 144 | | 111 |
| | 1931 | 2,586 | 2,280 | 988 | 3,379 | 496 | 220 | | 51 |
| Assam | 1921 | 5,434 | 2,896 | 17 | 1,479 | 168 | 1 | 5 | |
| | 1931 | 5,720 | 3,196 | 17 | 825 | 235 | 3 | 3 | 1 |
| Baluchistan | 1921 | 920 | 8,731 | 4 | | 159 | 182 | | 4 |
| | 1931 | 894 | 8,744 | 1 | 1 | 174 | 181 | 1 | 4 |
| Bengal | 1921 | 4,327 | 5,399 | 57 | 181 | 31 | | 3 | 2 |
| | 1931 | 4,304 | 5,487 | 63 | 105 | 36 | 2 | 2 | 1 |
| Bihar and Orissa | 1921 | 8,284 | 1,085 | | 553 | 76 | 1 | 1 | |
| | 1931 | 8,231 | 1,132 | | 544 | 91 | 1 | 1 | |
| Bombay | 1921 | 7,658 | 1,974 | 1 | 64 | 137 | 4 | 111 | 51 |

(Appendix X contd.)

(Appendix X contd.)

| *Province etc.* | *Year* | *Hindu* | *Muslim* | *Buddhist* | *Tribal* | *Christian* | *Sikh* | *Jain* | *Others* |
|---|---|---|---|---|---|---|---|---|---|
| *1* | *2* | *3* | *4* | *5* | *6* | *7* | *8* | *9* | *10* |
| | 1931 | 7,605 | 2,039 | 1 | 59 | 145 | 10 | 92 | 49 |
| Burma | 1921 | 368 | 380 | 8,506 | 534 | 195 | 4 | 1 | 12 |
| | 1931 | 390 | 399 | 8,430 | 444 | 226 | 7 | 1 | 103 |
| C.P. and Berar | 1921 | 8,354 | 405 | | 1,160 | 30 | 1 | 49 | 1 |
| | 1931 | 8,601 | 440 | | 872 | 33 | 3 | 50 | 1 |
| Coorg | 1921 | 7,733 | 795 | 1 | 1,265 | 194 | | 12 | |
| | 1931 | 8,939 | 844 | | | 210 | | 5 | 2 |
| Delhi | 1921 | 6,569 | 2,904 | | | 273 | 57 | 96 | 1 |
| | 1931 | 6,285 | 3,253 | 1 | | 267 | 101 | 84 | 9 |
| Madras | 1921 | 8,864 | 671 | | 137 | 322 | | 6 | |
| | 1931 | 8,831 | 707 | | 75 | 380 | | 7 | |
| N.W.F.P. | 1921 | 666 | 9,162 | | | 47 | 125 | | |
| | 1931 | 590 | 9,184 | | | 51 | 175 | | |
| Punjab | 1921 | 3,181 | 5,533 | 1 | | 159 | 1,109 | 17 | |
| | 1931 | 2,684 | 5,655 | 2 | | 176 | 1,299 | 15 | 169 |
| United Provinces | 1921 | 8,509 | 1,428 | | | 44 | 3 | 15 | 1 |
| | 1931 | 8,440 | 1,484 | | | 42 | 10 | 14 | |
| States | 1921 | 7,748 | 1,343 | 12 | 415 | 250 | 126 | 104 | 2 |
| | 1931 | 7.771 | 1.347 | 12 | 316 | 307 | 141 | 101 | 5 |

N.B.: A blank indicates that the number per 10,000 fractional; 0 indicates that none at all were returned. In the case of Assam the Khasi States are indicated in the 1921 figures; otherwise all States are excluded from Provinces. ”

## Notes

1. Please see Map 3.1 in Part I of this volume, p. 71.
2. Please see Map 3.2 in Part I of this volume, p. 75.
3. Please see Map 3.3 in Part I of this volume, p. 76.
4. Please see Map 3.4 in Part I of this volume, p. 78.
5. Please see Map 3.5 in Part I of this volume, p. 83.
6. See Appendix I, pp. 179–81.
7. See Appendix II, pp. 182–83.
8. This saying may be translated as, 'In the event of (possible) total ruin, the wise settle for half'.
9. Please see Map 3.5 in Part I of this volume, p. 83.

# VI

# On the States Reorganisation Bill, 1956

The States Reorganisation Bill was moved in the Rajya Sabha on 30 April 1956 by the Minister for Home Affairs (Govind Ballabh Pant). Though the Bill had some financial provisions, and according to the norms practised and the rules framed, such Bills ordinarily were to be referred only to a select committee consisting of the members of the Lok Sabha; taking in view the unique importance of this Bill, the Lok Sabha suspended the relevant rule and agreed that this Bill should be considered by the representatives of both Houses.

The SRC that was formed in 1953 submitted and published its report on 10 October 1955. The preliminary discussion on the report was held in almost all the states in November, followed by debate in the Lok Sabha and the Rajya Sabha in December. Ambedkar could not participate in the discussion in the Rajya Sabha due to his ill-health. He conveyed his views to the prime minister by sending a telegram where—speaking on behalf of Scheduled Caste Federation of India—he categorically objected the creation of 'monolithic monstrous States' such as UP, Bihar and Maharashtra. He added that the 'Federation feels these States not only are great dangers to Central Government, but will also be great dangers to minorities and Scheduled Castes. There be no protection to Scheduled Castes under aegis of State in which overwhelming majority is opposed to recognition of Scheduled Castes as human beings. Fear consequences might be very serious. Scheduled Castes are now without any political safeguard. Ambedkar wanted UP and Maharashtra to be divided into three states and Bihar into two states. And fearing that the SCs' 'desperation may take to any kind of violence', he requested the PM to pay serious attention to this question.[1]

The government announced its views on most of the matters with which the report dealt on 16 January 1956. But it then postponed its decision with regard to three matters, viz. those concerning Punjab, Bellary and Telangana. However, three months later on 6 March, the government came with the States Reorganisation Bill, that effected 12 out of the 17 (Part A and Part B) States in the country (the five that remained unaffected were Assam, Orissa, Bengal, Bihar and Uttar Pradesh). A number of amendments were proposed in the state legislatures and 97 (mostly of a minor character—only one or two concerned territorial redistributions) were adopted.

Ambedkar participated in the debate on 2 May 1956. However, he could not participate in the discussion until the last due to his ill-health. The motion was adopted in the Rajya Sabha on 3 May 1956. Six months later, the Lok Sabha finally passed the States Reorganisation (Amendment) Bill, 1956 on 21 November 1956, and the Rajya Sabha on 27 November 1956. Ambedkar during this period had gone to Sri Lanka to participate in the Fourth World Buddhist Conference at Khalinandu. He soon breathed his last on 6 December 1956.

***

Reproduced below are excerpts from *Dr. Babasaheb Ambedkar Writings and Speeches*, ed. Vasant Moon, vol. 15, 962–73 (Bombay: Government of Maharashtra, 1997).

## "SPEECH DELIVERED IN THE RAJYA SABHA ON 1 MAY 1956

The storm centre of the debate on this Bill as I see it from the papers is the position assigned to the City of Bombay. As is obvious from the Bill this City which was a premier city in the civic affairs of this country has been brought down to the level of Andaman and Nicobar Islands—what has been described in our Constitution as the territories of India. That means that these territories and now the City of Bombay will not have any Legislature or Executive. Nobody in his wildest dreams could have conceived of such madness. A city which has been in the forefront of India, which has taught politics of India, is now placed on the level of the Laccadive and Maldives Islands and the Nicobar Islands. I am sure that the Government which has fostered this proposal must have the strongest reasons, incontrovertible reasons, in order to justify the decision that they have taken.

There have been contestants to the claim for the City of Bombay. There are the Maharashtrians who claim that the city belongs to them. There are our Gujarati friends; I do not know on what basis they lay their claim, but they claim a kind of an easement over the city. They say that they will not allow the city to go into the possession of the Maharashtrains and the quarrel is going on. It has been admitted by no less a person than Mr. Morarji Desai that Bombay belongs to Maharashtra. I have read his speech which he delivered to the Gujarat Maha Pradesh· Congress; or something like that, in which he categorically made this statement that Bombay belongs to Maharashtra. If that is so, I am quite unable to understand what objection there can be for the city of Bombay to be given to Maharashtra.

Under the British regime when citizenship was common, any man could go anywhere and reside and the local people could not object. Under those circumstances various people from various Provinces have gone to cities located in other Provinces. They built up their interests and have lived there for generations. But in the redistribution that we are now making, I have not seen anybody non-Madrasi—living in Madras—raising objection to Madras being given to the Tamilian. Calcutta is equally a cosmopolitan city when I was the Labour Member, I had often to visit Calcutta in order to see the labour conditions there and I found that the Bengal people did not call the people living in Calcutta as, 'Bengali'. Their word was *"Calcut-tiya"* These are *"Calcuttiyas"*. That shows that they were not part of Bengali population, and it is a huge population. Notwithstanding this, our friends, the Congress Party people, have never raised any objection; nor the *Calcuttiyas,* have ever raised any objection to Calcutta being handed over to the Bengali.

My first question to my Friend, Mr. Pant, is this. If Calcutta can go to Bengali and Madras can go to Tamilian, what objection is there for Bombay to go to Maharashtra? That, I think, is a fundamental question which he must satisfy the Maharashtrians about. Yes, it is said that there is in Bombay a Gujarati population which amounts to not more than 15 per cent and that the Maharashtrians do not form a majority of the population. It is said that that is the reason which vitiates the claim of the Maharashtrians over Bombay. I wonder whether there are any cities in this country where the foreign population in the city is not 15 per cent and the position of Bombay, it is said, by reason of the fact that 15 per cent are Gujaratis is in a sense peculiar. How is it peculiar? One can give any number of illustrations to show that our cities are always a mixed quarter. No city can claim to have a uniform population of its own. And if notwithstanding this fact the other city can claim to belong to West Bengal, I am quite unable to understand why Bombay City should not make a similar claim. There are some people who have said that Bombay never belonged to Maharashtra. Well, I am surprised at the knowledge of those who made the statement, I am very much surprised.

Who were the first inhabitants of Bombay? They were the *Kolis*—the fishermen—and do the fishermen say that they are not Maharashtraians? I would like anyone to go and make enquiries and find out what is the opinion of the *kolis* who were the original inhabitants of Maharashtra. If those ladies and gentlemen who have indulged in these wild allegations want to know a little bit of its characteristics, I should like to tell them that even before the Portuguese acquired Bombay, Bombay belonged to a dowager queen called Lakshmi Bai and the Portuguese took it as a tenancy from her. It did not even belong to the Portuguese. The Portuguese never conquered it. They took it. The poor queen subsequently could do nothing. Ultimately, it was transferred to the British as a dowry to the wife of Charles II. It was so small that the dowry was not more than £10. That was because Bombay was what I shall call a place occupied by a few *kolis*. I have got with me the original print of the original Bombay when it transferred itself from the Portuguese to the British. Therefore, historically, geographically and logically, the logic which we have applied to other cities, I cannot see how anybody can dispute the claim of the Maharashtrians to have the city to themselves.

Of course, there is a wide difference of opinion between myself and the rest of the Maharashtrians. The rest of the Maharashtrians want Bombay as part of a United Maharashtra. Now, I am very much against this United Maharashtra. I do not understand why Maharashtrians should want a United Maharashtra and I am sure about it that in the course of future history, we are not going to war with U.P. nor are we going to war with any of the northern territories like Rajasthan. Why do you want a United Maharashtra? I am at one with Maharashtrians that Bombay belongs to Maharashtra. On that, I will fight tooth and nail. There can be no doubt on that point at all. And therefore I had suggested that the Government might give Bombay a separate status as a City State and call it the "Maharashtra City State" so that it will be part of Maharashtra and at the same time, it will enjoy the status of an 'A' class State. But since the Government, for some reason which it is very difficult for me to understand, is going to reduce the status of Bombay City to that of the Nicobar Islands, I tell them right now that I reverse my position and fight with them along with the rest of the Maharashstrians. Now that is what I want to say about Maharashtra.

With regard to the question that the Maharashtrians in Bombay City do not form a majority, I like to clear that idea. I think that there is a lot of misunderstanding. Some census figure has been dug out which said that the population of Maharashtrians in Bombay is 46 per cent or something like that. Therefore they are not in a majority. ... It is a complete misunderstanding. Any man who knows the census operation, who knows statistics and who knows the peculiar statistics of Bombay City would pay no attention to that figure. The census figure records the state of affairs on a particular day on which the census is taken. It does not indicate the common state of affairs. What happened on a particular day is taken as the typical example, but it is not typical at all.

Secondly, the important point to be noticed is that Bombay City is one of the cities which is most subjected to immigration and emigration. Unfortunately, in the year 1941 when the new census was taken, the Government of India, in order to shorten their labour, did not repeal the immigration and emigration report figures for the year 1931. But if one were to go into the figures given on immigration and emigration in the census of 1931, he will find what violent changes there are in the immigration and emigration position. I do not think that even the non-Maharashtrian population which appears to be in a majority is permanently there in a majority. Most of them come for seasonal labour. If they happen to be there on the day of census, their existence is recorded as 'resident's of Bombay'. On the next day, they might as well leave for their native places, because they have made enough money for their living. In these circumstances, can anybody accept the census figures as true figures of the citizens of Bombay? I deny that conclusion altogether. I have been a student of the census statistics. I have studied them considerably.

I know what they mean. Therefore, the claim that these figures show that the population of the Maharashtrians is less is absolutely ambiguous, if not bogus. It has no value. It only indicates what happened to be on a particular day on which the census was recorded.

Now, I have said that I did not agree with the majority of the Maharashtrians, if I may say so, that there should be a united Maharashtra. My contention is that there should not be. I am going to say the same thing about U.P., about Rajasthan and about these huge Hindi reptile provinces, which have been looming large before us. I shudder to see U.P. standing before me in that shape....[2]

I am surprised, I must say, that the Commission should have retained U.P. as it is, should have retained Rajasthan as it is, and should have linked up the two provinces of Vindhya Pradesh and Madhya Pradesh into one .... What does this (read Madhya Bharat) mean? I have made a little calculation. The area of U.P. is 1,14,323 sq. miles. Its population is 6,32,54,118. Bihar: The area is 70,368 sq. miles; its population is 4,02,18,916. Madhya Pradesh: Area is 2,01,633 sq. miles; its population is 3,28,46,971. I know I have to deduct something here for Vidarbha. Rajasthan: Area is 1,28,424 sq. miles; population is 1,52,97,979. The total area is 10 lakh[3] sq. miles and population is about 15 crores ....

The question that requires to be dealt with in my judgement is a very serious question. Are we to have one State for one language, or are we to have one language for one State? If this question had no political consequences, nobody would bother about it, but the trouble is that this question has very serious political consequences. In the United States, the population of the various States differs. In some States it is small, and in some States it is big. But the Americans do not mind it on account of the fact that the States have equal powers. The Lower House has the same power as the Upper House, and all the States have equal representation in the Upper House without reference to population. In the Senate they have equal representation. Here, what is the position? Under our Constitution, there is no such equality at all. Every State has not the same power, and the Upper Chamber has no powers at all, so far as finance is concerned.

It may happen—it is very likely—that the States in the northern area may combine together on an issue on which the southern States of India do not agree. What is likely to happen in that event? In that event, the north, if I may say, so, will over-ride every proposition in which the southern States are interested. If that happens, I fear that there may be civil war. I may be using some exaggerated sentiment, but such a thing has happened. It has happened in the United States. In the United States the origin of the Civil War was this inequality of power. In the earlier stages it was agreed that up to certain latitude the slave States might exist but that there would be no slavery above that latitude. It happened, I believe, that California was at one time a territory; it was not a State. It was later on decided to make it a State. The Southern States quarreled, because they felt that if California became a State, it would acquire the power of voting and that it would change the balance of voting. Notwithstanding that, the Northern States decided to convert California into a State. Thereby they got a majority of voting, and then with this majority of voting, they decided not to have slavery in the United States at all, which affected the political and economic interests of the Southern States. At once, the Southern States resisted. They said, "We would not remain part of the Union, if you are going to exercise that power for the abolition of slavery." Then, there was the Civil War. There are people here who fear the influence of the northern people.

One important example you could recently see was ....[4] Now there are plenty of things one can imagine on which the issue may be between the north and the south and if that happens and if the matter is taken to bloody conclusions, well, all the efforts that we have made in order to bring about unity will have been in vain. I therefore suggest that the United Provinces should be cut down into three provinces, Bihar should be cut down into two and Madhya Pradesh also should be cut down into two.[5]

Nothing is lost. It does not affect the linguistic principle at all. They all have the same language. What does it matter if U.P. is divided into three States, or if Madhya Pradesh is divided into two? I see no difference at all. My friend Mr. Pant, I remember to have read, once his statement had stated that he would have no objection to dividing the U.P. but he has never said a word about it in the course of the debate nor has he voluntarily suggested this self-sacrifice on his part. But I give a warning, I know the house is not going to listen to me, but it is my duty to say what I feel. With regard to Marathwada, I have very strong feelings and I very vehemently resist the United Maharashtra. I can speak more authoritatively about the Maharashtra than I can speak about other areas. What has been the state of affairs of this United Maharashtra? In Maharashtra I find that only that Marathas from the Satara district or that area are able to capture political offices. The rest of the people are just where they are. I do not understand how a Minister drawn from Satara can have any interest in for instance, the Ratnagiri district. I do not think any Minister has ever visited the Ratnagiri district ....

Areas and areas are completely neglected, what interest has a Maratha from the Satara district in the Ratnagiri district? What interest can a Brahmin, for instance, from Mahavidarbha have in the Satara district? I do not quite understand this mentality of huddling together. Is it like Bharat Milap? When Ram came from Lanka, Bharat embraced him. What for—for brotherly love and affection; nothing more than that. Why not allow such areas to develop their own interests, to pay attention to their own interests? Besides, as my friend Mr. Pant knows, I may be wrong, I suppose he is the last of the veterans. Who will succeed him, can he tell me? Who will succeed him as a Minister? I don't see anybody. Certainly I don't see anybody in the rank and file of the Congress. If any Minister of the towering personality of my friend Mr. Pant has to be looked for, it would have to be someone outside the Congress ranks. I am sure of that.[6]

...

Our primary concern is to raise and train politicians so that they can learn to take responsibility upon their own shoulders. We ought not to sit tight on one thing for ever. We ought to allow other people to take responsibility while we are alive so that if they commit any mistake, we may rectify it in time. If you have U.P. divided into three provinces, you will have probably 30 ministers trained in the art of administration, while if you have one, you will have just 10 ministers, nothing more than that. The same thing will happen in Bihar and the same thing will happen in these big provinces. Therefore, in my judgement, there is a great disadvantage to this country in keeping these large provinces as they are. My Friend may perhaps listen to this argument if he does not listen to the other. His argument, if I have heard correctly, is 'Oh! In a country where Ram and Krishna were both born, do not divide it.' That is the argument, I think, he used sometimes. But that is not an argument of a statesman. ... I was saying about the Marathwada people, I mean the Maharashstrians that the same thing is true of this Maharashtra. Maharashtra, except for a few Brahmins, is politically not upto the mark, I am sorry to say. I am not speaking with any personal venom of any kind. I know very well that I have had my full share of public life and I do not desire to compete with anyone for more. But I like that my State should be well administered and in order that it may be well administered, it must have competent people.

Now in a united Maharashtra you will not have more than five or six ministers. Some of them may be Brahmins and some of them may be non-Brahmins, is that going to be enough for the future of Maharashstra? Here you have a territory called Marathwada which has just been released from the reins of the Nizam. But you have only to just go and see the area in order to see its wretchedness, the condition of the people, with no clothes, hardly any food, and no education. There is no primary school even there. I was told that there was one primary school in which there was only one chair and all the teachers ran early in the morning in order to capture that chair so as not to allow any other teacher to sit on it. I like to know whether this most backward area which has no irrigation, no food, no clothes, no school or anything of that kind, will fare better.

For some reason or other, the Nizam spent all his love and affection on other people, not on Marathwada, I like to know whether my friend Kaka Gadgil, if he become[s] the Chief Minister of United Maharashtra would pay attention to the condition of the people of Marathwada or whether he would pay his attention to Poona and its inhabitants. Let us not talk nonsense. Let us see plain things as they are. Why not allow Marathwada to have a separate province or State and let Marathwada rule itself? It knows its interests best. I have been connected with Marathwada for the simple reason that I established a college there. But it is not a flourishing college and I am every year bearing a huge loss. I know that the Marathwada people would look after themselves much better than any of the Bombay people who talk about them. Particularly there is no education there at all. There is the danger that Marathwada may be attached to the Poona University. God only knows what will happen.[7]

...

In the case of Marathwada it is absolutely necessary that they should have a separate autonomous body to look after their education and they should not be tied down hand and foot to the Poona University. We won't have that at all.

There is one other point to which I would like to refer. As I have said, I may be wrong, but I have a feeling that there are many holes in this federation and it may crack. We are a cracking society. We have no union. We have no unity and any time this whole thing may crack. Therefore, we should, in time, take steps to see that it does not crack. I suggested one way and that was to reduce the Northern provinces to smaller areas so that the southern people may not suffer any heavy pressure. I also suggest another remedy and that remedy is to have two capitals for this country. I suggest that Hyderabad should be made the second capital of India. You can have your Delhi and for some seasons it may be good. But you must have a capital in Southern India, where people may feel that their Government is nearer to them.

I suggested at one time that Hyderabad should be made the second capital of India. It is one of the most beautiful towns that I have ever seen in India. It has got all the necessities and amenities which a capital may require. All that may be necessary would be to have a sort of Legislative Assembly and Council of State. If that is done, then the people in the South with whom I have had many talks, would feel that their Government is nearer, that it is not so far away as Delhi. Delhi to the Southern people is a kind of a foreign territory. It is hot and they do not want to stay for long. I hope my hon. friend will take these points into consideration.

... I am not in a condition to speak very long, nor have I got many other points to urge. But there is one thing that I would like to say. I had hoped that this Report of the S.R.C. would have been placed before, not merely the party people, but generally before all, and they should have obtained the common advice of all the citizens of India and should have given effect to their decision. ... it was my hope that what we would settle now, we would settle for ever, because it is a very foolish thing for a gardener to plant a tree today and to uproot it tomorrow, to see whether it has taken root. That way the plant will never live. I cannot help reminding my hon. friend of the statement of Tom Paine that whatever is wrongly settled is never permanently settled; it has to be resettled. If you are going to settle these things with the help of your party, remember that your party is not perpetual. You can see the signs of waning even now before your eyes. If whatever you do, you do without the consent of the Opposition, I have not the least doubt about it that when the Opposition would come into power, they would uproot the thing and replant it. Such a thing would be most dangerous for us.[8] ”

## Notes

1 Ambedkar's telegram to Jawaharlal Nehru regarding formation of linguistic states, dated 17 Janyary 1956. See Khairmode (2003: 56–57).

2. To this H. P. Saksena from Uttar Pradesh responded saying, 'God save your soul', but Ambedkar replied 'Do not pray for my soul. I have no soul. I am a Buddhist. Nobody need take the trouble of praying for my soul. I do not believe in God. I have no soul. I have spared you that trouble.'

3. This is the corrected figure. Ambedkar while speaking had said 10 crore square miles and that was corrected by T. Pande of Uttar Pradesh.

4. At this point he was interrupted by Kailash Bihari Lall (Bihar) and R. U. Agnibhoj (Madhya Pradesh).

5. Interrupted by R. U. Agnibhoj, 'You should have 600 States.'

6. Interruption by H. P. Saksena

7. Interruptions by B. B. Sharma (Uttar Pradesh) and Jaspat Roy Kapoor (Uttar Pradesh).

8. At this point C. P. Parikh of Bombay reportedly said, 'The hon. Member made an incorrect statement when he said that Morarji said at any time categorically, that Bombay belongs to Maharashstra. I think the hon. Member should make such statement with a sense of responsibility.' Ambedkar replied saying, 'It is in the *Times of India.*'

# VII

# Ambedkar's Recipe for Maharashtra: Voice of the People

In his speech in the Rajya Sabha, Ambedkar had made it quite clear that there was a wide difference of opinion between him and the rest of the Maharashtrians. While the rest of the Maharashtrians wanted Bombay as part of a United Maharashtra, he stood against this idea. There was confusion over whether Maharashtrians would constitute a majority in the Bombay City. Ambedkar tried to clear this confusion during his speech at the Rajya Sabha. But, when reports came in that Maharashtrians were not satisfied with the proposals made by Ambedkar in the Rajya Sabha, he made some changes in his proposal by way of addressing these concerns and wrote a small article in *Free Press Journal* on 31 May 1956. However, he still did not approve of the idea of a United Maharashtra.

* * *

Reproduced below is the *Free Press Journal* article by Ambedkar, published on 31 May 1956. These excerpts are from *Dr. Babasaheb Ambedkar Writings and Speeches*, ed. Vasant Moon, vol. 17, part II, 391–92 (Bombay: Government of Maharashtra, 2002).

"AMBEDKAR'S RECIPE FOR MAHARASHTRA: VOICE OF THE PEOPLE

The communications I have received indicate that the Maharashtrians are not quite satisfied with the proposals that I recently made in the Rajya Sabha over the Maharashtra-Bombay issue. They are afraid that in Bombay City they may not get the majority.

The Gujaratis, on the other hand, realise that with 15 per cent of Gujarati population in a house of 100 they would not have more than two to four seats. Both the communities will remain helpless and chafe at each other. I, therefore, make another suggestion.

The Maharashtra State, I suggest, should be divided into two States, one of which should consist of—(1) Greater Bombay; (2) Thana district; (3) Colaba; (4) Ratnagiri; (5) Kolhapur and (6) Marathi-speaking parts of Surat district, Belgaum and Karwar districts. The dividing line is Sahyadri Mountain.

The advantages of this division are: (1) it can give Maharashtrians majority over Bombay through North Bombay; (2) it is a separate cultural unit; (3) it is a separate linguistic unit and (4) the total area of this unit is 19,800 sq. miles with a total population of 9,067,413, which makes it a sizable State. The people are both maritime and martial.

I do not see why the Brahmins are insisting on United Maharashtra. Even then, there will be two rival claimants for power, Shri. B. S. Hiray and Shri Ramrao M. Deshmukh. Possibly, Dr. Punjabrao Deshmukh may have his own view. There is another point which is raising dificulty [*sic*] and that relates to the capital of the second division of Maharashtra. The Deccan Brahmins want Poona, while the present Madhya Pradesh Brahmins want Nagpur. Others suggest the third alternative of the Legislature's session being held alternately at these two cities. I condemn all the three alternatives. I am sure that under the name of United Maharashtra we are not calling Peshwai back. I suggest the capital of United Maharashtra be Aurangabad. Adjacent to it is Daulatabad which was the capital of Maharashtra until it was destroyed by the Muslims. It has a fine climate. The question must be decided immediately. Whatever the Congress High Command may say, there is not the slightest chance of a Gujarati voting for a Maharashtrian candidate and the Maharashtrian voting for the Gujarati Candidate.”

# VIII

# States and Minorities

Among the many problems the Constituent Assembly had to face, there were two, Ambedkar opined, that were admittedly most difficult. One was the problem of the minorities and the other was the problem of the Indian states. Despite being a champion of the problem of the Indian states—one who held some very definite and distinct views on the subject—the Constituent Assembly did not elect Ambedkar to the States Committee.

He had prepared a memorandum on the safeguards for the Scheduled Castes to present before the Constituent Assembly in 1947. Later, in order to make available to the general public, he decided to publish it in the form of a brochure. In detailing the safeguards, the brochure went a step beyond prescribed bounds and the dispensation issued on behalf of the 'high' and 'mighty Hindu majority'.

In this memorandum Ambedkar held that the SCs were more than a minority and that any protection given to the citizens and to the minorities would not be adequate for the SCs. In other words, it meant that their social, economic and educational condition was worse than that of the citizens and other minorities. Therefore, in addition to the protection that they would get as citizens and as minorities, they would also require special safeguards against the tyranny and discrimination of the majority. He compiled detailed notes and tables about the SC population in all states and its numerical minority status in relation to other communities.

The memorandum was drafted in the form of Articles for a constitution for a 'United States of India'. It is divided into five parts. The first part of the memorandum contains a preamble and Articles through which the states would be admitted to the federation. The remaining parts provide safeguards for minorities, particularly the SCs. It provides some special responsibilities towards SCs on the part of the Union and state governments, such as education—including college and foreign education, and training—special settlements or villages for SCs, a Settlement Commission to hold uncultivated lands belonging to the state in trust for settlement of the SCs in these separate villages, right to representation in the Legislature and the Cabinet in each state, etc.

The memorandum describes in detail the Fundamental Rights of all citizens of the Union and the judicial protection provided by courts against all forms of executive tyranny. It declares that any prior existing legislation, custom, disadvantage or disability which imposes any inequality on any citizen would cease to exist. Further, any person who prevents a citizen from enjoying any accommodation, advantages, facilities, privileges of inns, educational institutions, roads, paths, streets, tanks, wells and other watering places or public conveyances or places of amusement of convenience would be guilty of an offence. All citizens were also given the right to reside in any part of the country subject to the production of a certificate of citizenship from the state of his origin and no charge can be imposed on him. The right to reside can only be withdrawn from habitual criminals or those who try to alter the communal balance or due to any law made such as a person being capable of work. The state may make a distinction between settlement and residence for a period of time based on rules.

Special provisions are also provided for representation of minorities in the Legislature and the Executive with safeguards against the arbitrary removal of representatives of minorities. The memorandum also declares 'social boycott' of any group or person, or threat of a boycott, as an offence. It also appeals to guarantee representation to SCs in the Legislature, Executive and civil services in ratio to their number in the population. Regarding the method of election, it argues for adult franchise together with abolition of the Poona Pact and the introduction of the system of separate electorates. Most important, the Constitution of the United States of India would undertake to make the safeguards described, part of the Constitutional law of India. The memorandum held that the provisions for SCs should not be altered, amended or abrogated except in accordance with prescribed rules.

The detailed appendices that Ambedkar provided for 'States and Minorities' do not form part of this Compendium.

***

Reproduced below are excerpts from *Dr. Babasaheb Ambedkar Writings and Speeches*, ed. Vasant Moon, vol. 1, 381–452 (Bombay: Government of Maharashtra, 1979).

## " STATES AND MINORITIES: WHAT ARE THEIR RIGHTS AND HOW TO SECURE THEM IN THE CONSTITUTION OF FREE INDIA?

### Memorandum on the Safeguards for the Scheduled Castes submitted to the Constituent Assembly an behalf of the All India Scheduled Castes Federation, Bombay

#### CONSTITUTION OF THE UNITED STATES OF INDIA

#### PROPOSED PREAMBLE

We the people of the territories of British India distributed into administrative units called Provinces and Centrally Administered Areas and of the territories of the Indian States with a view to form a more perfect union of these territories do—ordain that the Provinces and the Centrally Administered Areas (to be hereafter designated as States) and the Indian States shall be joined together into a Body Politic for Legislative, Executive and Administrative purposes under the style The United States of India and that the union so formed shall be indissoluble and that with a view:

(i) to secure the blessings both of self-government and good government throughout the united States of India to ourselves and to out posterity,
(ii) to maintain the right of every subject to life, liberty and pursuit of happiness and to free speech and free exercise of religion,
(iii) to remove social, political and economic inequality by providing better opportunities to the submerged classes,
(iv) to make it possible for every subject to enjoy freedom from want and freedom from fear, and
(v) to provide against internal disorder and external aggression, establish this Constitution for the United States of India.

**PROPOSED ARTICLES**

### Article I, Section I—Admission of Indian States into the Union:

Clause 1: Qualified Indian States and their admission into the Union.
Clause 2: Relation of Qualified Indian States which have not entered the Union and of the Disqualified Indian States to the United States of India.
Clause 3: Power of the United States of India to reorganise the territory of the Disqualified Indian States into suitable Administrative Units with a view to qualify them for admission into the Union as States of the Union.
Clause 4: Formation of new States within the Union.

## Explanatory Notes

### Clause 1

The United States of India may, on application and on fulfillment of the terms prescribed by an Enabling Act of the Union Legislature laying down the form of the Constitution admit an Indian State into the Union provided the Indian State seeking admission is a Qualified State.

For the purposes of this clause a list of Qualified Indian States shall be drawn up. A State shall not be deemed to be a Qualified State unless it is proved that it is of a standard size prescribed by the Union Legislature and is endowed with natural resources capable of supporting a descent standard of living for its people and can, by reason of its revenues and population function as an autonomous State, protect itself against external aggression, maintain Law and Order against internal disturbance and guarantee to its subjects minimum standards of administration and welfare which are expected from a modern State.

### Clause 2

The territory of an Indian State which is a Qualified State but which has not entered the Union and the territory of the Indian States which are disqualified shall be treated as incorporated territories of the United States of India and shall at all times form integral parts thereof and shall be subject to such parts of the Constitution of the United States of India as may be prescribed by the Union Legislature.

### Clause 3

The United States of India shall have power to reform, rearrange, redistribute and amalgamate the territories of Disqualified Indian States into suitable Administrative Units for admission into the Union as States of the Union.

### Clause 4

After a State has been admitted into the Union as a State no new State shall be formed or created within its jurisdiction nor any new State shall be formed by the junction of two or more States or parts of States without the consent of the Legislatures of the States concerned as well as of the Union Legislature.

## Article I, Section II—United States of India and New Territory:

Clause 1: Incorporation of Foreign States into the Union.
Clause 2: Acquisition of new territory by the United States of India and its retention as unincorporated territory of the Union.

### Explanatory Notes

### Clause 1

The United States of India may admit into the Union any territory which forms a natural part of India or which is on the border of India on terms and conditions mutually agreed upon. Provided that the terms shall not be inconsistent with the Constitution of the United States of India and the admission is recommended by the Legislatures of one half of the States comprising the United States of India in the form of a resolution.

### Clause 2

The United States of India may acquire territory and may treat it as unincorporated territory. The provisions of the Constitution of the United States of India shall not apply to the unincorporated territory unless a provision to the contrary is made by the Legislature of the United States of India.

## Article II, Section I—Fundamental Rights of Citizens.

The Constitution of the United States of India shall recognize the following as Fundamental Rights of citizenship:

(1) All persons born or naturalised within its territories are citizens of the United States of India and of the State wherein they reside. Any privilege or disability arising out of rank, birth, person, family, religion or religious usage and custom is abolished.

(2) No State shall make or enforce any law or custom which shall abridge the privileges or immunities of citizens; nor shall any State, deprive any person of life, liberty and property without due process of law; nor deny to any person within its jurisdiction equal protection of law.

(3) All citizens are equal before the law and possess equal civic rights. Any existing enactment, regulation, order, custom or interpretation of law by which any penalty, disadvantage or disability is imposed upon or any discrimination is made against any citizen shall, as from the day on which this Constitution comes into operation, cease to have any effect.

(4) Whoever denies to any person, except for reasons by law applicable to persons of all classes and regardless of their social status, the full enjoyment of any of the accommodations, advantages, facilities, privileges of inns, educational institutions, roads, paths, streets, tanks, wells and other watering places, public conveyances on land, air or water, theatres or other places of public amusement, resort or convenience, whether they are dedicated to or maintained or licensed for the use of the public, shall be guilty of an offence.

(5) All citizens shall have equal access to all institutions, conveniences and amenities maintained by or for the public.

(6) No citizen shall be disqualified to hold any public office or exercise any trade or calling by reason of his or her religion, caste, creed, sex or social status.

(7) (i) Every citizen has the right to reside in any part of India. No law shall be made abridging the right of a citizen to reside except for consideration of public order and morality.

(ii) Every citizen has the right to settle in any part of India, subject to the production of a certificate of citizenship from the State of his origin. The permission to settle shall not be refused or withdrawn except on grounds specified in sub-clause (iv) of this clause.

(iii) The State in which a citizen wishes to settle may not impose any special charge upon him in respect of such settlement other than the charge imposed upon its own inhabitants. The maximum fees chargeable in respect of permits for settlement shall be determined by laws made by the Union Legislature.

(iv) the permission to settle may be refused or withdrawn by a State from persons—

(a) who have been habitual criminals;

(b) whose intention to settle is to alter the communal balance of the State;

(c) who cannot prove to the satisfaction of the State in which they wish to settle that they have an assured means of subsistence and who are likely to became or have become a permanent burden upon public charity;
(d) whose State of origin refuses to provide adequate assistance for them when requested to do so,

(v) Permission to settle may be made conditional upon the applicant being capable of work and not having been a permanent charge upon public charity in the place of his origin, and able to give security against unemployment.
(vi) Every expulsion must be confirmed by the Union Government.
(vii) Union Legislature shall define the difference between settlement and residence and at the same time, prescribe regulations governing the political and civil rights of persons during their residence.

(8) The Union Government shall guarantee protection against persecution of a community as well as against internal disorder or violence arising in any part of India.
(9) Subjecting a person to forced labour or to involuntary servitude shall be an offence.
(10) The right of the people to be secure in their persons, houses, papers and effects against unreasonable searches and seizures, shall not be violated, and no warrants shall issue, but upon probable cause, supported by oath or affirmation, and particularly describing the place to be searched, and the persons or things to be seized.
(11) The right of a citizen to vote shall not be denied or abridged on any account other than immaturity, imprisonment and insanity.
(12) No law shall be made abridging the freedom of Speech, of the Press, of Association and of Assembly except for consideration of public order and morality.
(13) No Bill of attainder or ex post facto law shall be passed.
(14) The State shall guarantee to every Indian citizen liberty of conscience and the free exercise of his religion including the right to profess, to preach and to convert within limits compatible with public order and morality.
(15) No person shall be compelled to become a member of any religious association, submit to any religious instruction or perform any act of religion. Subject to the foregoing provision, parents and guardians shall be entitled to determine the religious education of children up to the age of 16 years.
(16) No person shall incur any penalties of any kind whatsoever by reason of his caste, creed or religion nor shall any person be permitted to refuse to fulfil any obligation of citizenship on the ground of caste, creed or religion.
(17) The State shall not recognise any religion as State religion.

(18) Persons following a religion shall be guaranteed freedom of association and shall have, if they so desire, the right to call upon the State to pass legislation in terms approved by them making them into a body corporate.
(19) Every religious association shall be free to regulate and administer its affairs, within the limits of the laws applicable to all.
(20) Religious associations shall be entitled to levy contributions on their members who are willing to pay them if their law of incorporation permits them to do so. No person may be compelled to pay taxes the proceeds of which are specifically appropriated for the use of any religious community of which he is not a member.
(21) Ail offences under this section shall be deemed to be cognizable offences. The Union Legislature shall make laws to give effect to such provisions as require legislation for that purpose and to prescribe punishment for those acts which are declared to be offences.

### Article II, Section II—Remedies against Invasion of Fundamental Rights:

Clause 1. Judicial Protection.
Clause 2. Protection against Unequal Treatment.
Clause 3. Protection against Discrimination.
Clause 4. Protection against Economic Exploitation.

### Explanatory Notes

The United States of India shall provide:

### Clause 1

(1) That the Judicial Power of India shall be vested in a Supreme Court.
(2) The Supreme Court shall have the power of superintendence over all other Courts or officers exercising the powers of a Court, whether or not such Courts or officers are subject to its appellate or revisional jurisdiction.
(3) The Supreme Court shall have the power on the application of an aggrieved party to issue what are called prerogative writs such as Hebeas Corpus, Quo Warranto Prohibition, Certiorari and Mandamus, etc. For purposes of such writs the Supreme Court shall be a Court of general jurisdiction throughout India.
(4) The right to apply for a writ shall not be abridged or suspended unless when in cases of rebellion or invasion the public safety may require it.

### Clause 2

That the Authority of the Legislature and the Executive of the Union as well as of every State throughout India shall be subject to the following limitations:

It shall not be competent for any Legislature or Executive in India to pass a law or issue an order, rule or regulation so as to violate the following rights of the subjects of the State:

(1) to make and enforce contrasts, to sue, be parties, and give evidence, to inherit, purchase, lease, sell, hold and convey real and personal property.
(2) to be eligible for entry into the civil and military employ and to all educational institutions except for such conditions and limitations as may be necessary to provide for the due and adequate representation of all classes of the subjects of the State.
(3) to be entitled to the full and equal enjoyment of the accommodations, advantages, facilities, educational institutions, privileges of inns, rivers, streams, wells, tanks, roads, paths, streets, public conveyances on land, air and water, theatres and other places of public resort or amusement except for such conditions and limitations applicable alike to all subjects of every race, class, caste, colour or creed.
(4) to be deemed fit for and capable of sharing without distinction the benefits of any religious or charitable trust dedicated to or created, maintained or licensed for the general public or for persons of the same faith and religion.
(5) to claim full and equal benefit of all laws and proceedings for the security of persons and property as is enjoyed by other subjects regardless of any usage or custom or usage or custom based on religion and be subject to like punishment, pains and penalties and to none other.

## Clause 3

(1) Discrimination against citizens by Government officers in Public administration or by private employers in factories and commercial concerns on the ground of race or creed or social status shall be treated as an offence. The jurisdiction to try such cases shall be vested in a tribunal to be created for the purpose.
(2) The Union Legislature shall have the right as well as the obligation to give effect to this provision by appropriate legislation.

## Clause 4

The United States of India shall declare as a part of the law of its constitution—

(1) That industries which are key industries or which may be declared to be key industries shall be owned and run by the State;
(2) That industries which are not key industries but which are basic industries shall be owned by the State and shall be run by the State or by Corporations established by the State;

(3) That Insurance shall be a monopoly of the State and that the State shall compel every adult citizen to take out a life insurance policy commensurate with his wages as may be prescribed by the Legislature;

(4) That agriculture shall be State Industry;

(5) That State shall acquire the subsisting rights in such industries, insurance and agricultural land held by private individuals, whether us owners, tenants or mortgagees and pay them compensation in the form of debenture equal to the value of his or her right in the land. Provided that in reckoning the value of land, plant or security no account shall be taken of any rise therein due to emergency, of any potential or unearned value or any value for compulsory acquisition;

(6) The State shall determine how and when the debenture holder shall be entitled to claim cash payment;

(7) The debenture shall be transferable and inheritable property but neither the debenture holder nor the transferee from the original holder nor his heir shall be entitled to claim the return of the land or interest in any industrial concern acquired by the State or be entitled to deal with it in any way;

(8) The debenture-holder shall be entitled to interest on his debenture at such rate as may be defined by law, to be paid by the State in cash or in kind as the State may deem fit;

(9) Agricultural industry shall be organized on the following basis:

- (i) The State shall divide the land acquired into farms of standard size and let out the farms for cultivation to residents of the village as tenants (made up of group of families) to cultivate on the following conditions:
  - (a) The farm shall be cultivated as a collective farm;
  - (b) The farm shall be cultivated in accordance with rules and directions issued by Government;
  - (c) The tenants shall share among themselves in the manner prescribed the produce of the farm left after the payment of charges properly leviable on the farm;
- (ii) The land shall be let out to villagers without distinction of caste or creed and in such manner that there will be no landlord, no tenant and no landless labourer;
- (iii) It shall be the obligation of the State to finance the cultivation of the collective farms by the supply of water, draft animals, implements, manure, seeds, etc.;
- (iv) The State shall be entitled to—
  - (a) to levy the following charges on the produce of the farm: (i) a portion for land revenue; (ii) a portion to pay the debenture-holders; and (iii) a portion to pay for the use of capital goods supplied; and
  - (b) to prescribe penalties against tenants who break the conditions of tenancy or wilfully neglect to make the best use of the

means of cultivation offered by the State or otherwise act prejudicially to the scheme of collective farming;

(10) The scheme shall be brought into operation as early as possible bat in no case shall the period extend beyond the tenth year from the date of the Constitution coming into operation.

## Article II, Section III—Provisions for the protection of minorities:

The Constitution of the United States of India shall provide:

Clause 1. Protection against Communal Executive.

Clause 2. Protection against Social end Official Tyranny.

Clause 3. Protection against Social Boycott.

Clause 4. Authority and obligation of the Union and State Governments to spend money for public purposes including purposes beneficial to Minorities.

## Explanatory Notes

### Clause 1

(1) That the Executive-Union or State—shall be non-parliamentary in the sense that it shall not be removable before the term of the Legislature.

(2) Members of the Executive if they are not members of the Legislature shall have the right to sit in the Legislature, speak, vote and answer questions.

(3) The Prime Minister shall be elected by the whole House by single transferable vote.

(4) The representatives or the different minorities in the Cabinet shall be elected by members of each minority community in the Legislature by single transferable vote.

(5) The representatives of the majority community in the Executive shall be elected by the whole House by single transferable vote.

(6) A member of the Cabinet may resign his post on a censure motion or otherwise but shall not be liable to be removed except on impeachment by the House on the ground of corruption or treason.

### Clause 2

(1) That there shall be appointed an Officer to be called the Superintendent of Minority Affairs.

(2) His status shall be similar to that of the Auditor General appointed under section 166 of the Government of India Act of 1935 and removable in like manner sad [*sic*] on the like grounds as a Judge of the Supreme Court.

(3) It shall be the duty of the Superintendent to prepare an annual report on the treatment of minorities by the public, as well as by the Governments, Union and State and of any transgressions of safeguards or any miscarriage of justice due to communal bias by Governments or their Officers.

(4) The Annual Report of the Superintendent shall be placed on the Table of the Legislatures—Union and State, and the Governments—Union and State, shall be bound to provide time for the discussion of the Report.

## Clause 3

That Social Boycott, Promoting or Instigating a Social Boycott or Threatening a Social Boycott as defined below shall be declared to be an offence:

(i) Boycott Defined.—A person shall be deemed to boycott another who—
   (a) refuses to let or use or occupy any house or land, or to deal with, work for hire, or do business with another person, or to render to him or receive from him any service, or refuses to do any of the said things on the terms on which such things should commonly be done in the ordinary course of business, or
   (b) abstains from such social, professional or business relations as he would, having regard to such existing customs in the community which are not inconsistent with any fundamental right or other rights of citizenship declared in the Constitution, ordinarily maintain with such person, or
   (c) in any way injures, annoys or interferes with such other person in the exercise of his lawful rights.

(ii) Offence of Boycotting—Whoever, in consequence of any person having done any act which he was legally entitled to do or of his having omitted to do any act which he was legally entitled to omit to do, or with intent to cause any person to do any act which he is not legally bound to do or to omit to do any act which he is legally entitled to do, or with intent to cause harm to such person in body, mind, reputation or property, or in his business or means of living, boycotts such person or any person in whom such person, is interested, shall be guilty of offence of boycotting.

Provided that no offence shall be deemed to have been committed under this Section, if the Court is satisfied that the accused person has not acted at the instigation of or in collusion with any other person or in pursuance of any conspiracy or of any agreement or combination to boycott.

(iii) Offence of Instigating or Promoting a Boycott—
Whoever-
   (a) publicly makes or publishes or circulates a proposal for, or
   (b) makes, publishes or circulates any statement, rumour or report with intent to, or which he has reason to believe to be likely to cause, or

(c) in any other way instigates or promotes the boycotting of any person or class of persons, shall be guilty of the offence of instigating or promoting a boycott.

Explanation— An offence under this clause shall be deemed to have been committed although the person affected or likely to be affected by any action of the nature referred to herein is not designated by name or class but only by his acting or abstaining from acting in some specified manner.

(iv) Offence of Threatening a Boycott—Whoever, in consequence of any person having done any act which he was legally entitled to do or of his having omitted to do any act which he was legally entitled to omit to do or with intent to cause any person to do any act which he is not legally bound to do, or to omit to do any act which he is legally entitled to do threatens to cause such person or any person in whom such person is interested, to be boycotted shall be guilty of the offence threatening a boycott.

Exception.—It is not boycott—

(i) to do any act in furtherance of a bona fide labour dispute;
(ii) to do any act in the ordinary course of business competition.
(2) All these offences shall be deemed to be cognizable offences. The Union Legislature shall make laws prescribing punishment for these offences.

## Clause 4

That the Power of the Central and Provincial Governments to make grants for any purpose, notwithstanding that the purpose is not one for which the Union or State Legislature as the case may be make laws, shall not be abridged or taken away.

## Article II, Section IV—Safeguards for the Scheduled Castes.

Part I—Guarantees:

Clause 1: Right to Representation in the Legislature and in the Local Bodies.

Clause 2: Right to Representation in the Executive.

Clause 3. Right to Representation in Services.

## Explanatory Notes

Right to Representation in the Legislature.

The Constitution of the United States of India shall guarantee to the Scheduled Castes the following Rights :

## Clause 1

(1) Quantum of Representation.—

(a) (i) The Scheduled Castes shall have minimum representation in the Legislature—Union and State—and if there be a group Constitution then in the group Legislature equal to the ratio of their population to the total population. Provided that no other minority is allowed to claim more representation than what is due to it on the basis of its population.

(ii) The Scheduled Castes of Sind and N.W.F. Provinces shall be given their due share of representation.

(iii) Weightage where it becomes necessary to reduce a huge communal majority to reasonable dimensions shall come out of the share of the majority. In no case shall it be at the cost of another minority community.

(iv) Weightage carved out from the share of majority shall not be assigned to one community only. But the same shall be divided among all minority communities equally or in inverse proportion to their—

(1) economic position,

(2) social status, and

(3) educational advance.

(b) There should be no representation to special interests. But if the same is allowed it must be taken out of the share of representation given to that community to which the special interest belongs.

(2) Method of Election—

(A) For Legislative Bodies

(a) The system of election introduced by the Poona Pact shall be abolished.

(b) In its place, the system of Separate Electorates shall be substituted.

(c) Franchise shall be adult franchise.

(d) The system of voting shall be cumulative.

(B) For Local Bodies

The principles for determining the quantum of representation and the Method of election for Municipalities and Local Boards shall be the same as that adopted for the Union and State Legislatures.

## Clause 2

For explanation see Explanatory Notes

(1) The Scheduled Castes shall have minimum representation in the Executive—Union and State—and if there, be a group Constitution then in the group Executive equal to the ratio of their population that no minority community is allowed to claim more than its population ratio.

(2) Weightage where it becomes necessary to reduce a huge majority to reasonable dimensions shall come out of the share of the majority community. In no case shall it be at the cost of another minority community.

(3) Weightage carved out from the share of the majority shall not be assigned to one community only. But the same shall be divided among all minorities equally or in inverse proportion to:
   (i) their economic position.
   (ii) social status, and
   (iii) educational advance.

## Clause 3

(a) The quantum of representation of the Scheduled Castes in the Services shall be as follows :
   (i) In the Union Services.—In proportion to the ratio of their population to the total population in India or British India as the case may be.
   (ii) In the State and Group Services.—in proportion to their population in the State or Union.
   (iii.) In the Municipal and Local Board Services.—In proportion to their population in the Municipal and Local Boards areas :
   Provided that no minority community is allowed to claim more than its population ratio of representation, in the Services.
      (b) Their right to representation in the Services shall not be curtailed except by conditions relating to minimum qualifications, education, age, etc.
      (c) The conditions prescribed for entry in Services shall not abrogate any of the concessions given to the Scheduled Castes by the Government of India in their Resolutions of 1942 and 1945.
      (d) The method of filling up the vacancies shall conform to the rules prescribed in the Government of India Resolutions of 1942 and 1946.
      (e) On every Public Services Commission or a. Committee constituted for filling vacancies, the Scheduled Castes shall have at least one representative.

Part II—Special Responsibilities: Provisions for Higher Education
Part II—Special Responsibilities:
Clause 1: For Higher Education.
Clause 2. For Separate Settlements.

## Explanations:

That the United States of India shall undertake the following special responsibilities for the betterment of the Scheduled Castes:

### Clause 1

(1) Governments—Union and State—shall be required to assume financial responsibility for the education of the Scheduled Castes and shall be required to make adequate provisions in their budgets. Such Provisions shall form the first charge on the Education Budget of the Union and State Government.

(2) The responsibility for finding money for secondary and college education of the Scheduled Castes in India shall be upon the State Governments and the different States shall make a provision in their annual budgets for the said purpose in proportion to the population of the Scheduled Castes to the total budget of the States.

(3) The responsibility for finding money for foreign education of the Scheduled Castes shall be the responsibility of the Union Government and the Union Government shall make a provision of rupees 10 lakhs per year in its annual budget in that behalf.

(4) These special grants shall be without prejudice to the right of the Scheduled Castes to share in the expenditure incurred by the State Government for the advancement of primary education for the people of the State.

### Clause 2

1. The following provision shall be made in the Constitution of the Union Government:
   (i) There shall be a Settlement Commission under the new Constitution to hold uncultivated lands belonging to the State in trust for Settlement of the Scheduled Castes in separate villages.
   (ii) The Union Government shall set apart annually a fund of Rs. 5 crores for the purpose of promoting the scheme of settlement.
   (iii) That the Commission shall have the power to purchase any land offered for sale and use it for the said purpose.
2. The Union Government shall from time to time pass such legislation as may be necessary for the Commission to carry out its functions.

Part III—Sanction for Safeguards and Amendment of Safeguards
Clause 1. Safeguards to be embodied in the Constitution.
Clause 2. Amendment of Safeguards.

### Explanation:

### Clause 1

The Constitution of the United States shall provide that—

The United States of India undertakes to give the safeguards contained in Article II Section IV a place in the Constitution and make them a part of the Constitutional Law of India.

## Clause 2

The provisions for the Scheduled Castes shall not be altered, amended or abrogated except in the following manner:

Any amendment or abrogation of Section IV of Article II or any part thereof relating to the Scheduled Castes shall only be made by a Resolution passed in the manner prescribed below by the more Popular Chamber of the Union Legislature:

(i) Any proposal for amendment or abrogation shall be initiated in the form of a Resolution in the more Popular Chamber of the Union Legislature.

(ii) No such Resolution shall be moved—
   (a) unless 25 years have elapsed after the Constitution has come into operation and has been worked; and
   (b) unless six months' notice has been given to the House by the mover of his intention to move such a Resolution.

(iii) On the passing of such a Resolution, the Legislature shall be dissolved and a new election held.

(iv) The original Resolution in the form in which it was passed by the previous Legislature shall be moved afresh in the same House of the newly elected Union Legislature.

(v) The Resolution shall not be deemed to have been carried unless it is passed by a majority of two-thirds of the members of the House and also two-thirds of members of the Scheduled Castes who have been returned through separate electorates.

Part IV— Protection of Scheduled Castes in the Indian States

The Constitution of the United States shall provide that the admission of the Indian States into the Union shall be subject to the Scheduled Castes following condition:

All provisions relating to the Scheduled Castes contained in Section IV of Article II of the Constitution of the United States of India shall be extended to the Scheduled Castes in the Indian Slates. Such a provision in the Constitution of an Indian States shall be a condition precedent for its admission into the Union.

Part V—Interpretation

I. For the purposes of Article II the Scheduled Castes, as defined in the Government of India Scheduled Caste Order, 1936, issued under the Government of India Act, 1935, shall be deemed to be a minority.
Scheduled Castes and change of Domicile

II. For the purposes of Article II a Caste which is a Scheduled Caste in one State shall be treated as Scheduled Caste in all States of the Union. ”

# References

## Books and Articles

Ambedkar, B. R. 1956a [1997]. 'Speech delivered in the Rajya Sabha on 1 May 1956'. In *Dr. Babasaheb Ambedkar Writings and Speeches*, ed. Vasant Moon, vol. 15, 962–73. Bombay: Government of Maharashtra.

———. 1956b [2002]. 'Ambedkar's Recipe For Maharashtra: Voice Of The People'. *The Free Press Journal*. 31 May. In *Dr. Babasaheb Ambedkar Writings and Speeches*, ed. Vasant Moon, vol. 17, part II, 391–92. Bombay: Government of Maharashtra.

———. 1955 [1979]. 'Thoughts on Linguistic States'. In *Dr. Babasaheb Ambedkar Writings and Speeches*, ed. Vasant Moon, vol. 1, 137–204. Bombay: Government of Maharashtra.

———. 1953a [1979]. 'Need for Checks and Balances'. *The Times of India*. 23 April. In *Dr. Babasaheb Ambedkar Writings and Speeches*, ed. Vasant Moon, vol. 1, 129–36. Bombay: Government of Maharashtra.

———. 1953b [1997]. 'Speech delivered in the Rajya Sabha on 2 September 1953'. In *Dr. Babasaheb Ambedkar Writings and Speeches*, ed. Vasant Moon, vol. 15, 851–64. Bombay: Government of Maharashtra.

———. 1948 [1979]. 'Maharashtra as a Linguistic Province: Statement Submitted to the Linguistic Provinces Commission'. In *Dr. Babasaheb Ambedkar Writings and Speeches*, ed. Vasant Moon, vol. 1, 99–128. Bombay: Government of Maharashtra.

———. 1947 [1979]. 'States and Minorities: What are their Rights and how to secure them in the Constitution of Free India, Memorandum on the Safeguards for the Scheduled Castes submitted to the Constituent Assembly on behalf of the All India Scheduled Castes Federation, Bombay'. In *Dr. Babasaheb Ambedkar Writings and Speeches*, ed. Vasant Moon, vol. 1, 381–452. Bombay: Government of Maharashtra.

———. 1945 [1990]. *Pakistan or the Partition of India*. In *Dr. Babasaheb Ambedkar Writings and Speeches*, ed. Vasant Moon, vol. 8. Bombay: Government of Maharashtra (Originally published by Thackeray and Company, Bombay).

———. 1938 [1982]. 'Speech Delivered in the Bombay Legislative Assembly on April 4, 1938'. In *Dr. Babasaheb Ambedkar Writings and Speeches*, ed. Vasant Moon, vol. 2, 188–96. Bombay: Government of Maharashtra.

Annamalai, E. n.d. *Language Movements in India*. Manasgangotri, Mysore: Central Institute of Indian Languages. Available at http://www.ciil-ebooks.net/html/langMove/samyukta.html (accessed 3 April 2012)

Austin, Granville. 1967. *The Indian Constitution: Cornerstone of a Nation*. New Delhi: Oxford University Press.

Bandyopadhyay, Sekhar. 2000. 'Transfer of Power and the Crisis of Dalit Politics in India, 1945–47'. *Modern Asian Studies* 34 (4): 893–942. October.

Bhargava, G. S. 1956. 'India is a Multi-lingual Nation—Not a Multi-national State'. *The Economic Weekly* 8 (9): 269–70, 277. 3 March.

Bondurant, Joan. 1958. *Regionalism Versus Provincialism: A Study in Problems of Indian National Unity*. Indian Press Digest, Monograph No. 4, December. Berkeley: University of California.

Brecher, Michael. 1959. *Nehru: A Political Biography*. Toronto: Oxford University Press.

Chatterjee, Partha. 2006. 'B. R. Ambedkar and the Troubled Times of Citizenship'. In *History of Science, Philosophy and Culture in Indian Civilization* 10, part 7, *Political Ideas in Modern India: Thematic Explorations*, eds V. R. Mehta and Thomas Pantham, 73–90. New Delhi: Sage Publications.

Das, B., ed. 1980. *Thus Spoke Ambedkar*. Vols 1–4. Banglore: Ambedkar Sahitya Prakashan.

Editorial. 1953. 'Tyranny of Languages: Demand for New States'. *Economic and Political Weekly* 5 (4–5): 79–80. 26 January.

Forrester, Duncan B. 1970. 'Subregionalism in India: The Case of Telangana'. *Pacific Affairs* 43 (1): 5–21. Spring.

Gangan, Surendra. 2010. 'Mouthpieces of the Movement Emerged from Within'. *DNA*. 1 May. Mumbai edition.

Gopal, S., and Uma Iyengar, eds. 2003. *The Essential Writings of J. Nehru*. New Delhi: Oxford University Press.

Gore, M. S. 1993. *The Social Context of an Ideology: Ambedkar's Political and Social Thought*. New Delhi: Sage Publications.

Guha, Ramachandra. 2007. *India After Gandhi*. London: Macmillan.

Harrison, Selig S. 1960. *India: The Most Dangerous Decades*. Washington: Oxford University Press.

*Hindu, The*. 2006. "The Struggle for Andhra". 1 November. Available at http://www.hindu.com/2006/11/01/stories/2006110101690200.htm (accessed 12 May 2012)

Jaffrelot, C. 2004. *Dr Ambedkar and Untouchability: Analysing and Fighting Caste*. New Delhi: Orient Longman.

JVP (Jawaharlal Nehru, Vallabhbhai Patel and Pattabhi Sitaramayya). 1949. 'Report of the Linguistic Provinces Committee'. New Delhi: AICC.

Keer, D. 1994 [1964]. *Dr. Ambedkar Life and Mission*. Bombay: Popular Prakashan.

Khapre, Shubhangi. 2010. 'Maharashtrians Originated from Different Palettes'. *DNA*. 1 May. Mumbai edition.

Khairmode, C. B. 2003. *Dr Bhimrao Ramji Ambedkar: Charitra*. Vol. 10. Third edition. Pune: Sughava Prakasan.

Kodesia, K. 1969. *The Problem of Linguistic States in India*. New Delhi: Sterling Publications.

Kolhatkar, Neeta. 2010. 'Experiment of an Assimilative State by Nehru'. *DNA*. 1 May. Mumbai edition.

Kumar, Avinash. 2011. 'Splitting UP Not A Bad Idea'. *The Hindu Businessline*. 18 November.

Majeed, Akhtar. 2003. 'The Changing Politics of States' Reorganization'. *Publius: The Journal of Federalism* 33 (4): 83–98.

Mallik, Pradeep. 2005. 'Demand for a "Dalitstan" Raises its Head'. *DNA*. 12 October.

Mishra, K. K. 1972. 'Linguistic Nationalities in India'. *Social Scientist* 1 (3): 20–33. October.

Mukerji, Krishna P., and Suhasini Ramaswamy. 1955. *Reorganisation of Indian States*. Bombay: Popular Book Depot.

Nag, Sajal. 1993. 'Multiplication of Nations: Political Economy of Sub-Nationalism in India'. *Economic and Political Weekly* 28 (29/30): 1521–32.

Noorani, A. G. 2010. 'Linguism Trap'. *Frontline* 27 (08).

———. 2002. 'Nehru and Linguistic States'. *Frontline* 19 (16).

Omvedt, Gail. 2003. *Buddhism in India: Challenging Brahmanism and Caste*. New Delhi: Sage Publications.

———. 1994. *Dalits and the Democratic Revolution: Dr. Ambedkar and the Dalit Movement in Colonial India*. New Delhi: Thousand Oaks; California: Sage Publications.

Pai, Sudha, ed. 2013. *Handbook on Politics in the Indian States: Regions, Parties and Economic Reforms*. New Delhi: Oxford University Press.

———. 2007. 'Reorganisation of States'. In *Ambedkar in Retrospect: Essays on Economics, Politics and Society*, ed. Sukhadeo Thorat and Aryama, 195–210. Jaipur: Rawat Publications.

Parkash, Prem. 2002. *Ambedkar: Politics and the Scheduled Castes*. New Delhi: Ashish Publishing House.

Patra, S. C. 1979. *Formation of the Province of Orissa: The Success of the First Linguistic Movement in India*. Calcutta: Punthi Pustak.

Pattanayak, A. K. 1988. 'The Formation of the Province of Orissa'. In *Government and Politics in Orissa*, ed. B. B. Jena and J. K. Baral. Lucknow: Print House (India).

Prasad, H. Y. Sharada, and A. K. Damodaran. 2002. *Selected Works of Jawaharlal Nehru, Second Series, 1 September – 17 November 1955*, vol. 30. New Delhi: Oxford University Press.

Rao, Anupama. 2009. *The Caste Question: Dalits and the Politics of Modern India*. Berkeley: University of California Press.

Rao, B. Shiva, ed. 1968. *The Framing of India's Constitution: A Study*, vol. 5. New Delhi: Universal Law Publishing Co. Pvt. Ltd.

———, ed. 1967a. *The Framing of India's Constitution: Select Documents*, vol. 1. New Delhi: Universal Law Publishing Co. Pvt. Ltd.

———, ed. 1967b. *The Framing of India's Constitution: Select Documents*, vol. 2. New Delhi: Universal Law Publishing Co. Pvt. Ltd.

———, ed. 1967c. *The Framing of India's Constitution: Select Documents*, vol. 3. New Delhi: Universal Law Publishing Co. Pvt. Ltd.

———, ed. 1967d. *The Framing of India's Constitution: Select Documents*, vol. 4. New Delhi: Universal Law Publishing Co. Pvt. Ltd.

Rao, P Kodanda. (1953). 'Linguistic States', *The Economic Weekly*, February 14, pp. 183–85.

Reddy, Ram, and B. A. V. Sharma, eds. 1979. *State Politics: Andhra Pradesh*. New Delhi: Sterling.
Rodrigues, Valerian. 2002. *B. R. Ambedkar: Essential Writings*. New Delhi: Oxford University Press.
Sangharakshita. 1986. *Ambedkar and Buddhism*. Glasgow: Windhorse Publications.
Sarangi, Asha. 2006. 'Ambedkar and the Linguistic States: A Case for Maharashtra'. *Economic and Political Weekly* 41 (2): 151–57. 14 January.
Sarangi, Asha, and Sudha Pai. 2011. *Interrogating Reorganisation of States: Culture, Identity and Politics in India*. New Delhi: Routledge.
Shah, N. A. 1955. 'Reorganisation of States'. *The Economic Weekly* 7 (23): 665–66. 4 June.
Tare, Kiran. 2010. 'Samyukta Maharashtra movement United All Opponents Against the Congress'. *DNA*. 1 May. Mumbai edition.
Thirumali, Inukonda. 2013. *Telangana-Andhra: Castes, Regions and Politics in Andhra Pradesh*. New Delhi: Aakar Books.
Tillin, Louise. 2014. *Remapping India New States and their Political Origins*. New Delhi: Oxford University Press.
*Times News Network* (*TNN*). 2009. 'Demand for Creation of 10 New States before Home Ministry'. 29 June.
Verghese, B. G. 2011. 'Foreword' to *Interrogating Reorganisation of States: Culture, Identity and Politics in India*, eds Asha Sarangi and Sudha Pai, vii–xxii. New Delhi: Routledge
Vundru, Rajasekhar. 2012. 'Voting Rights for All, No Mean Achievement'. *The Hindu Businessline*. 14 May.
———. 2010. 'Ambedkar and Small States'. *The Hindustan Times*. 31 January.
Wadhwa, K. K. 1975. *Minority Safeguards in India: Constitutional Safeguards and their Implementation*. New Delhi: Thomson Press (*India*).
Wilkinson, T. S., and M. M. Thomas, eds. 1972. *Ambedkar and the Neo-Buddhist Movement*. Madras: Christian Literary Society.
Windmiller, Marshall. 1956. 'The Politics of States Reorganization in India: The Case of Bombay'. *Far Eastern Survey* 25 (9): 129–43. September.
———. 1954. 'Linguistic Regionalism in India'. *Pacific Affairs* 27 (4): 291–318. December.
Zelliot, E. 1996. *From Untouchable to Dalit: Essays on the Ambedkar Movement*. New Delhi: Manohar Publications.
———. 1977. 'The Psychological Dimension of the Buddhist Movement in India'. In *Religious Conversions and Religious Movements in South Asia in Medieval and Modern Times*, ed. G. A. Oddie, 191–214. New Delhi: Manohar Publications.
———. 1972. 'Gandhi and Ambedkar'. In *The Untouchables in Contemporary India*, ed. J. M. Mahar, 69–99. Tuscon: The University of Arizona Press.

## Government Reports

Bombay Legislative Council Debates, 1956, vol. 34.
Census of India, Paper No. 1, 1954. New Delhi: Government of India Press.
Constituent Assembly of India Debates Proceedings (CAD), vol. 7, Wednesday, 17 November 1948.

Government of India (GoI). 2010. 'Report of the Committee for the Consultations on the Situation in Andhra Pradesh, 2010'. New Delhi: Government of India. Also known as 'Srikrishna Committee Report'.

———. 1955. 'Report of the States Reorganisation Commission'. New Delhi: States Reorganisation Commission, GoI.

———. 1948. 'Linguistic Provinces Commission, 1948—Report'. New Delhi: Constituent Assembly of India. Also known as Dar Commission report.

# Index